McILVANNEY ON HORSERACING

McILVANNEY ON HORSERACING

HUGH McILVANNEY

Foreword by Peter O'Sullevan

MAINSTREAM
PUBLISHING

EDINBURGH AND LONDON

First published in Great Britain in 1995 by
MAINSTREAM PUBLISHING COMPANY (EDINBURGH) LTD
7 Albany Street
Edinburgh EH1 3UG

ISBN 1 85158 733 0

A catalogue record for this book is available from the British Library

Typeset in Palatino
Printed and bound in Great Britain by Butler and Tanner Ltd, Frome

Contents

Foreword

THIS IS A BOOK of pure, breathtaking delight. The work of Hugh McIlvanney needs about as much introduction and commendation as that of Ludwig van Beethoven, with whom he shares a magical capacity to raise and refresh the spirit and to heighten the quality of human perception.

Were the world-renowned sportswriter to turn up at the racecourse ('a place where everyday reality is suspended in favour of a theatrically heightened version') bearing the medals which his remarkable talent has accumulated, he'd be carrying enough overweight to anchor Pegasus in the stalls; yet he'd still be odds-on to outperform the opposition with embarrassing facility. I guess one of the happiest features of the McIlvanney magic is that, as with Lester Piggott ('a volcano trapped in an iceberg'), his fellow professionals accept him for what he is – superior.

Racing's most perceptive and articulate interpreter refers to 'the irresistible qualities of a game which, at its best, is one of the most attractive and natural metaphors for life that sport has to offer'. Racing is also like farming – it is invariably in a situation of reasonably affluent crisis with the principal performer often receiving less consideration than his due. In 1992 a decision to produce a book in aid of the International League for the Protection of Horses resulted in a collection of previously unpublished articles contributed gratuitously by hippographists (A.J. Liebling's favoured noun for race writers) on both sides of the Atlantic. Demands on the services of H. McIlvanney, the only sportswriter, incidentally, to be voted Journalist of the Year, are such that he is not renowned for delivering copy sufficiently in advance of the deadline to avoid a 'photo'. On this occasion the camera was about to be activated when, to the accompaniment of widespread relief,

the magic words were produced in the press room at Cheltenham –
the arena which has inspired some of the maestro's most
memorable *chefs d'oeuvre*.

As co-editor of the book, which was to be called *That's Racing*, I
had the privilege of being the first to relish the last of 40
submissions. A few desks away sat my ample and erudite colleague
Chris Poole, himself a valued contributor and no mean handler of
both the written and spoken word – as readers of the *Evening
Standard* and listeners to the BBC World Service would happily
testify. Knowing that Chris would share my delight, I wandered
over and placed the offering before him. Head bowed in homage
and temporarily ignoring the action which accounted for our
presence, he chuckled his way from start to finish before returning
the pages with a vehement injunction: 'For God's sake, don't put
my piece anywhere near it.' He added resignedly: 'No man should
be allowed to write as well as that.'

It is as near to a certainty as you can get that readers of the
following pages will fully share the big man's sense of wonder,
admiration and enchantment.

Peter O'Sullevan

Introduction

IT IS TO BE hoped that no one will be put off by the wild cheek that seems to be implicit in the title of this book. I have less right to hold forth on horse racing than I have to pontificate on quantum theory, as the scars I have carried out of the betting ring insistently testify.

As I have taken pains to explain previously, in relation to collections of my pieces that appeared as *McIlvanney on Boxing* and *McIlvanney on Football*, the form of words used in the titling has nothing to do with delusions of authority on my part. It was chosen by the publishers and they overrode my doubts with the argument that its simple purpose was to emphasise that these books represent one privileged observer's view of several sports over the past 30-odd years. In the case of racing, the subjectivity (certainly in the area of wagering) was often extreme, some would say surreal. I yield to no one when it comes to originality in interpreting the form book. But I hope that, when there was serious chronicling to be done, I retained enough objectivity and conscientiousness as a reporter to do some measure of justice to the great occasions and great performers, great men and great horses I have encountered.

The competitive essence of racing could not be more basic but there is something mysterious about the depth of pleasure millions of us take from it. I have said elsewhere that I don't think it is too fanciful to suggest there is an element of folk memory in the excitement stirred by the sight of the running horse. Until the invention of the steam engine, humans who wanted to rise beyond their own rate of locomotion on dry land had, broadly speaking, the choice of employing a kind of sledge, jumping off a cliff or riding an animal. Since the horse was by far the most widespread means of effecting such an extension of our possibilities, isn't it natural that a special attachment to this beautiful creature should be buried deep in our collective subconscious? All right, so you sometimes feel, as the gloaming of the damned gathers around you at Epsom or Ascot or Cheltenham, that jumping off a cliff might have been a better option. And folk memories don't help much when the men with brass knuckles are at the door. Still, it does no harm to justify our addictions with a little speculative anthropology.

Racing's hold on me has obviously been strengthened over the years by the extraordinary access my job has given me to its most compelling performers, equine and human. Many of the horses have been dazzling. If I tried to compile a list of those that have thrilled me to the core, the names would spill over a page or two. Alongside Arkle and Sea Bird II and Nijinsky, Sir Ivor and Mill Reef and Secretariat, and all the other giants, there would be a number of much more obscure animals whose lack of celebrity did not prevent them from brightening at least one day of my life. A heartfelt tribute to a horse of that kind, a modest hurdler called Overall, is included in these pages and he might have been joined by many another humble hero. To all those gallopers, fast and slow, genuine and dubious, I am grateful. Without their help, I might never have learned that getting poorer by the minute can be marvellous fun.

Of course, the horses represent only half the appeal of racing. The people who work with them can be every bit as entertaining and, unlike their four-legged allies, they can often justify the word enriching. The term is plainly an understatement when applied to the opportunities I have had to spend priceless hours in one-to-one conversations with Vincent O'Brien, Lester Piggott, Jonjo O'Neill and other masters. Even they were never likely to make me wiser in the ways of the Turf but they did enlarge my appreciation of its magic.

So too, in their own way, did a multitude of anonymous devotees of the game with whom I have shared the battle for survival in places as scattered as Ludlow and Melbourne, Caracas and Moscow, Musselburgh and Chantilly and Santa Anita. The bond we forged may have been ephemeral but it was real enough. Race trains are like troop trains without the dread. We have camaraderie and coarse humour, an adrenaline flood that sharpens the senses and boosts the appetite for living. But running through it all is the blissful reassurance that the conflict we are approaching is make-believe, an arena in which everyday reality is suspended in favour of a theatrically heightened version. Obviously, if the betting arm is allowed to get out of control, reality of the old-fashioned kind may reassert itself by way of the bailiffs or collectors whose methods are less formal. If we keep a grip on the fantasies, however, we have a licence to enjoy thousands of adventure playgrounds all over the globe.

My attempt to put into book form my own enjoyment of these pleasures across three or four decades has been assisted by innumerable acts of kindness. The tolerance and generosity of my extended family (extended, frequently, close to breaking point) have again been miraculous, and pestered journalistic colleagues have responded with their usual smiling patience. More generally, the newspapers and magazines for which the material reprinted here was originally written will always have my gratitude, as payers of the rent as well as suppliers of the badges.

Everyone at Mainstream has been so unfailingly helpful that mention of individual names would be wrong. They deserve a team prize – say, a guarantee that they won't ever again have to suffer me as a lodger in their offices. But they cannot have that promise.

There are two or three individuals who must be singled out for special thanks. My old friend John Watt is one. There are many reasons for being grateful to him but perhaps the simplest is his capacity for dredging up arcane facts and figures with a conjuror's facility. Mike Dillon, who is not only an invaluable pillar of the Ladbrokes organisation but an indispensable asset to the racing press room, is a man who has done me more favours than could be repaid in a couple of lifetimes (and, believe me, that statement has nothing to do with betting, concerning which God couldn't do me a favour). One of Mike's great friends is Peter O'Sullevan and I am proud to think that The Voice is also a friend of mine. His foreword to this book is impossibly generous but I am moved to find that he felt able to write it.

Finally, and vitally, I wish to thank Geoffrey Irvine and Angie Bainbridge of the Bagenal Harvey Organisation for the boundless warmth and support they have always provided for their most tiresome client. If they could just give me a winner, I would start campaigning for their canonisation straight away.

Hugh McIlvanney

The Horseman Even Arkle
Must Respect

I have chosen to start with something I wrote nearly 30 years ago about a great Irishman and the unforgettable horse he partnered.

PAT TAAFFE IS one of the few horsemen in the world who can look Arkle in the eye without feeling inferior. He has ridden the nine-year-old bay gelding to 21 of the 23 victories that have established him as the greatest steeplechaser in the history of racing, and has ridden Arkle's younger stable companion Flyingbolt to all of the 13 wins that have made him a possible heir to the title.

Taaffe says seriously that he considers himself lucky to be alive and riding at a time when these two great champions are available to him, but most experts agree that the arrangement is just as fortunate for the horses. Tom Dreaper, who trains both at Kilsallaghan, County Dublin, a few miles from Taaffe's home, sees the situation simply: 'Pat is the best there is. Apart from his achievements as a jockey, he is the most beautiful horseman you could hope to see. Even for the greatest of horses it is a privilege to be ridden by such a man.'

Yet, on at least two counts, it is astonishing that Taaffe should be riding professionally at all. For a start, he is six feet tall, which makes him almost as much of a freak among jockeys as a five-foot centre forward in the First Division. However, he is naturally slim and narrow-shouldered and even after giving up smoking his weight stays down to a reasonable 10st 7lb without strict dieting. He has the pleasant, weather-reddened face of an Irish farmer, which is what he is, and at 36 his hair is thinning in front and greying at the sides. His only remarkable physical feature is one you notice immediately when he greets you on the steps of the farmhouse at Straffan where he lives with his wife and five young children. The handshake is relaxed but powerful. His hands are large, with long, thick fingers that would be a great advantage in golf and can be no drawback when it comes to restraining an exuberant jumper. The tips of the second and third fingers of his right hand are missing, having been sliced off when they were jammed between a wall and a falling drum of treacle. 'It was a nice clean job,' he said with a smile. 'I didn't even have to have the ends trimmed away.'

He is not given to exaggerating mishaps. When I asked him if he had had the National Hunt rider's normal experience of injuries he said he thought he had been luckier than most. Had there been any serious injuries then? 'Well, I broke an arm and a leg and I've done a few ribs . . . oh, yes, and I fractured my skull when a horse called Ireland threw me at Kilbeggan in August of 1956.'

In fact, that injury was serious enough to have put many another man out of the game. Taaffe was in hospital for five weeks and when he came back in November his second mount at Naas dropped him at the ditch and he had to have six stitches in a thigh wound. He feels that what happened at that point probably had a crucial effect on his career. 'Mr Dreaper had two going at Manchester but I said, "Don't you think you'd better get somebody else to ride them?" You know what it's like after something like that, you don't really know where you are some of the time. But Mr Dreaper said, "If you don't ride them we won't run them". So I rode them and they both went in.'

In the dining-room, which is large with plain, handsome furniture and the expected paintings of horses on the walls, Taaffe served drinks from a silver tray presented to him by local admirers when Arkle won his first Gold Cup in 1964. It was impossible to hold back the memory of that beautiful clear day in Cheltenham when Mill House led him by 10 lengths round the far side of the course and knowing watchers wanted to lay any price against Arkle. Then as Taaffe, who had planned it all that way, began to close on the turn at the top of the hill, the incredible Irish support, the farmers and stableboys and priests, roared in unison: 'Here he comes.' It was like a beleaguered army greeting the hero who brings relief. He came all right, to run the heart out of Mill House, and that great horse was never the same again.

'It was losing to Mill House in the Hennessy at Newbury earlier on that made that race so important to all of us. I knew well enough that Mill House was a heck of a horse, a born jumper, for I had ridden him once to win a maiden hurdle over here in 1961. He could stand off from his fences and still get over them easily. Yet I let my fellow jump with him in the Hennessy, and Arkle was taking off along with him and, of course, in the end we slipped up on landing and lost the race. But I knew we could murder Mill House for speed, so I decided we'd beat him between the fences. I told the Duchess: "Don't worry, we'll trot up in the Gold Cup".'

Taaffe has a vast respect for Anne Duchess of Westminster, the owner of Arkle, because she shares his love of horses to the extent of insisting on a firmly defined annual holiday for her champion, when he is put out in a paddock that is specially laid and rolled for him and is forbidden ground to all other animals. 'That's why Arkle won't be taking up the invitations to go to America or France and she thinks too much of him to risk him in the National, although I've got my own ideas about what he could do to that race. We'll concentrate on beating Golden Miller's record of five wins in the Cheltenham Gold Cup.'

Seeing horses as something more than racing machines is an attitude that appeals to him. He is sometimes accused of being suspect in tight finishes and, though he does not accept the criticism entirely, he understands its basis. 'It's not my strong point. I don't like punching a horse that much. I prefer to use the things I think are my biggest assets – knowing how to keep out of trouble, judging the pace accurately – so that I can have the race settled at the last jump. Anyway, a length gained at the last is worth a hundred yards on the run-in, for it takes a hundred yards to make it up.'

Taaffe was born only four miles from his present home. 'We're a horsey family. Mammy is a Nugent. Daddy got on a boat for Australia when he was about 12, was lost for about four years, then turned up and did a bit of training over there. But he came back and established himself here. My brother Tos has taken over from Daddy now and he's doing well. He's had seven winners this year.'

Pat Taaffe first learned to ride at the age of eight at Lt.-Colonel Hume Dudgeon's famous school near Dublin, did some show jumping, rode a winner in a point-to-point at 17 and in the same season won his first bumper race on Ballincorona. He turned pro in 1950 and has now headed the National Hunt jockeys' list in Ireland four times, a record that would certainly be improved if he undertook more rides. His programme is crowded with the responsibilities of the farm, where he keeps about 80 sheep, nearly 30 cattle and a handful of brood mares, but he still manages to ride to hounds most weeks. He thinks hunting is wonderful training in horsemanship ('they never jump the same way twice') and particularly relevant to the Grand National, which he won on Quare Times in 1955. 'You just hunt them round and keep out of trouble, then you can ride your race when you get on to the racecourse.'

The only one of the jumping classics he has still to win is the Champion Hurdle but Flyingbolt, the less gentlemanly of his great partners ('I daren't go into his box – he'd kick the eye out of your head'), can put that right at Cheltenham on 16 March. Even if he does, however, it may not be Flyingbolt or even the incomparable Arkle that Taaffe will remember longest. It may be an undistinguished animal called Foinavon, which he thinks is the only horse that ever took a rise out of him. 'He fell with me at Baldoyle,' he said, shaking his head incredulously at the memory. 'And when I looked round to see if he was all right, he was lying there eating grass.'

The Observer, 20 February 1966

Foinavon's impertinence put him into history in 1967, when he skirted unbelievable mayhem at the 23rd fence to win the Grand National at 100-1.

Home and Terribly Dry
in the Derby

THE DRAMA THAT has shaken English racing in the past week stirred a few ghosts in a handsome white manor house on the edge of a Surrey golf course.

The lord of Pachesham Manor at Leatherhead is a short, stocky man whose pugnacious features and brisk, assertive gestures might mark him as a former professional fighter. As it happens, Charlie Smirke has boxed for money in his time but his most notable victories have been won on the racecourses of Europe. He rode the winner of the Epsom Derby four times and had a total of 11 wins in the English Classics, as well as winning a clutch of great races in France and elsewhere. He was one of the finest race riders ever seen and he was at his best when the stakes were highest.

However, last week, as Ryan Price and Josh Gifford waited tensely for the stewards of the National Hunt Committee to adjudicate on the running of Hill House in the Schweppes Hurdle, Smirke was not thinking of his successes. He was remembering the bitter day in 1928 when his jockey's licence was withdrawn after he had failed to make a heavily backed favourite named Welcome Gift jump off from the starting gate at Gatwick, where take-offs are more predictable these days. He does not think Gifford or Price has done anything to deserve such punishment. But, for that matter, he insists that he did not deserve it either. 'That sod Welcome Gift did the same in India afterwards. Just refused to start. But that didn't help me. I was off, and without any idea of when I'd get back. That's the inhuman thing about it. If they took your licence away and said you were off for a year or two years you'd know where you were. You could take a job, resign yourself to waiting out your time. I applied twice a year for renewal but for a long time it looked as if I'd never be back.

'I was only a kid of 22 then and all I had was a lousy 12,000 quid and that didn't last all that long. I did all sorts of jobs. My father had had a fish and fruit business in Battersea and I could stack a ton of potatoes in hundredweight bags by the time I was ten, so I knew what it was to work. But with the uncertainty of it all I couldn't settle into a proper job. I worked on the beach at Brighton, had a few pro fights, did all sorts of things. I was offered £1,000 a year to ride gallops on the course in America, but they wouldn't let me go. Eventually, after five years I was told I'd never be allowed back. Then some lobbying was done for me among the top people and in the finish the Prince of Wales intervened. I had my licence back within three weeks. I think the regulations should be changed so that a jockey or a trainer who is stood down knows the length of his sentence. Even a fellow that's been done for murder knows that. If he's going to be hung he knows that too. In racing you don't know whether you are being hung or not.'

When Smirke did come back after five years, he wasted no time in proving that the lay-off had blunted neither his ambition nor his reflexes. In 1934 he won the Derby and the St Leger on Windsor Lad. 'Without a doubt he was the best horse I ever sat on,' he says. 'And I don't just say that because of what those wins meant to me at that stage. The thing about him was that he had real class. He could win at six furlongs or six miles. A lot of people don't believe me when I say that the second-best horse I ever rode was Never Say Die.' Strangely, it was the suspension of Lester Piggott in 1954 which gave Smirke the St Leger ride on Never Say Die. He won by 12 lengths.

'Tulyar was the most difficult of my Derby winners because he stopped if you went in front with him too soon and that is a terrible problem to have in a Classic horse. He wasn't such a great one anyway. Just a good little horse that didn't beat anything marvellous. I always said the same about Bahram. Naturally the Aga always thought a hell of a lot of him, for he won the Triple Crown. But I told him Bahram had never beaten anything very good.'

Smirke's greatest years were in association with the Aga Khan (who used to send a private plane to fly him to Deauville to discuss plans) and his son Aly. 'No jock ever had guvnors to equal the Aga and Aly. There could never be anybody like them again.' This wistfulness is in almost everything Smirke says about racing now. He has not attended a meeting for four-and-a-half years, though the Epsom course is only a quarter-of-an-hour's drive from his home. When the weather is good he plays golf on the fairways that surround the house or strides out, wearing a wool-collared windcheater and carrying a walking-stick, to exercise his two dogs. For the rest of the time, apart from having a drink with his pals at Leatherhead Golf Club, of which he is a director, he potters around at home, watching more television in a day than Maurice Richardson is likely to see in a week. 'I'm potty about it,' he admitted, recalling what Harry Carr had said: 'I'm bad, but Charlie is worse. He'll watch anything – the Flowerpot Men, the test card, anything.'

There is a paradox inherent in all this, because Smirke, at 60, is not by any means burnt out. When stimulated, he still displays the old ebullience, he is still full of ideas and opinions; the brown eyes are no less challenging. (He has remained very much the cockney, saying 'My life' and 'It's the God's truth' to pledge the veracity of his own statements, winking and lifting his eyebrows like Frankie Howerd while he mouths silent endorsement of a story being told by someone else.) He says he would not mind going to help one of his friends in a stable but is afraid he would be accused of trying to take over. The truth, however, is probably that he feels alienated by the changes that have taken place in racing. Both he and his second wife, Ruth, refer constantly to the growth of commercialism in the game and for a time this is puzzling, for Smirke never lacked enthusiasm for hard currency. After a while it emerges that what they mean is simply that people are much more conscious of spending money these days.

The age of the Aga Khan and the aristocratic owners who did not have to worry about a few thousand here or there has given way to an era when ownership is diversified and expenditure is anxiously watched. The revolution has been just as much of a wrench for his wife as for Smirke. She worked for the late Dorothy Paget, the eccentric millionairess who used to keep her trainers and advisers hanging around racecourses for hours after racing so that she could conduct a post-mortem, sometimes concluding it in the ladies' cloakroom at 11 p.m. 'I have put £20,000 on a horse for D.P. and on a loser at that,' she says. 'That kind of betting is unheard of now.'

One thing that has not changed in racing is the agony of wasting, which dominates the lives of jockeys who have become too heavy for their trade. I had gone to see Smirke with Jack Leach, who rode with him at one time and subsequently trained some good horses that were ridden by him. Both had terrible weight trouble and their conversation began with nostalgic reminiscences about the Turkish baths that had disappeared from London ('Remember that wonderful place, The Hammam, in Jermyn Street?').

Smirke should have weighed more than 10 stone but he was dehydrated to ride at 8st 6lb. Some of it was done with pills and injections. 'I used to get this injection in Wimpole Street and go to the pictures and I'd wee-wee 5lb off in four hours.' But mainly it came down to brutal sacrifice, going without food and drink. 'Food isn't so bad, but you go mad for liquid. My wife used to have to snatch bottles of milk away from me. You'd be driving to the races and a Tizer lorry or a Schweppes lorry would pass you and it would knock you potty. I used to have this dream that when I gave up riding I'd have this big tank at the side of my bed with a tube attached and I'd drink and drink until I blew out. It's all had a permanent effect, of course. Even now I can stand up at a bar and drink without ever having to go to the lavatory. And because of all that wasting my hair won't grow and my fingernails won't grow.'

Smirke's riding equipment was trimmed down as severely as his body. The colours he wore on Tulyar were so flimsy that they weighed only one ounce. He had heel-less riding boots so thin that they tore if he pulled them off too firmly. He wore ladies' silk stockings and as a substitute for the compulsory skull-cap he had the crown cut from a bowler hat. His entire equipment, including saddle, stirrup irons, surcingle (a sort of girth), breeches, boots, stockings, safety cap and colours, weighed only a pound and three-quarters. 'I thought I had reached the limit and mine weighed two pounds,' said Jack Leach.

A jockey is allowed to weigh-in at two pounds over his horse's stipulated weight after a race. 'So on wet days I'd change into the stronger boots after weighing-out. Those light ones murdered my feet and you could get away with the others when it was raining. You'd be well over when you came back, of course, but the Stewards would say: "Look at him, he's soaked through and covered with mud".'

Now all those disciplines are behind Smirke. Above all, he can eat and drink what he likes. 'But it's a funny thing,' he says sadly, 'I'm just not interested.'

The Observer, 26 February 1967

Steering Clear of the Idiots

We are still in the Sixties, with one of the National Hunt giants of the century.

FRED WINTER'S PREPARATIONS for the Grand National on 8 April have introduced a new factor into form calculations: the Securicor Rating.

When Winter trained Jay Trump, the outstanding American steeplechaser, to win at Aintree two years ago, he engaged Securicor to post an all-night guard on his stables for some time before the race. Last year his challenger was Anglo and Winter was sufficiently realistic about the chestnut's prospects to decide that extra security would be unnecessary. Intending nobblers, he felt, would have more inviting targets. Anglo's pride may have been hurt but if he bore a grudge he showed no evidence of it at Aintree, where he came home full of running at 50-1, 20 lengths ahead of the remnants of the field. His performances since then have been indifferent but Winter knows better than to underestimate his National chances again. A Securicor guard will move into the yard at Lambourn a week before the event and Winter will be happy to pay 17 shillings an hour – a total of £60 or £70 – for the additional protection from those whose financial commitments might encourage them to do a little unofficial veterinary work. Two of Anglo's neighbours, Solbina and Magnetic Rock, are also in the National but the stable's hopes are concentrated on last year's winner.

'Solbina at his best is different class, maybe 2 pounds better than Anglo,' said Winter. 'In fact Anglo is really rather a bad horse. Always has been. He's slow and it's a real effort for him to lie up in a three-mile chase. But it's different at Liverpool. Everything is different at Liverpool. The National is like no other race. And Anglo is not a bad horse in the National – he's a very good one. He was an easier winner than any I've seen or ridden. If Solbina was right, then at the weights he should thrash Anglo. But does Solbina get the trip, will he jump the course? Anglo has proved he can do both. He's tough and he stays forever. Last year when my wife Di saw how far back he was at one stage out in the country she thought we had no chance. But I saw that Josh Gifford was behind our fellow and if Josh was happy to be there I wasn't worried. Little Tim Norman rode a perfect race for me, did everything I said. I told him not to bother about being well back. "Yours won't get any better," I said. "But the others will get worse. And when they start coming back you'll go on." That's how it was.

'Now people are looking at Anglo's form since then and writing him off. But this is stupid. These races he's been running in are not the kind I'd expect him to do well in anyway. He's been carrying a stone more than he's really up to carrying. I don't know why the handicapper has done this to him unless it's got something to do with the fact that he won 20,000 quid.' Winter's characteristic smile is slightly mocking in a friendly way, as if the joke is on you, him and everyone else. It suits his face, which is creased and has a worldly puckishness. The hair is dark and combed back, fairly thick at the neck. In his loose sweater he is rather round-shouldered, which is not uncommon among former jockeys, especially those who have known what it is to waste hard. He is sociable and modest but there is an underlying toughness. The overall impression is of a man who knows his way around but does not feel it is necessary to be rough on other people to prove it.

He has more to say about the misinterpretation of Anglo's recent record: 'When he finished fourth to Kilburn and Highland Wedding he was 20 lengths behind them but he was flying at the finish. He was the fresh horse. That was three miles. If it had been four the others would have been kippered and he'd have been going as strong as ever. With reasonable luck he's got to have a hell of a chance at Aintree. If he'd gone back in the last year, if he'd told me he'd had enough it would be another story. But he hasn't. He's the same horse. He's shown what he can do at Liverpool. So they'll all have to worry about him. Of course I have a lot of respect for quite a few of the others – for Kilburn, Different Class, Freddie, Highland Wedding. Freddie's a great Aintree horse but his chance

may have gone and I think the one I'd have to fancy apart from my
own is Highland Wedding. But he couldn't do it last year and even
at the difference in weights I don't see why he should do it this
year.'

Winter insists that the strain of training a runner for the
National is far greater than that of riding in it. 'A jockey thinks from
day to day and, although the National is a race on its own, to some
extent it's just another ride. As a trainer you're under strain for at
least three months before the race. Each time you watch the horse
work or you go into the box at evening stables and feel his legs you
suffer some tension.'

He survived the tension well enough to win the race twice in
his first two years as a trainer, a feat which, as Jack Leach says, is
'just not on'. Winter won it twice as a jockey, on Sundew in 1957 and
Kilmore in 1962, but he had a long career as a rider and was top of
the National Hunt table four times, establishing a record total of
121 winners in 1953. He rode in the National about a dozen times.
'But I only remember half of them. Di used to come out and meet
me in some strange places on that course. Dandy Shot is one I won't
forget. He just flew over the first few fences. He was jumping far
too well. We got past Becher's but when we reached the Canal Turn
he had to think for the first time. He gave it a great belt and that was
that.'

Each ride at Aintree taught Winter something but the lessons he
learned with Sundew were special. 'I never considered myself
much of a horseman and when I went to Liverpool I asked the old
hands what it was all about, how you coped with those big fences.
They said "Give 'em a kick in the belly, and make them take off
before they get too close. You've got to stand back here." But when I
applied that with Sundew first time he came down. He was so tall
he could afford to go in close to the jump. All he had to do was pull
his knees up and he popped over.

'Later I noticed that Pat Taaffe used to try to get them back on
their hocks going into the fences. And, let's face it, you couldn't ask
for much better than Taaffe at Aintree. Anyway, the second time
Sundew won by eight lengths. We made most of the running too,
but that was the exception that proves the rule. Usually you want to
settle your horse in behind in the National. There may be 40
runners in the race and a lot of them are ridden by idiots. I don't
want to be rude but the occasion takes over and so many of those

fellows lose their brains. They think they're not going a proper gallop and they push their horses on. By the time the field has gone two miles half of them have had it, maybe 10 of them have blown up and 10 of them have fallen. At three miles, 80 per cent of them have gone or have no chance. So it all comes down to four or five animals. When you've got one like Anglo you're happy to go round quietly and keep out of trouble, let the maniacs murder one another.

'When I won on Kilmore, I settled him well behind and when I was moving up I asked John Lawrence to ease over and give me some room. "Do you mean there's actually somebody behind me?" John said. "Yes," I told him, "and there's something behind me."' Not all Winter's races were as smooth as that one. A painting above the fireplace in his sitting-room shows seven riderless horses leaping a fence. It is called 'Jockey's Nightmare' and symbolises an experience he has gone through often enough.

When he went to ride in America he had to undergo a medical examination. 'I'd been a jockey for 15 years but I had to have it. "Cough" and the lot. A nurse who was filling out a form asked me if I'd broken any bones. "Everything," I said. She said she wasn't joking. I said: "Neither am I. Do you want to start above or below the waist?" In fact, I had a very good run in the game. But I cracked my skull twice and lost two whole years, one with a broken back and one with a broken leg.'

Winter's most legendary achievement was winning the Grand Steeplechase of Paris on Mandarin after the bit had broken in the little horse's mouth. Typically, he plays it down. 'I still had a little control. The bridle stayed over his ears.' That made the task about as easy as walking a tightrope across Niagara in miner's boots.

He kept his nerve and fitness much longer than a National Hunt jockey can hope to keep them. But in 1964, at the age of 37, he decided that he was not giving the service his employers had a right to expect from him. 'It was partly middle-age spread and I hadn't quite as much guts. At my peak I feared nobody, though I worried about Harry Sprague in a finish. As I got older I thought more about horses putting me on the floor. The last time I really rode to my best was at Newbury. I was on Vultrix, and going to the last Jeff King was ahead of me with the race won. He was confident because there was no danger. But suddenly going into that fence I got all the old drive back. I got the bit between my teeth and I gave

Vultrix a clatter and we went flying into that last one. Before Jeff knew what was happening we were past him and had won half a length. I rode four winners that day but I never rode like that again. It was my last season.'

Remembering such moments, Winter is amused by a letter he received from a boy who said he was 20, weighed 10st 6lb, had never ridden anything but beach donkeys but wanted to be a jockey. 'He said his great asset was the strength of his arms. He had been toting around heavy coils of steel wire. I don't know what he thought that had to do with riding horses.'

'Perhaps he thought you wanted a few stopped,' said Jack Leach.

Other people will have to worry about stopping Anglo from winning his second Grand National in succession on Saturday week. As Anglo goes out to defend his title, he could be reassured by the knowledge that he has a useful man in his corner.

The Observer, 26 March 1967

Greatness Against the Odds

In this piece from 1967, Lester Piggott says some interesting things about intending to retire early.

NEARLY EVERYBODY IN Britain knows something about Lester Piggott, but hardly anybody knows very much. At 31 he is securely established as one of the greatest jockeys in the history of horse racing. Millions refer to him simply as Lester. Yet racing men who have been in regular contact with him for almost 20 years admit that they have never got beyond the most superficial knowledge of him.

Some, perhaps defensively cynical, suggest that the part of Piggott on view to the world is all that is worth knowing – that the rest of the iceberg is just ice. But most admit that it is rather more complicated. 'Ask me what makes Lester tick,' says one of them, 'and I could say money, because he has a respect for the green stuff that amounts almost to religion. Or I could say it is a drive to prove himself because he was born with a cleft palate – or whatever that minor impediment is – and a little deaf. But obviously this is all too glib and doesn't get anywhere near the whole truth. Lester is a complex man.'

The point about Piggott's complexity is that it is self-perpetuating. It produces a quality of remoteness that would make a Henry James heroine appear as obtrusively cordial as Hughie Green. He even looks remote. The lank, fairish hair is combed straight back from the pale, thin face. The eyes are light and cool. The mouth is usually pursed in an expression which may not be hostile but is certainly not likely to encourage casual exchanges. He is tall for a flat-race jockey (5 ft 7½ in). On a racecourse, as he walks from the weighing room to the paddock, slim and straight among his shorter, squatter rivals, the impression of aloofness, of a man apart, is strengthened. Even when you are alone with him, he is liable to seem far away.

A big part of the problem is simple shyness, probably stemming originally from the slight abnormality in his speech. He has now overcome this to a great extent (though the voice is still heavily nasal), but his conversation remains ingeniously economical. Involved, 200-word questions will be answered with one syllable. No doubt this is what people who ask involved, 200-word questions deserve. One-syllable questions, however, are likely to get a similar response.

What he does say is invariably relevant. 'Every time he opens his mouth to say something it's worth listening to,' says Jimmy Lindley, himself one of the most intelligent and articulate of English jockeys. 'He can talk sense on any subject and he won't speak at all unless he has a contribution to make.' Everyone who knows Piggott at all well tends to make this vigorous rebuttal of the popular fallacy that he does not say very much because he does not think very much. Richard Baerlein, *The Observer*'s racing correspondent, says that the best way to get a rational account of what happened at a crucial point in a hectic race is to ask Piggott. 'He knows exactly what is happening all the time, where the others are and how they are going.'

Throughout his career the others have rarely been going as well as he has. He was 12 when he rode his first winner, The Chase, on 18 August 1948 at Haydock, and since then he has repeated the performance more than 2,000 times, often in more exotic places from Australia to the Americas to Scandinavia.

He has proved himself a great rider practically wherever horse racing is taken seriously. Several of the famous foreign races he has won more than once and the repetition is even more impressive in his staggering record of success in England. He was only 18 when he first won the Derby on Never Say Die and by the time he was 24 he had won it twice more. The only Classic that has eluded him is the One Thousand Guineas, which is for three-year-old fillies and not one of the categories in which his principal employer over the last 10 years, Noel Murless, has specialised. Piggott has won the St Leger twice and the Oaks three times. He is a prodigy who has stayed the course and he has done it against formidable odds.

Above all, he has overcome the worst disadvantage that can

plague a Flat-race jockey: too much weight. If he lived a normal life he would probably weigh at least 10 stone. By sustained, almost uninterrupted wasting he manages to ride regularly at 8st 6lb, and occasionally for an important assignment, he gets down to 8st 4lb. Despite the physical and mental strain imposed by this discipline, he has been champion jockey for the last three seasons, and last year rode 191 winners, which is appreciably more than the brilliant and much lighter Australian, Scobie Breasley, achieved in any of the four years when he was champion. 'I'll bet if I hadn't taken so many days off to ride in France and so on I could have ridden 200 winners without trying too hard,' Piggott says without conceit. It depends, of course, on what you mean by trying hard.

A former apprentice, Colin Lake, once told me about getting a lift home from the races with him. 'He wore a sweat suit under his clothes in the car and whenever he got in he turned the heater up full,' Lake recalled. 'He reckoned to lose 4 or 5lb by the time he got home. Greville Starkey was in the car with us and we stopped to get some orange to drink but Lester wouldn't hear of it. He's real dedicated.'

Harry Carr, the tough Yorkshireman who was the Queen's jockey for years and could be considered Lester's closest friend on the Turf until he retired, puts it another way: 'He's bloody well killing himself. I've never seen a man take so little liquid into his system. I had a lot of difficulty with weight myself and I had to have an operation for kidney trouble. Lindley is the same. We had to drink special water because of the danger to the kidneys. Lester goes further than any of us at the wasting business. He never lets up. Even in winter he hardly lets his weight go at all. When the rest of the boys are off relaxing somewhere, living pretty well, he's abroad riding in Florida or some place. Even on race days I would always have a couple of lagers afterwards. If we had an afternoon meeting and then a night meeting I'd have a hamper with me and on the plane coming home I'd get settled down with it between my knees and tuck in. Maybe I'd have half a chicken and a half bottle of champagne. Lester would be sitting there beside me with a little drop of black coffee in the bottom of a cup and a sliver of salami between two bits of toast you could hardly see. He'd look across at what I was having and I'd say, "Come on, have something." He'd take one nibble or one sip and go back to his black coffee.'

Piggott himself is philosophical about his weight. 'Wasting's not much fun but maybe it's just as bad being a big fat man. That's not very good either, is it? Naturally, now and again you feel like saying "To hell with it", and I know I won't be able to go on into my fifties the way Gordon Richards and Scobie Breasley could. I know I can't have many more years at the top. I'd certainly expect to pack it in before I'm out of my thirties. But at the moment I feel strong at the weight.' It has begun to seem almost natural until he adds with a smile: 'When I want a really good feed I go up to London.'

His eating habits could obviously be a source of anxiety and frustration for his wife, but Susan Piggott is the daughter of the successful trainer Fred Armstrong and she was brought up to understand the peculiar demands of racing. In the huge, plain kitchen of their unpretentious house near the centre of Newmarket (named Florizel, presumably after the sire of the first Derby winner) Susan has half a dozen cookery books on a shelf, but she refuses to go into detail about the food she cooks for her husband. That is part of his professional life and she insists curtly that it should be discussed with him.

Susan is trim, darkly attractive, exuding the outdoor vitality that helped her ride two winners of the Newmarket Town Plate, the most celebrated Flat race for women riders. But she stays resolutely in the background while Piggott is seeing anyone who has the faintest connection with his work, appearing now and again to retrieve Maureen (six) or Tracy (two) when they threaten to exploit their father's willingness to have them climbing over him. Maureen already rides and has been known to tell her father at a party that he should not have another glass of champagne because he has to make 8st 4lb the next day.

On the morning of a race day, Piggott's mood, as far as the visitor to Florizel can see, is one of almost meditative calm. This morning may be particularly relaxing, for he is going to Beverley, which is in Yorkshire and a long way from Ascot whichever way you look at it. He sits in the front room of the house wearing twill trousers, black buckled shoes, a blue shirt, dark pullover and a jacket of a blue suit. It is a well-used, comfortable room with potted plants in the fireplace, cushion covers that testify to the destructive energy of the children and an assortment of the racing photographs, equestrian statuettes, plaques and other mementoes that spill through the house, including the walls of the nursery.

Piggott is smoking a Havana cigar and looking at the *Sporting*

Life. English and French form books are to hand. It is a mild contradiction of his friends' claim that his usual morning reading is the *Financial Times*. 'When you are away from home with him and at a hotel and you go in early in the morning you find him with that pink paper up in front of his face, a pot of black coffee beside the bed and one of those big cigars in his mouth,' says Carr. 'He lives on those bloody cigars. He can tell you the exchange rate in any part of the world. Jimmy Lindley says if Lester hadn't been champion jockey he'd have been Prime Minister, but that's wrong. He would have been Chancellor of the Exchequer.'

Challenged now with the suggestions that he is a financial genius and has accumulated a million to prove it, Piggott smiles his slow, full smile. 'I only wish I was sharper. How would a jockey make a million? How can you earn a million? I don't think even Gordon Richards with his fantastic career could have done it. Men who sell companies, businessmen, they make the millions. The Government gets too much off us and you don't half spend a bit getting around. We are taxed two years behind, like film stars, so I can't afford to have a bad year.'

Most people believe that Piggott's earnings are also in the film-star bracket. The standard riding fee of £7 per mount ceased to concern him a long time ago. His decision to ride Valoris to win last year's Oaks for the Irish trainer Vincent O'Brien precipitated a break with Noel Murless, the training partner in Piggott's most spectacular successes. So he will be a freelance this year, but his earnings, with gifts from winning owners, will no doubt still be several times the salary of the Prime Minister. And he has a reputation for being able to hold on to what he makes. Other jockeys tell the story of how someone paid Lester a large debt on the racecourse, giving him a huge wad of ready money. Going into the jockeys' room afterwards, Lester turned to a fellow rider and said: 'Lend me a fiver, I'm a bit short.' 'What about that lot you just collected?' the man asked incredulously. 'Oh, I don't want to break into that.'

Piggott is now at the window looking at the sky. He is to be flown to Beverley if the weather holds. If he goes by road to the races he is driven there by a friend or by his wife. A series of brushes with the police over motoring offences has encouraged him to curtail his driving, to replace his Jaguar with a more sedate Austin Westminster. 'Racing people are the best drivers,' he says, 'but they tend to go too fast because they are always in a hurry. Riding races, you get used to judging relative speeds, so you can gauge distances accurately on the road.'

Those who have driven with him agree that his handling of a car is incredible. Someone who has driven with both Fangio and Stirling Moss says that on the road Piggott was more impressive than either. But again it is Carr who is the most interesting cross-reference. His admiration and affection for Piggott are immense ('For my money, he's just the best rider who ever got up on a horse, anywhere, any time – I'm all for Lester'), but he views the younger man with the mildly amused eye of experience. 'Lester used to be a magnificent, insane driver. He took years off my life driving me to the races. It was like going by jet. I'm a good reader in a car and the faster he went the lower I slid down behind my book. But he got to be too much even for me. You had the feeling that he was liable to go round the wrong side of a lamp-post or do a U-turn on a motorway if it saved time. You'd be 75 miles from Birmingham racecourse with an hour to do it and Lester would say we would stroll it. His control was marvellous but in the finish my heart wouldn't stand it. When he said, "I'll drive you to the races," I said, "No, I'll drive you," and that's what we did.'

Piggott has decided that he will be able to fly to Beverley but he is still preoccupied, drifting round the room, looking at letters, reaching to answer the telephone every few minutes with laconic, scarcely audible responses. He conducts almost all his own business, arranging rides and terms from week to week. He usually goes abroad alone. He may be seen at an airport on a Sunday morning, a solitary figure with a riding whip protruding from his travelling bag.

At last he sits down on a settee with his cigar and begins to talk quietly about what riding means to him. 'My father was a jockey and a trainer; my grandfather was a jockey and a trainer. I had no option. I had to ride early. I started when I was about four. If I had been too heavy to ride on the Flat I'd have been a jump jockey. That's all there is to it.' He speaks with an unquestioning sincerity that conveys a sense of destiny. It is understandable, for he was bred to ride horses. His grandfather won the Grand National three times; his father was a first-class National Hunt rider before he took up training. On his mother's side he is a Rickaby: his uncle won the One Thousand Guineas four times; the jockey Bill Rickaby is a cousin.

True to his father's traditions, Lester prefers the jumping side of the sport and whenever he gets a chance he watches it avidly on television. It is widely accepted that Keith Piggott's rugged attitudes gave his son the determined will to win which put him in trouble with the stewards early in his career. 'I got a bad name. I did some things I shouldn't have done, but I got blamed for things I didn't do. I tried too hard to win. Some of the older riders were a bit resentful, but that was natural. They've got to look after themselves.'

He is much more restrained now, but he is not a man anyone would trifle with. For all his icily composed exterior, there is a hint of potential turbulence about him. In his bachelor days he came back from Scandinavia to be met by a swarm of journalists and photographers who had heard whispers of a romance. Again Carr is the witness: 'He went crazy. If he'd got hold of some of those fellows he'd have killed them. He was using words I didn't even think he knew.'

On the course, Piggott has suffered his own share of turbulence in the form of falls. He broke a leg and his collar bone in a bad one at Lingfield, and before that he had broken the collar bone as well as cracking a shoulder riding jumps. His nose has been fractured three times. 'But it doesn't show much,' he says, fingering the bone.

Unexpectedly, he becomes technical: 'I ride rather short, with my stirrup leathers shortened. People say they can tell how well I'm going by how far my behind is stuck up in the air. It's just that I'm a big person, bigger than most of the other jockeys. I can't roll myself up into a ball. In any case, you can't copy great jockeys. The best I've seen are Gordon Richards here, Eddie Arcaro in America and Yves St Martin in France. All completely different. The thing people say about me knowing how the other jockeys are going comes with experience, from having ridden against them often. It's like playing football with the same people. You get to know roughly what they will do in a given situation. I don't talk to horses, but I do try to humour them if they don't want to go. When you really ask them to go they either do or they don't. Lots of them don't want to try. It's a mystery why they don't. It's a nonsense to say I treat them as machines to win races. Jockeys in this country are a lot more considerate than the riders abroad.'

Piggott likes water-skiing and shooting and lately he has been trying to take up golf. But he hardly has time for anything but racing. 'Anyway, there is nothing like the excitement of race riding. It's like nothing else in the world.'

'You know, Lester has this dream,' says Harry Carr. 'Says that when he retires from riding he's going to have a villa in the South of France and a yacht and lie in the sun to make up for all the years of sacrifice. But that is only a dream. Lester could never stay away from horses.'

The Observer, 9 April 1967

All Right Jack!

FORTY YEARS AGO this weekend Jack Leach, having shed protesting flesh by means about as painless as cutting it off with a butcher's knife, weighed eight-and-a-half stone and was riding work on Newmarket Heath. He was looking forward to partnering a lightly built, rather leggy colt named Adam's Apple in the Two Thousand Guineas the following Wednesday, if only because all colts in the race are set to carry the undemanding weight of nine stone.

The other day in Skindles Hotel, which is a straight five furlongs from his home in Maidenhead (if you happen to have a sprinter that can jump the Thames), Jack stimulated the memory of those wasting days by inflicting spectacular damage on a formidable lunch. He is 65 now but he looks fresher than a few who will be given a leg up at Newmarket shortly after three o'clock on Wednesday. And his mind still goes a good gallop over any ground.

Of course, it needs no encouragement to go back to Adam's Apple. He jumped off in front, was never more than four lengths behind the leader and came out of The Dip with a splendid rush to beat Call Boy, the Guineas favourite and future Derby winner, by a short head. 'The first thing I remember seeing when I came back to the unsaddling enclosure was Fred Astaire grinning all over his face and jumping about like a wild man,' Leach recalled. 'He'd been staying with me and insisted he was going to back mine, but I said: "Don't be a mug all your life – Call Boy's a certainty." When I came out of the weighing-room after the race, he said: "You don't think I'd listen to you, do you? I had a tenner on you at twenties."

'Mind you, I should have known we had a hell of a chance after riding Adam's Apple in his final gallop. I'd never sat on him until Harry Cottrill, Humphrey's father, got me down to Lambourn 10 days before the Guineas. We tried him over a severe bit of ground called The Farringdon Road Gallop and at the end of about six-and-a-half furlongs I thought that was it and eased him up. He had won the gallop easily.

'Then I suddenly noticed Cottrill standing about another furlong and a half further on, up a bloody steep hill. I had to get Adam's Apple going again but he still won easily. I didn't tell Harry about my blunder in case it had done the horse some harm. In fact it did the opposite, for he was as fit as a flea for the Guineas. He was some miler that day, the best mover I ever rode apart from Nothing Venture, and he could run on anything from that road outside to mud up to the earholes. One of the great things about Adam's Apple was that he settled down so easily. And he did a thing I'd never known any other horse do. He had a good look at the uprights of the other starting gates, easing up a shade as he passed them and giving himself just the slightest breather each time. It made him a perfect ride. Not like Hot Night, who went far too freely for Harry Wragg's liking. If he went like that with Harry I don't know what he'd have done with anyone else because Harry was the best I've ever known at settling them down.

'He damn near stole the Guineas on Mirza, and it never did get more than six furlongs. He waited and waited, past the Bushes, down into The Dip and out of it again and he was still waiting. Then, with a hundred yards to go, he slipped out from behind the leader and went. I said, "Christ, he's going to wish this one home". But Mirza died on him just before the line. As it was, Harry had performed a miracle. It just wasn't on for Mirza to be with them at that stage. He was a bloody magician, that Wragg. He's the sort of man I'd like to see on Prendergast's colt Bold Lad. The last time I saw that one he ran much too freely and the jockey had to pull and haul him about in the early stages of the race. He won because he was much the best horse, but in my opinion those tactics are wrong – if a horse won't settle down it's better to let him run along for a bit, then he may settle without struggling and I believe that you can pull a horse slow if you fight against him.

'I don't think Bold Lad will win the Guineas. There's a doubt about his stamina and don't let anybody tell you that the Rowley Mile is for sprinters. It takes all the getting. That last rise up to the post may not look much from the stands but when you're on one that doesn't quite get the trip it looks like a bloody mountain.

'I think Noel Murless will win it with Royal Palace. They say he's not really being trained for the Guineas but for the Derby. If a horse is going to win the Derby he's bloody well got to be fit to go a mile by Guineas time. I think this one could be a bit like Crepello, and he won both. Crepello was another case that strengthened my feeling that modern trainers go too easy on their horses. Noel wouldn't run him in the King George VI and Queen Elizabeth at Ascot because he thought the going was a little dubious, then the horse broke down at home a fortnight later. He'd have been as well breaking down running for brass, as old Matt Peacock would have said.

'Of course, if their legs aren't sound they'll break down eventually whatever you do. You can take it easy on them at home, cantering them four or five miles rather than risking hard gallops, even swimming them as I did with one I trained that had dicky legs. I asked old Reg Day how long I should swim him and he said 15 or 20 minutes, but when I asked Frank Bullock he said: "A minute – if you swim him a minute and a half he'll be weary; if you swim him three minutes he'll be drowned." Reg, of course, was thinking about sea swimming. But Frank knew I was going to a lake near Thetford. Anyway, when we went out in a boat with the horse on a great long lunging rein, he nearly drowned us. He decided to get in the boat with us and he was a bit too big for that. However, it all worked. The swimming saved him two gallops a week and we got him to the races sound.'

I will be with Jack at the races next Wednesday and I don't think I will be taking any bets on which of us is the sounder. Certainly not if Fred Astaire is around.

The Observer, 30 April 1967

Golden Day for a Deserving Case

IF PAUL KELLEWAY'S bank manager is still celebrating the result of the Cheltenham Gold Cup it is not merely because he had a pound each way on What a Myth.

'That one was needed, I'll tell you – bloody financially,' Kelleway said with a sideways grimace as he drove towards a single modest ride at Lingfield on the morning after his old ally had taken full advantage of Domacorn's insistence on hitting every available obstacle. 'What with the weather, and me being a second-string jockey anyway, I've had 23 rides since the middle of December and at 12 quid a time, plus 10 per cent of the stakes for any winners, it doesn't add up to a rich living. It's a tough old game, this racing.'

National Hunt racing happens to be a tougher game for Paul Kelleway than for many less talented riders. The briefest scrutiny of his career shows that Thursday's thrilling victory, and his share of the £8,000 prize, could not have gone to a more deserving case. Having been introduced to stable routine as an evacuee in Doncaster, he suffered the disappointment of finding his apprenticeship as a Flat jockey with Harry Wragg at Newmarket ended by growing weight and then had the misfortune to arrive in Ryan Price's Sussex yard at the same time as Josh Gifford. 'I actually rode three winners for the old man before Josh got one home but he had made a bit of a name on the Flat and that was that. Josh became second in line to Freddie Winter and I had to be content with the leavings.'

Even for an Islington-born Yorkshireman of Anglo-Irish and Welsh stock it was a discouraging situation, but Kelleway stuck six years of it before packing his bag. 'In 1963, after that terrible freeze-up, I rang Britt Gallup and said, "Hey, do you want your head lad back?" My wife Jill had been his head lad before we got married the previous June. So I said, "You can have your head lad back and a bloody jockey as well." I rode about 10 winners for him, including that horse Tunbridge Wells that was owned by the town. But I think maybe Gallup took us on more because of the wife than me. She's wonderful with horses. In fact, she's the best rider I know, my wife. She sits a horse better than I do.'

His pride in his wife is understandable. She remains beautifully slim after bearing him three children and her vivacious, delicate features contradict the ancient canard about the effect that a fanatical affection for horses has on a woman's appearance. There is, too, good and recent cause for him to respect her skill on horseback. It concerns Cracker Box, a semi-retired show jumper of vast seniority who shares Kelleway's 12 acres near Findon with a handful of racehorses he is nursing back to soundness for their owners. When the BBC sponsored a televised show-jumping competition for National Hunt jockeys the other week Mrs Kelleway was sure that Cracker Box had only to make the long journey to Stoneleigh in Warwickshire to collect the money. 'She had won just about everything she had gone in for with him, right up to a ladies' Flat race at Horsham Show, and she couldn't see how I could lose,' he recalls shamefacedly. 'But he's a free old sod and I had always got the impression that he was pissing off with the missus, so I decided to steady him. I steadied him so much that he refused at the first. She went spare, the wife did. And the other boys in the changing-room at the racecourse have kidded me rotten. It was the joke of the year. No horse had ever refused with me on the racecourse in my life. I won't come without them. I've got a reputation for handling awkward horses, for being difficult to shift from the saddle and really kicking them into their fences, for being willing to have a go at anything.'

It was Kelleway's knack of establishing a profitable relationship with unco-operative horses – something that had been developing since the days when Eddie Magner was patiently helping him to master the basics of riding technique back in Doncaster – which persuaded Captain Price to approach him, in February 1965, to ride What a Myth at Wincanton. They took second place there and by the November of that year Kelleway had left Syd Dale to rejoin Price's stable at Findon. He had been away slightly more than two years.

His partnership with What a Myth, which has been by far the most rewarding episode in his riding career, was incredibly successful in the 1965–66 season. The chestnut gelding won five races in a row, including the valuable Rhymney Breweries Chase at Chepstow, and then recovered magnificently from a taxing run in the Grand National (he fell at Becher's second time round when going well) to win the Whitbread Gold Cup. The story of the following season was mainly one of honourable failure behind such as Arkle, Mill House and Stalbridge Colonist, who just ran him out of second place in the Gold Cup won by Woodland Venture.

Victories at Plumpton and Huntingdon were all that could be achieved in 1967–68 and when Price was content to let the 12-year-old dominate a couple of hunter chases earlier this year it seemed that he had no future in the major events. But as the Gold Cup drew near and the ground became softer and softer, Kelleway urged his trainer to let What a Myth make another challenge. Price was not hard to convince. He had never lost faith in the horse's ability to land him his first Gold Cup. In doing so, What a Myth took his own total of successes to 21 (10 under Kelleway) and his gross winnings to around £40,000. 'And the great thing is that we got the big one with a lot less trouble than we've had in moderate races. He used to hit the odd fence so hard that his jock was fired up round his neck or beyond. But he gave me a wonderful ride on Thursday. Of course, it's the first time for ages that the ground has been really right for him. He likes mud up to the withers.

'The only anxious moment I had in the Gold Cup was when Stalbridge Colonist fell. The old horse took the dead needle when he saw Stalbridge go. He started pulling faces and jerking his head back and one ear lay down in a funny way. I slapped him on the right side of the neck with one open hand, then on the left side with the other. "Go on, you old bugger," I said and he straightened up and got on with it.'

Kelleway admires jockeys who can get the best out of their mounts by using their hands and heels, 'by coaxing and kidding them'. He thinks Freddie Winter and Bill Rees are probably the finest National Hunt riders he has seen, considers Jeff King outstanding among those who are most prominent today. His general prejudice against amateurs ('A lot of them couldn't sit up in bed straight') becomes particularly contemptuous when he talks about their vigour with the whip. 'You see them charge into a fence with that stick up in the clouds. It's idiotic. That old stick is all right but as Harry Wragg used to say, if they don't go for one good belt they won't go for 20.'

A short, sturdy man of 28 who crams a lot into his 10 stones, Kelleway has strong black hair, and dark eyes and an aggressive chin that give immediate warning of bluntness. 'I'm not a fanny merchant. I don't give owners or trainers the tale. If a horse is a bastard I say so. I may not get the ride next time but we know where we stand.'

His ambition is to train but before he turns to that he hopes to add considerably to the 161 winners he has ridden. That perfect ending to What a Myth's racing career may have marked a new beginning for Paul Kelleway. If there is any justice in the world, his bank manager should continue to smile.

The Observer, 23 March 1969

Irish Switch on the Sun

FOR A LONG time at Cheltenham last week it seemed that the Irish horses had declared a truce to leave room for an English initiative. It was a situation that worried many people, not least a man in the bar opposite the paddock who wore a lapel badge identifying him as a member of the Northern Ireland Former Boxers' Association. Any unlikely doubts about his hardness were dispelled when he ordered a large sherry with a lager chaser, then readily held out the beer to have it charged with a hefty injection of champagne. 'This is the worst bunch of Irish horses I've ever seen here,' he said, strengthening the condemnation with the rawness of the Belfast accent. 'If things keep going like this we'll have to leave a special parcel among those bookmakers on the rails.'

The bitterness behind the macabre joke had been fed by a Tuesday afternoon on which the Irish could find nothing to praise but the weather. They had smiled indulgently when the two moderate hurdlers they entered in the first race of the meeting were left among the debris. But there was noisy concern when Straight Fort, from the stable that sent Arkle out to make good steeple-chasers look like dray-horses, staggered in as an odds-on third in the National Hunt Champion Chase. And the oaths multiplied when Sea Brief, another who treads the fields that nourished Arkle, was backed down to 6-4 in the big race of the day and then ran as if he were going towards the edge of a cliff. By the last race on Tuesday, even the priests who invade Cheltenham like a holy army were losing faith in Ireland's cause. There was a five-year-old gelding from across the water called Noble Life in the Gloucester Hurdle but his colours were black and tan and what Irishman in his right mind would support such a combination? Noble Life was left at a neglected 16-1 but that did not prevent him from lunging into contention a few yards from the winning post. The public address system announced that he was in a photo-finish with Comedy of Errors but those of us who had backed Comedy of Errors felt a fearful certainty about the result. 'What do you lay Noble Life in the photo?' we asked John Banks. 'Next race,' he said.

Coming away from the course, we were in no danger of agreeing with the American who declared that Ireland should be towed out to a point south-west of the Azores and quietly torpedoed. Poverty is no excuse for racism.

On the way from Cirencester to Cheltenham on the Wednesday morning we noticed for the first time a signpost to Kilkenny. One could only assume that it was a settlement formed by Irish punters who were left without the homeward fare. The first race on Wednesday was bound to be full of hope and nostalgia. It was the Arkle Challenge Trophy and J.T.R. Dreaper, the son of the man who trained that miraculous animal, was represented by Colebridge, winner of his last three races and widely held to be a remarkable talent. 'He's flying now,' an optimistic Irish voice yelled as they came down the hill into the straight. 'I tell you, he's another Arkle.'

'I'll tell you what he is,' said a less ecstatic brogue beside the shouter. 'He's a million to one.' He was, for the English Pendil was cruising in as comfortably as a pleasure steamer approaching a pier. Fred Winter trains Pendil, but he could afford to regard the seven-year-old's success as his secondary pleasure on Wednesday. His principal satisfaction came from Bula, the best hurdler in the world. Bula went through the field in the Champion Hurdle as though they were going the other way. He is a beautiful, irresistible machine and he deserved every decibel of the Cup Final cheers that accompanied his surge up the hill to the line. For a few hours impoverishment seemed unimportant and our spirits were raised further in the Queen's Hotel by a tiny, bald priest who said he was a Limerick man and kept producing ribald rhymes to prove it. 'I've got to have dinner tonight with a terrible pious woman,' he said. 'And I'm not feeling at all pious. What the hell can I tell her?'

We suggested that he should tell her the winner of the next day's Gold Cup. As it happened, we could have told her that, for our faith in Glencarrig Lady, who fell last year when she appeared to be carrying our money to victory, was about to be vindicated. The Lady outfought The Dikler up that exhausting gradient to the line and stayed resolutely ahead of Royal Toss. Her gallantry entitled her to survive the turmoil of objections that followed the race. We were on her at sixes and suddenly the sun was several degrees warmer.

It was Chesterton who said that the great Gaels of Ireland are the race that God made mad, 'for all their wars are merry, and all their songs are sad'. No fight is merrier than Ireland's three-day war with the Cheltenham bookmakers and the song we were singing at the end of it was not at all sad.

The Observer, 19 March 1972

After all the Vitriol,
What a Winner

This account of the Derby of 1972 was written on deadline for the Daily Express.

WHEN ALL THE vitriol had been spilled, the finish had been fought, the inquiry held, and the booty divided, the one inevitable winner at Epsom yesterday was the Derby itself. It remains the greatest stayer in racing, the big one that never lets you down. And its excitement and fascination are only increased by little things like an American millionaire's willingness to slap Bill Williamson in the face in order to let Lester Piggott slap a horse called Roberto on the rump.

Bitterness left by the abrupt unseating of Williamson, one of the most brilliant and popular jockeys ever to come out of Australia, may have muted the cheers that met Roberto as he came back into the winner's enclosure, but even those who begrudged Piggott his sixth Epsom Derby (a record equalled only by Jem Robinson between 1817 and 1836) were glad they were there to see the deed done, whether they regarded it as historic or merely dirty. Williamson and his admirers had adequate consolation. Willie, who sometimes looks about as cheerful as a man trying to get a cyanide capsule out from behind his teeth, allowed his thin face to be invaded by a smile before the end of the meeting. He had watched Piggott earn him £6,000 and then gone on to beat two short-priced favourites ridden by the Englishman. To win on his only two rides of the day was a fair performance for a man who had lost his Derby mount because he was considered to be still shakily convalescent after a fall. 'I'm happy for all of us,' Williamson said cryptically.

There could have been no more sensible reaction, for most of the informed watchers in the stands yesterday had to agree that no jockey ever born could have ridden the bay colt better, however much they disapproved of the way Piggott came to ride Roberto. In matters of subtlety and refinement of balance and timing, Williamson yields to no jockey, but he does not drive with the almost terrible strength of Piggott and it was driving that Roberto required. After Rheingold had gone about a neck in front 300 yards out, he seemed to be moving well enough to stay there. But on the run to the line Piggott rode like a man possessed. Roberto, who is named after Roberto Clemente, one of the biggest hitters in American baseball, could have been forgiven at that point for thinking his namesake was on his back, complete with bat. But the horse responded magnificently and at the post he was the width of a distended nostril in front of Rheingold.

Having suffered the tension of one of the closest finishes the Derby has known, Mr John Galbreath, the owner whose change of riding arrangements had caused so much acrimony, had to wait for the result of a stewards' inquiry. He and his Irish trainer, Vincent O'Brien, a horseman of genius who could pass for a country doctor, spent the time making diplomatic noises about the decision to replace Williamson. 'I have had a lot of experience of athletes,' said Mr Galbreath. 'The baseball team I own, the Pittsburgh Pirates, has just won the World Series. I know something about fitness and I am convinced that no sportsman who has been completely out of action for about 10 days, as Williamson was, can be 100 per cent fit. It was that factor and nothing else that brought about the switch.'

O'Brien, squinting into the sun that was winning its running fight with clouds and rain, concurred and added a simple tribute: 'Lester Piggott gave Roberto a beautiful race.'

Mr Galbreath, ignoring assurances that his horse had been innocent of any felony in the straight, had begun to worry about what the stewards were doing. 'The longer it goes the scareder I get,' he said. But the alert, brown face under the grey top hat looked impressively composed. He is a 74-year-old who is not easily flustered. 'I'm not going to say whether the World Series gave me more of a thrill than this has,' said Mr Galbreath. 'But what I will say is that anyone who doesn't consider the Epsom Derby one of the greatest sports events in the world must be out of his mind.'

He was not about to get an argument from me. The Derby is one of the last genuine folk festivals left to us. We used to have quite a number of events in sport that had that quality, but most of them have been diminished, mainly by television. With each succeeding Cup Final, Wembley Stadium becomes more and more like a TV studio and the same process is taking place elsewhere throughout the sporting year. But there is no lens wide enough or screen big enough to take in the uniqueness of the Derby, the ritual and razzmatazz and throbbing public excitement of it all. A comparison with Ascot makes the point. Ascot, for all the magnificence of the racing, often suffers the disadvantages of an open-air cocktail party. It is coiffured, decorated and deodorised, its stuffiness jealously protected by an army of belligerent gatemen and petty officials. Those men, who give the impression of having nearly made sergeant-major, seem to divide their time between touching forelocks to the privileged and feeling the collar of anyone who looks as if he has less than 50 grand in the biscuit tin. Epsom has a sprinkling of top hats and morning suits, but the wholesome, happy coarseness of the crowd wins through. Here the people take over. Whether they are drinking champagne on the tops of buses or scrummaging for light ales, watching the two-headed dwarf or being conned by tipsters who couldn't have backed a winner in the Six-Day War, the quarter of a million who go to the Downs on Derby day are somehow bound together by the experience. The people matter more than the clothes at the Derby. It is an occasion with sweat in its armpits.

No wonder the result was officially posted in Daily Orders during the Crimean War, no wonder an MP once moved in the Commons that the House should adjourn for the Derby. He and Mr Galbreath would have got on well together. Mr Galbreath would not get on badly with John Banks either. Banks, the Glasgow bookmaker and failed recluse, looked at me when I had £1 on Our Mirage as if I had just backed myself to ride over Niagara Falls in a plastic mac. When I had rather more on Yaroslav and Lyphard, he was no more impressed. He was right, of course, and after the race one had to endorse his eulogies of the Long Fellow, Lester Piggott. 'There's so much rubbish talked about what happened over that ride,' said Banks. 'You saw the proof today in that last furlong. Old Bill is a great jockey but he couldn't have done that job. No one but Lester could.'

Lester did not have to say anything about his own performance. As soon as the field came round Tattenham Corner, with the vivid silks strung out in the sunshine like a Harlequin's laundry, Lester was ready to make his statement. As so often before, there was no answer to it.

Daily Express, 8 June 1972

The Shropshire Nag

Oh I have been to Ludlow Fair
And left my necktie God knows where

MR A.E. HOUSMAN should have gone to Ludlow races, and tried holding on to his shirt. The poet's ashes, resting in a nearby churchyard, may have stirred gently in sympathy around three o'clock on Wednesday afternoon as Marungu, backed to 5-2 on in a three-horse steeplechase, came home a weary, once-paced second. An hour before, an 11-year-old called The Spaniard, also asked to beat two opponents, had been made 11-4 on to do the job. He went under by a short head to Jimmy Bourke on Miss Dorothy Squires's Esban and even that lady's traditional reception of her heroes, which involves scattering kisses like moistened buckshot, could not drown the groaning of the wounded.

By the time Marungu's failure had taken its toll, the misty Shropshire air was loud with talk of atrocities and strong men were wondering if the Geneva Convention could be applied to National Hunt racing. Some of the worst sufferers were battle-toughened punters from the urban Midlands. At an ordinary Flat race meeting the invisible handcuffs forged by long experience would have kept them from laying such dubious odds – odds that were made even less attractive by the inroads of betting tax. But here in the friendly and historic countryside, under a tiny stand with the pillared and fretted facade of a Victorian railway station, they succumbed to the rustic charm of it all. For a few light-headed moments they seemed to imagine that they were at one of those point-to-points where odds-on favourites are safe from practically all hazards short of a well-aimed hand grenade. So they went over the top and were mown down while the more venerable of the local farmers, rosy and whiskered and dateless, watched them with the ambivalent sympathy a fox might give to a lemming.

On past form, I should have been with the lemmings but this day was different. I had not gone to Ludlow as a mug. I had gone as an owner. Well, as a surrogate owner, second class. To come clean, two friends of mine own a hurdler called Overall and, since one of them was in the Canaries and the other was showing a moving sense of duty by staying at his desk in the *Daily Express* office, I was elected travelling representative.

Looking up Ludlow on the map, one had the impression that the trip would take about three hours in a Boeing 747. But the prospect was irresistible. Apart from all its other attractions, this sortie would keep me away from some of the predictable temptations of my first week back in sports writing, such as running off at the mouth and the ballpoint about Brian Clough, that alternately admirable and exasperating man whose dramas have become slightly less riveting than the music of Syncopating Sandy, the marathon piano player. Anyway, I reflected on the drive up through stone-built villages that make grey seem the warmest colour in the world, the Flat was ending this weekend. National Hunt racing was about to resume its winter monopoly, to demonstrate again its popularity and confirm that it holds an important place among the sporting pleasures of the nation. Before we reached Worcester I was musing on all the statistics that made a journey to Ludlow on an overcast Wednesday in October an essential contribution to any serious analysis of leisure activities in the early Seventies. Had not the man at William Hill's assured me that their volume of betting, which once diminished spectacularly at the close of the Flat, is now reduced by a mere 15 or 20 per cent when the jumpers take over? Had not the Racing Information Bureau reported that attendances at National Hunt meetings in 1972 numbered 1,419,971 despite the competition of 16,000 betting shops and endless coverage of the sport on television? Yes, they had.

But by the time we pulled into Ludlow racecourse, I had owned up. My presence in Shropshire had nothing to do with facts and figures or the rising status of National Hunt racing. I had been towed there by a fantasy. Ever since I learned to read a form line (surely one of the vital uses of literacy that Richard Hoggart neglected) I have fantasised privately about being an owner. Now, for a day, I had a licence to play the game in public. Most of my daydreams have had Epsom as their setting, with Lester and my champion three-year-old treating the Derby field as a shark might treat a shoal of mackerel. Overall is a four-year-old gelding and he was running in a novice hurdle worth £204 to the winner, but I was happy enough to carry his banner. Wearing my owner's badge like a breastplate, I was testing the ground before I was halfway out of the car. Overall doesn't like the firm and I was relieved to find my heel sinking in an inch or so. 'This will do us,' I said professionally. 'Yes,' said my companion, 'if they run the race through the car park he's a good thing.'

I gave him a brief glare and went in search of Richard Smith, who was to ride for me, I mean us or even them. Smith, a farmer's son who was champion amateur rider before he started bringing in winners for money, is thin-faced and intense and not inclined to be garrulous. The ground was a shade firmish, he said, but it wouldn't be a problem. I began to flex my punting hand as I went to meet Jenny Kennard, the wife of Overall's trainer. Les Kennard had urgent business at the Newmarket sales and had delegated Jenny to bring the horse up from Taunton. She turned out to be a pleasant, lively lady with much of the West Country practicality and horse sense that have made her husband a telling force around the circuit. Still wearing her smart mauve coat and white fur hat, she moved in briskly to prepare Overall for his work. The little, light-framed horse stood with the dignity of a bullfighter being dressed for the ring while the saddle was strapped on him and the girths were tightened. He looked reserved, but no more humble than he had a right to be after winning the second of his two previous hurdle races by 12 lengths at Wincanton. He is no scrubber and Mrs Kennard agreed that he should be able to give weight and a beating to the 18 hurdlers against him. She gave his face a last wipe with a wet sponge, then squeezed it in his mouth, saying with a laugh: 'A drop of gin and tonic before you go.'

I telephoned my friend in Fleet Street with the reassurance and we made our concerted assault on the enemy. We took a little 2-1, a little 15-8 and quite a lot of 7-4 and left the masses with the evens. I am inclined to describe every stride of the two miles, one furlong and 20 yards of the race but we triumphant owners must preserve a sense of modesty. It is enough to say that when Overall came to the line Richard Smith was holding sufficient leather to make a pair of training gloves for Muhammad Ali, and it would have taken the Jodrell Bank telescope to find the rest of the field.

Mrs Kennard, Mrs Smith and the rest of us who could be considered what Richard Baerlein loves to call 'the connections' swilled a little champagne, as connections do, and set off happily for home. On the way I had to be forcibly restrained from stopping to make phone calls to Vincent O'Brien and John Mulcahy. I would like to make them aware that if they need someone to lead in Apalachee when the colt wins next year's Guineas and Derby, I am their man.

The Observer, 4 November 1973

Apalachee went wrong, but that day with Overall remains perfect in the memory.

Calling the Horses Home

PETER O'SULLEVAN IS widely accepted as the best horse-racing commentator in the history of broadcasting and possibly the most accomplished reader of action operating on any sport in the English-speaking world. His admirers are convinced that had he been on the rails at Balaclava he would have kept pace with the Charge of the Light Brigade, listing the fallers in precise order and describing the riders' injuries before they hit the ground.

'Compared with him,' said Lester Piggott, 'all the rest are amateurs.' Obviously it would be naive to expect a contrary opinion from Brian Cowgill, Head of BBC Sport and Outside Broadcasts, who has fought long and successfully to guard his star against the wooing attentions of Independent Television. But Cowgill's enthusiasm is of a kind that cannot be explained by self-interest. He sounds as close to being awed as a Lancastrian could be when he says: 'I've worked with O'Sullevan, man and boy, for 25 years and I've never known the bugger to be wrong. The man is an experts' expert. There are many others who have more to say before and after a race but while the horses are running he is on his own, without a rival. Between the starting stalls and the winning line Peter is Holy Writ. I tell you the bugger's just never wrong.'

On hearing such a tribute at second-hand, O'Sullevan winces behind the heavy rims of his glasses. 'It's marvellous that one's guvnor should say things like that, and I won't be sending any letters of protest to Brian but, of course, it's all bull really. My own awareness of just how fallible I am makes me try like hell to take out insurance against disaster. I go to all sorts of lengths to get a proof of the race card the night before a meeting, then I paste it on to cardboard and draw in the silks of the owners in coloured pencil opposite each horse. In some races over the jumps, where the fields are large and many of the animals and their riders comparatively unknown, the process of memorising can be desperate. Maybe I overdo the homework but I don't want to leave myself any excuse for a balls-up. I'm terrible for forgetting people's names at parties but I always say that if they came in wearing crossbelts and a spotted cap I'd get them right without any trouble.'

Neither his own thoroughness nor the absolute faith of those who work with him can relieve O'Sullevan of the nervous agony that has always accompanied his preparation for major commentaries. He no longer has the severe attacks of diarrhoea he once endured, often right up to starting time, but says he is not beyond having a mild case of the trots, especially before a Grand National. 'That one always gets me choked up, far more so than a Derby or anything else on the Flat. Mind you, it would be impossible for me not to get excited watching any horse race. I think it is so beautiful, so dramatic. That's one reason I'm glad to have a special viewing apparatus with a powerful pair of naval binoculars fixed into metal supports and angled lenses that allow me to stand and look down into them. I always read a race direct through glasses, not from a screen, but if I tried to hold a pair of bins they would vibrate in my hands as if electricity was going through them.'

Fortunately for everyone interested in racing, he keeps coming up for the next ordeal, and not merely because of the £175 a day the BBC pay him on a minimum of 40 working days a year. As a prodigiously informed and experienced racing journalist (his partnership with Clive Graham in the *Daily Express* is reckoned by our own award-winner Richard Baerlein to represent the highest standard of work in the field) he shares the frustrations of many another newspaperman and says that broadcasting offers an excellent release. The technicians who find themselves targets for O'Sullevan's impatience are rewarded by his almost flawless performances, consoled by the certainty that he is harder on himself than on anyone else. He goes on his twice-yearly holidays in the knowledge that his last few nights away from commentating will be marred by recurring nightmares about his return. 'In my dreams a race is suddenly being led by a horse that should not be there, one I have never seen before. Or it may be worse and I will see 20 totally unfamiliar horses, 20 anonymous sets of riding silks coming towards me. I wake up in a sweat.' These glimpses of a black apprehension will astonish many among the millions of racing enthusiasts who regard him as Mr Cool, a man whose voice can stay calm, mellifluous and charged with relevant information in the most hectic finish – and did so even when his own great sprinter Be Friendly was getting up to win £5,000 by a short head. But Peter O'Sullevan has been in deeper tunnels, darker places, than those provided by dreams.

Seeing him now at 55, a tall, slim, handsome figure, with his silver hair swept back from a strong profile and down on to the velvet collar of his overcoat, a man who catches the eye of most women and instantly commands the deferential attentions of waiters, it is hard to believe there were years when he sought the shadows as resolutely as the Phantom of the Opera. Those years, when his face and his confidence were blighted by a virulent form of acne, shaped his view of life. They created the paradox of an apparently remote personality, a natural loner who drives from the racecourse in his Jaguar almost before the sweat has dried on the horses and yet is vibrant company for anyone who penetrates the outer stockade. Strangely, considering that it was ability on the football field that swung his admission into Charterhouse, he suffered from asthma even before leaving his birthplace in County Kerry. At the age of 16 he was taken to Switzerland, where he acquired the French that has been so useful to him ever since and found some ease from asthma. Sadly, the nervous implications of that disease culminated in the outbreak of acne. It became so bad that he spent most of one year in the Middlesex Hospital.

'They wanted me to leave because they couldn't do any more for me but I didn't want to go. Once out of the hospital, I used to find the coffee bars and milk bars where the lights were dimmest. I could still take on most taxi drivers when it comes to knowledge of London. That was an indescribably painful period of my life but I am convinced that a serious illness, for anyone who comes out of it in reasonable shape, can be a profoundly enriching experience. It forces you back on your own resources, makes you examine yourself and your life more honestly than you might otherwise do. My experiences, for instance, took me further into literature than I might ever have been and taught me an appreciation of the visual arts which may not be acute but is an important sustaining element in my life. Having no direct communication with fellow human beings, I resorted to inanimate forms of communication such as painting. I still find visiting galleries a marvellous restorative, far better than going for a drink. And I say that as someone who loves wine.'

The love of wine and the love of art are equally in evidence in the flat in Chelsea where O'Sullevan lives with his wife Pat and their poodle. Some of his favourite pictures he bought from his friend John Skeaping after they got skint at White City dogs 32 years ago. He met Pat rather later, in 1946, long after what happened to him as an ambulance driver with the Rescue Service during the blitz had begun his progress towards a cure. 'I was rated as a daredevil but the truth is that at first I didn't care whether or not a bomb or building fell on me. Then I realised that other people could be nervous, that I could have the respect of other people, and I began to come out and lead a full life.'

He has certainly done that in the last 20 years. His career as a racing journalist, which he had already decided upon by the age of eight, and as a broadcaster, which he jeopardised by tossing a bemused BBC executive double or nothing over the terms of his first contract, have both flourished. As a racehorse owner (an interest that developed naturally when he realised he wasn't the greatest rider in the world) he graduated from a succession of hilarious mishaps to a partnership in Be Friendly. That flyer won 11 races, dead-heated for another, collected £44,000 in prizes, brought O'Sullevan half as much when he sold a quarter share and has given the compulsive punter in him quite a few bonuses. Be Friendly is now a high-earning stallion. 'My luck with him,' says the part-owner, 'has been miraculous.'

O'Sullevan, however, will be remembered as someone who describes other people's triumphs, as the man whose voice is the most precise focusing mechanism in sport, the perfect instrument for putting names and personalities to the blurred rainbow of a big racing field. But there is a strong spirit behind the voice, as some drunken critics of Lester Piggott discovered at Longchamp when they accosted O'Sullevan after Nijinsky's defeat in the Arc. 'Well, Peter, did Lester make a boo-boo?' they asked. He had just seen a great friend and a great racehorse beaten and his customary affability deserted him. So did his microphone voice. '"Fuck off," I said. And I felt better for it.'

Most of us feel better for hearing Peter O'Sullevan, but maybe those fellows were an exception.

The Observer, 12 December 1973

Bull's-eye Philosophy

When it is remembered that the long interview which forms the basis of this article took place 20 years ago, I think most readers will agree that the ideas presented came from one of the best minds ever applied to sport in this country.

IF THE MOST dramatic figure in British racing since the Second World War has been Lester Piggott, surely the most lastingly influential has been Phil Bull. By force of personality and intellect he has done more than even the most progressive of his contemporaries to bring a stubbornly anachronistic sporting industry face to face with the realities of its current situation. Along the way, he has been a considerable and distinguished owner of racehorses and a breeder of international standing, he has made a substantial fortune for himself and, through his Timeform publications, he has provided a lifeline of scientific analysis that must have saved many a groping punter from the abyss. It is not a bad record for a man who remembers his father soaping away coal-dust in a zinc bath in front of the living-room fire and whose first connection with a bank was that his mother had to scrub one to ensure that he and his sisters did not lack comforts or opportunities. Bull is inclined to snort at the frequency with which the poor-boy-makes-good element in his story is emphasised by journalists, not because he has any trace of embarrassment about his origins but because he views such an approach as a corny route to irrelevance.

Anyone interviewing him is unlikely to be offered a stream of cosy reminiscences. His conversation is almost always polemical, hardly ever anecdotal, reflecting his insistence that ideas form the primary substance of his life. Yet if he is nudged persistently enough towards memories of his early days the recollections that emerge are affectionate, vivid and entertaining. He was born 65 years ago in the Yorkshire mining community of Hemsworth, son of a man sufficiently remarkable to embrace, in chronological order, the careers of captain in the Salvation Army, collier and sanitary inspector. Bull senior was, in addition, a voracious reader (Carlyle, Ruskin, William Morris were among his favourites) and a left-wing thinker and activist who might well have inherited the vast Labour majority at Hemsworth instead of advancing the political education of the brother-in-law who did take over the parliamentary seat.

According to his famous son, this unusual father developed an enthusiasm for racing rather abruptly in 1901 at a time when he was given to making evangelical excursions for the purpose of daubing religious messages and exhortations in places where they were likely to be seen by large crowds of people. On a wall in Doncaster he slapped the question: 'What shall we do to be saved?' Then he found that underneath someone had written: 'Back Doricles for the St Leger.' That joker was presumably the spiritual ancestor of the one on Merseyside who reacted to the Wayside Pulpit's inquiry, 'What would you do if Christ came to Liverpool?' by scrawling: 'Play St John at inside-forward.' Ian St John was a winner for Bill Shankly in his time and Doricles proved no less on Town Moor three-quarters of a century ago. He beat the Derby winner, Volodyovski, after a turbulent race and survived an objection to give a return of 40-1 to his backers, who included a certain travelling salvationist whose search for souls was subsequently less zealous than his pursuit of winners.

So it was that the young Phil Bull found himself raised in a household where the plentiful reading matter constantly available included not only the classics of serious literature and the thoughts of radical politicians but Racing Up-to-Date and the Sporting Pink. He responded to all of it. Today he will tell you that he is happier discussing the works of Noam Chomsky and Professor Freddie Ayer or the political philosophies of Mao and Castro than the relative merits of Ribot, Sea Bird II and Mill Reef. He says it would be no great deprivation for him if he never had another bet in his life, no disaster if he never saw another horse. However, although he is not a man who tosses remarks around glibly, such utterances seem to relate not to a sense of disillusionment but to a dread that he should ever be suspected of the kind of narrow obsession that gives so many people in racing their depressing insularity. His enthusiasm for the game is real and deep but he does not want anyone to imagine that it has ever blinkered his mind against the larger world beyond, where the losers suffer harsher indignities than tearing up tickets and walking home broke. He claims that his description of racing as 'a magnificent triviality' has often been misrepresented by those who fail to appreciate that his definition of it as trivial is comparative, but the basic ring of its meaning is clear and must be acceptable to most of us.

Naturally, Bull's awareness of the wider priorities has increased with age. One moment he will talk spiritedly of the recharging of interest brought about by the installation of a £20,000 computer at the Timeform offices in Halifax, a mechanical ally that will enable him to go back to making the most refined interpretations of horses' times, to calculating and relating all the measurable factors down to the precise effect of windspeeds, even on round courses. He did this by sheer mental effort until shortage of time obliged him to abandon it a few years ago. Now the computer will permit him to apply the process again, perhaps more thoroughly than before, and he means to test the results with his own money for a season before deciding whether to incorporate them in the data supplied by the Timeform publications. The thought seems to excite him for a moment. Then he gives a sudden, dismissive grunt. 'Still, it's all a lark. We'll be dead in a few years, and then how important will all this be?'

These words are a provocation, not a lament. His dark blue eyes shine mischievously behind his glasses as he speaks and he bites a shade more aggressively on the cigar that protrudes from his face as naturally, and almost as constantly, as the celebrated whiskers. The beard is not quite the orange battle standard it once was but it remains virile enough, as indeed does its owner despite his mild complaints about the accumulation of the years. 'Sixty-five – I'm not too happy about it, in fact I object to it,' he said lightheartedly as we drove back to Halifax in his Daimler after a pleasant lunch on the outskirts of the town. There was, I pointed out, little chance of a stewards' inquiry. 'The trouble is, there are no stewards,' he said, laughing. 'They don't exist. I'd be happier if they did. But the life we have here is the only one we're going to know, so it's up to us to make the most of it. Looking back does no good and regret is a waste of time.'

Nevertheless, it is possible to detect some regret when he talks about the extent to which his overwhelming concern with ideas has in the past made him 'careless of people'. This, he says, is as much a legacy from his father as are his mental capabilities and passionate faith in rationalism. 'He was so taken up with his causes and his ideas that he was often inconsiderate of the feelings of other people and I must admit that I have had the same tendency. I have not made much of a success of marriage for instance. But in recent years I have come to attach more and more importance to personal relationships.' Perhaps his loss has been racing's gain, because a man with a less rigorously intellectual attitude would have been unlikely to accomplish so much on so many fronts in his chosen area of professional activity. He came to the task very well armed after his ability to collect scholarships had carried him through grammar school to a BSc degree in mathematics at Leeds University.

After leaving university he entered a phase of his life that was at least as important. It took him to London as a teacher and into the stimulating atmosphere of the City Literary Institute. Chess was his introduction there. He had been the student champion at Leeds and was good enough during his spell in the South to play blindfold against three opponents simultaneously and manage two wins and a draw. That kind of challenge would be too much for him now, he says, adding that although he has stayed unbeaten on the board for 25 years that fact tells more about the opposition than his own skill. 'Still, I'll never lose my love of chess. It is the greatest of games. If I ever went blind, I'd get someone to read to me from all those books on the subject I have studied over the years so that I could re-learn the game. That's how I'd spend my time and, believe me, I'd be quite content.'

Talk of blindness comes strangely from someone who is still a deadly adversary on the snooker table. At The Hollins – the 250-year-old house near Halifax where his own taste in design and the eccentricities of the original owner, a Mr Murgatroyd, co-exist charmingly – guests enter the billiards room with trepidation. 'If you are playing Phil for 50p you are all right,' says Richard Baerlein, the distinguished racing correspondent, who is a friend and admirer of long standing. 'But when the money goes on it is murder.' Even the master, Joe Davis, who has been one of Bull's favourite companions for 40 years or so, knows how difficult it is to beat the host at The Hollins off a level start. There was a time when Bull was happy to compete at golf and other games but now snooker is his 'only time-wasting activity'.

In those youthful days around the City Literary Institute in London, Bull, much influenced by Shaw, made a bold if brief lunge into dramatic writing. It was racing, however, that was to be the natural arena for his talents. He had been exposed to the unique appeal of the racecourse at the age of seven or eight, when he was taken to Pontefract, and half-a-dozen years later he watched from the Silver Ring as the great Mumtaz Mahal won the Champagne Stakes at Doncaster. That was a sight to put a permanent tingle in the blood. He had played with model courses as a child and by the time he reached university his interest had become so sophisticated that he was able to name the first four in correct order in Blenheim's Derby, a prognostication that he made available to fellow students but failed to exploit himself because he was absorbed by examinations on the big day.

At first glance there might appear to be something contra-dictory in the way his London experience, with its widening of cultural and intellectual horizons, was followed by his departure from school teaching and entry into horse racing. But it is only a superficial contradiction, because racing provided an ideal context in which to express his combination of cerebral gifts and extreme competitiveness. 'It was the perfect battleground for me,' he says. 'This was an exhilarating place where you could put your abilities and your nerve against those of everyone else – because that is what it amounts to, every punter against every other punter – and only the best-equipped would survive. I wanted an arena and here was one ready-made for me, with all the elements for testing myself already created and a marvellously varied and fascinating cast of characters.' The rest of the story is racing history. His success as an owner has been prodigious. He has had something like 350 animals in his time and has made sure that they paid their way. Big races that have fallen to him include the Gimcrack, the Jubilee, the Wokingham and the City and Suburban. He has bred winners of practically all the major Flat events apart from the Classics and even a Derby might have come his way if two most hopeful contenders had stayed sound and well through to Epsom.

He likes to be vague about the amount of money he has won from betting, but estimates of £400,000 are probably not outrageous. It is a nice irony that one of his greatest friends was William Hill, the bookmaker. 'I phoned him one day to complain because I had heard he was closing the account of one of my clients. He asked me to call on him at his office. I had a great red beard down to my navel and when he saw me I am sure he said to himself: "I'll soon get rid of this bugger." The bugger stayed until two in the morning and for the next 30 years I was never very far away. I gave the address at Bill's memorial service at St Martin's-in-the-Fields church in London. An atheist punter giving tribute to a religious bookmaker – how far can your imagination stretch?'

Bull's views on the breeding of thoroughbreds have long been on record and testify to his contempt for the higher gobbledygook that so infests the subject. 'There is practically nothing in print worth reading,' he has said. 'The few books on the subject have as much relation to the realities of the matter as astrology has to astronomy – tap roots, inbreeding, outcrossing, sires' lines, prepotency, etc, overlaid with a dressing of genetics, mostly misunderstood – it is a world of fantasy.' Mating the best with the best has been the essence of his own policy and its effectiveness is there to be seen.

The direct and vigorous logic he applies to breeding runs through every other area of Bull's involvement with the sport. By the time he had established his racing publications (*Best Horses of the Year* was soon followed by *Timeform* and its immensely authoritative stablemates) he had developed his system of detailed analysis of horses' performances to the stage where it had not only brought great benefit to every level of the betting public, but was bound to have an impact on the basic structure of the game, specifically on the structure of the two-year-old season. One of his essential concerns when he set out to interpret results, and separate the principal factors that produced them, was to ascertain the relative maturity of the horses competing. This obliged him to make a total re-examination of the weight-for-age scale. He admits to being impressed by the degree to which the principles laid down by Admiral Rous were valid but stresses that there were nevertheless crucial anomalies. To identify these precisely he drew up mathematical graphs showing by means of progressive curves the rate at which horses matured during their two-year-old, three-year-old and (in terms of extreme distances) four-year-old seasons. Probably the most significant lesson to come out of his investigation was that the tradition of never running two-year-olds beyond six furlongs until September was not only illogical but positively damaging. His evidence to the Rosebery Committee showed that this arrangement simply made a present of most two-year-old races to sprint-bred horses. It was calculated to harm the horses bred to stay because it forced them into end to end contests with their speedier contemporaries at a time when they were not mature enough to do themselves justice at the short distances and would have benefited far more from longer races in which they were allowed to settle down and run in the style appropriate to their stock.

The Committee did not alter the programme as substantially as Bull had asked but they did agree to institute seven-furlong races in August and mile races in September. The symbol of his wisdom on this issue is the tremendous relevance to Classic form of the mile race he initiated at Doncaster, which began as the Timeform Gold Cup and is now the Observer Gold Cup. This contribution is only one of dozens that he has made towards improvement and modernisation of horse racing in Britain. As a member of the Council of the Racehorse Owners' Association, he has often caused the raising of voices as well as eyebrows by his willingness to set aside the vested interests of himself and others in favour of what he considers to be the objective needs of a situation. He has produced a resentful stir among some of his fellow owners recently with his pronouncements on the present state of British racing and his suggestions on where the solutions lie. 'In the beginning this game was an exercise for those people, namely the aristocracy, who rode down to the course on their hacks,' he reminds us. 'It was almost a kind of circus in the Roman sense with the riff-raff allowed to attend on sufferance. Then courses were built and enclosures made and there was a charge to go in. In the Twenties and Thirties it was viable as a circus. The Establishment ran it. Admittedly there had been some penetration of racing by the nouveau riche, fellows like the Joels, and by the odd Aga Khan or two. But by and large it was still in the hands of the aristocracy. The public attended in enormous numbers, a quarter million on Town Moor, even more at Epsom and really healthy crowds at the smaller meetings too. It was a business proposition on the basis of what came through the turnstiles. Then television arrived and killed it as a business proposition. The income at the turnstiles diminished to the point where it was no longer enough. But with the legalising of betting shops a new source of revenue opened up. The only reason that racing remains viable at all is the support it gets from the taxing of betting shop punters. The Chancellor takes 10/11ths of the tax and the remainder is just enough to keep the game going.

'What is so sad and so alarming regarding the future of racing is the refusal to admit the obvious, that the vital audience for the sport is no longer on the course but in the betting shops and that it is absolutely wrong to go on claiming that the interests of racing and the interests of owners and breeders are synonymous. This is, above all, an entertainment industry and it is the audience that matters. If private owners ceased to exist that need not mean the end of racing. The Levy Board could own horses, commercial companies could own them, groups of people could own them, the alternatives are numerous enough. Those people in the betting shops must be looked after and given the consideration they deserve as the ones who can guarantee the future of racing. Their facilities should be improved. There should be TV in the shops, for instance. The Jockey Club should reorientate its thinking in favour of the punters, and there should be a relaxation of the controls applied to the ownership of horses so that firms can run them in their own names, working men's clubs can own them, and so on. There must be a liberal and progressive attitude to this. Given the rocketing costs of keeping horses, it is clear that measures such as these will be necessary if we are to have sufficient animals in training in three or four years' time.

'Another thing the Jockey Club should be doing is organising itself to resist the Chancellor's attempts to take more money from the punter in the betting shops. This constant milking could have a fatally discouraging effect. The Chancellor may think that because you can double the tax on beer and spirits and tobacco and still have people buying the same volume of those commodities you can do much the same with betting. But this is a fallacy. With betting, there is no real article you are selling to a man. What you are selling him is the prospect of profit, or at least the illusion that he may profit. If you raise the tax to the point where you destroy the illusion then you kill his incentive to bet. The Chancellor must be made to realise that betting is a different kind of goose, one that could easily be choked.'

If racing itself is to avoid being choked, the voice of Phil Bull will have to be heeded yet again.

Pacemaker, April 1975

A Modest Sidestep into History

THE WIND THAT blew across Ayr racecourse on Friday was cruel enough to make Muriel Naughton think twice about making history. It was the kind of wind that seemed to peel the flesh off your bones and come back for the marrow, but as she walked through it towards the first fence two hours before racing, Mrs Naughton was thinking less of her own comfort than of the wellbeing of a 12-year-old steeplechaser called Ballycasey. She had hoped that a softening of the weather during the day would ease the frost out of the ground and bring the yielding going that allows Ballycasey to forget all the painful abuse the tendons of his forelegs have suffered over the years.

But the afternoon remained beautifully raw, with a flawless blue sky offering sunlight as pale as malt whisky and much less warming. As she stamped a foot on the unfriendly surface of the home straight, the putative heroine suggested quietly that perhaps all the fuss had been for nothing, maybe the reporters and the press photographers and the television crews had wasted their time assembling in the West of Scotland. Maybe they would have to wait for another day and another place to see a woman ride for the first time in public competition with men over a National Hunt course. 'I know there has been quite a build-up to this,' she said, 'and I hate the idea of letting anybody down. But that old horse Casey means a lot to me, and I wouldn't risk doing him serious harm for the sake of a little bit of personal glory.'

Happily for all of us, she and her husband, Michael Naughton, who trains Ballycasey, decided after a lot more plunging of heels that conditions were sufficiently reasonable to permit the historic partnership to start out on the three miles of the Spittal Hill Amateur Riders' Handicap. And their polite warning that the chestnut gelding would be pulled up if he did not relish his work never had to be implemented. The Naughtons had made their point, however, and it was one that left a wholesome taste in the mouth. The lady who rode through that hole in racing tradition opened up by the Sex Discrimination Act was not infatuated with the idea of being a pioneer. Nor did she see herself as a frustrated champion, an exceptional talent caged too long by outmoded regulations and ready now to assert herself at men's expense up and down the country. If she seemed to come charging on to the racecourse almost before the ink had dried on the rider's licence granted to her by the Jockey Club last Tuesday, it was simply because there happened to be a vacancy aboard Ballycasey, one of the three jumpers she and Michael own. Muriel's intrusion into history was almost an incidental in another busy day at the races for this happily dedicated pair of Yorkshire people. If the weather had frozen her out of the headlines and the news bulletins, they would hardly have been desolate. 'I don't come here brimming with ambitions,' she said at Ayr. 'There's no great urge to make a name for myself in the Grand National or anything like that. I'd have been delighted to slip on to the scene unnoticed, ride my horses, have some fun, perhaps pick up a few prizes, go back to my five-year-old daughter, and leave it at that.'

Fortunately for those of us who could not leave it at that, noticing her is no hardship at any time. Even in a working outfit of anorak, lilac corduroys and clumpy shoes, she made an appealing, feminine figure. The wind, having tried unsuccessfully to scrape the light make-up from above her attractive eyes, concentrated on blowing the short brown hair into thick bunches about a face that mirrors the liveliness and contained strength of her nature. She is small, but not at all frail, with square, capable hands adorned with a wedding ring as broad as a bangle. Once the decision about running Ballycasey had been taken, any hint of agitation left her demeanour. Neither she nor Michael expected her to come to any harm on the course. 'I think this can be a far safer game than point-to-pointing, where Muriel has been doing her competitive riding,' he said. 'The main attraction for her in racing under Rules is that she'll get better ground and fences that are better sited. You never really meet a badly sited fence on a racecourse.'

'And I won't be riding rubbishy horses, the kind that are likely to get you hurt,' she added. 'I won't be getting up four or five times a day, taking all sorts of chance rides like the men who have to make a living at the game. The animals under me will be our own or ones we know, things that have proved themselves sound jumpers. That's where the danger is cut down tremendously. If Casey doesn't fancy the conditions today we'll drop out quietly. He won't do anything wild. When he gave me my first race in public in the Tynedale point-to-point about a couple of years back he treated me like a passenger and we won handily. He likes to please himself, running up near the front when he's in the mood. But he's a marvellous jumper and with that kind of partner I may be able to maintain my record of never having had a really nasty fall. I mean, I've come off hard enough, I know what it is to hit the deck, but I've had nothing worse than bruising, nothing to make me think, "God, I'm never going to do this again".'

Mick Naughton has a different experience of injuries. Being bumped through the rails at Market Rasen on Easter Monday, 1967, broke a leg badly enough to end a National Hunt riding career that had produced 17 winners in two seasons. While recuperating, he stayed on the stud farm that was managed by Muriel's father and was taken over by her on her father's death. Soon a new racing double act was being formed, one that is now flourishing as a 16-horse yard near Richmond in the North Riding of Yorkshire – a yard from which the Naughtons have sent out 20 National Hunt and two Flat winners in their first three seasons of training.

Ballycasey scarcely threatened to add to the total around 2.15 on Friday, but he did jump a perfect first circuit in second place before tiring into sixth on the second, and he certainly gave his jockey the opportunity to impress the sternest judges with the solid quality of her skills. Afterwards only Muriel Naughton thought it extraordinary that owners of the better-class horses in the stable should want to put her in the saddle. Earlier she had shied away, almost blushing, when Mr Percy Raine offered her the mount on Fine Fellow, the highly talented seven-year-old that was to be narrowly beaten in the feature race of the afternoon. But she was worth that tribute, just as she is worth the promise of a future ride on the star of the Naughton yard, Collingwood, who has been a close second in the Hennessy Gold Cup and is now being aimed at the Scottish National in April. 'I'm so glad Muriel is getting the pleasure of riding on the racecourse, because she works so hard with the horses at home,' said Mick. 'Collingwood is an example of the fantastic job she does. When he came to us he was practically a nervous wreck, had no confidence in himself at all. Muriel has spent hours and hours with him, hunting him, and she has made him a new horse. He has kept on winning for us, and although he's getting on a bit I really believe he's still improving. Because Muriel is alongside me, I can afford to take on horses that other people would reckon doubtful, or even hopeless, because I can bank on her to bring them round. She's a bit of a marvel.'

That view was not being noisily contested at Ayr on Friday.

The Observer, 1 February 1976

Racing's Vintage Era

HE IS STILL slight enough to be accommodated by a racing saddle, and an ordinary armchair encloses him like a small cave. Beyond the upper edge of the chair, through the large windows of the ground-floor flat, can be seen the entrance to Edgware Road tube station and the subdued mid-morning traffic of that area of west London. But the cool, shadowed room is steadily invaded by the sights and sounds and smells of another place, another world.

Charlie Elliott is talking about the Derby and, though the pitch of his conversation is undramatic, almost downbeat, the depth and authenticity of his experience of the greatest horse race in the world fill the listener's mind with images of a score of summer afternoons on Epsom Downs. He rode 29 times in the Derby between 1922 and 1953 (if we include a handful of the substitutes run at Newmarket during World War Two) and he won three, was second in two and was fourth in three. His place in the lore of the race is made additionally secure by the peculiar coincidence that his three victories punctuated the advance of the Derby into the technological age. When he brought Call Boy home two lengths clear in a field of 23 in 1927, the year after the General Strike, the BBC were broadcasting the event on radio for the first time. The introduction of television coverage in 1938 found him equally well placed to widen his circle of admirers when his mount, Bois Roussel, devoured all opposition in the straight and won by a rapidly increasing four lengths. In the year 1949 the photo-finish camera was used for the first time to decide the outcome of the Derby and, with what had come to seem an instinctive sense of theatre, it was Elliott on Nimbus who emerged on the print as having edged out Amour Drake and Swallow Tail by a head and a head. Nimbus had won by an even smaller margin in the Two

Thousand Guineas from the blindingly fast grey, Abernant, exploiting his bottomless courage against the ebbing stamina of the 5-4 favourite on the finishing ascent from The Dip, and forcing himself a short-head in front in the last stride.

'It was a Mr and Mrs Glenister that owned Nimbus,' Elliott recalls. 'They were pretty new to racing and the ordeal of those two photo-finishes put a hell of a strain on them. I remember one of them fainted on Guineas day and the other one fainted on Derby day. I can't be sure now which one flaked out on which day but I know they did the double.'

Few jockeys in the history of the game have been less susceptible to the vapours than E.C. Elliott. 'You've got to be ice when you go out there to ride, whether it's Epsom or a seller at Bath,' he says, and develops the theme with an insistence that makes it clear that inviolable coolness and self-belief are high, perhaps highest, on the list of qualities he sees as separating the good from the truly exceptional race-rider. 'You have to be convinced that you are as good as the next man and maybe better. I think it's true to a large extent that great jockeys are born, not made, that the ability to communicate with a horse so that he'll run for you, give you his maximum, is some kind of natural gift. But you've got to work to develop it and you've got to have a lot of self-confidence to make the most of it on the big occasion.

'What it is that makes one jockey so much better than another at getting a racehorse to do his best, maybe to do better than the horse ever thought he could do, is something that cannot be explained. I defy anybody to define it. You can talk about strength and balance and having good hands and a good seat and there's some sense in all of it but at the end of the day there's a bit of a mystery. There's something strange and marvellous happens between the horse and certain men who get on his back and you can't explain it. You can only demonstrate it by getting up on the animal.

'Lester Piggott does phenomenal things and they come off for him. If nine out of ten jockeys, even very good ones, tried to do what he does they would get beaten a head but he wins a head. Gordon Richards looked to be doing all sorts of things wrong but there was no argument with his results. Steve Donoghue, Gordon, Lester – men like those are a law unto themselves. I watch my racing here on the box now and I get some of my friends coming in and they say this or that about Piggott. I don't stand for any kind of carping. The fella's proved what he is. His record speaks for itself. It's unanswerable. He belongs right up there with the best the game's ever seen. And round Epsom there's no one among this generation of jockeys who can touch him – just as, when I was coming up, Steve was the master of the Derby.'

Elliott was still apprenticed to Jack Jarvis when he shared the jockeys' championship with Donoghue in 1923 and when he displaced that legend as champion the following year, and his talent had stamina to match its precociousness. He was an undisputed star throughout those inter-war years when British racing had greater quality in depth among its riders than it had ever known previously or, surely, can ever hope to boast again. When Elliott came down the hill to Tattenham Corner on Call Boy he had as company, apart from Donoghue, such as Brownie Carslake, Charlie Smirke, Fred Fox, Joe Childs, Gordon Richards and Tommy Weston and, by the time he was making a procession of the Derby on Bois Roussel, Harry Wragg, Michael Beary, Tommy Lowrey and the like had added their competition.

'There are quite a number of outstanding riders these days,' he says. 'As well as Piggott, you've got Eddery and Mercer, Lewis, Taylor, Carson, Hide, those fellas, and I particularly like Bond and Fox of the young lads coming through, but the list is nowhere near as long as it was in our day. Whether you're talking about the men who were established when I got to the fore just after the First World War or those who were working their way through as apprentices along with me, the string of names would take your breath away.

'My generation were helped tremendously by having first-class guvnors, like me with Jarvis and Smirke with Stanley Wootton. They told you firmly enough where you went wrong but they didn't give you a rousting when you made a mistake. What's the point of bawling and shouting at a boy. It just means that he'll have less confidence in himself the next time he goes out and a jockey without confidence isn't much good to anybody. All through my career I always had the confidence to admit when I had ridden a bad race. That's the way it has to be if the trainer is going to know where he stands, if he's going to be able to judge accurately what his horse's performance is worth. On the same basis, I never worried if I was taken off an animal so that somebody else could have a go. Sometimes a horse will perform for one jockey better than he will for another. I had the self-confidence not to feel slighted if a switch was made. In fact, sometimes I suggested that a change should be tried. It was simply the professional way to behave.'

He is into his seventies now, only slightly hunched in his dark sweater and cardigan and scarcely heavier than he was when he wore the rainbow jackets of some of the most influential owners on the Turf. His hair is combed back and close to his head in a style that is a date-stamp in itself and the intent alertness of the face gives it a mildly querulous expression. There is, however, little that is cutting in what he has to say except about some who comment on the race coverage he watches on television. Peter O'Sullevan and the late Clive Graham are carefully exempted from his strictures. Of the utterances of most of the others, he says that 'housewives and people who don't know anything about racing may be kidded but to anyone who knows the game most of it is balls'.

What he knows about the game does not appear to have been softened or blurred by the years. His objectivity has a matter-of-factness that comes across at times as harsh, even – almost especially – when he talks of his own exploits and those of the horses with whom he has been associated. In describing Bois Roussel's Derby, a distinguished writer, Roger Mortimer, tells us that 'once in the straight he fairly flew', and elaborates: 'He passed horse after horse, and swooping on Scottish Union with just under a furlong to go, he finished so strongly that he had four lengths to spare when the winning post was reached. In another furlong he would probably have been a hundred yards clear, and it was certainly one of the most remarkable and spectacular victories in the history of the race.' Elliott's encapsulation of the drama, accompanied by a dismissive gesture of the strikingly small hands, is succinct: 'Bois Roussel wasn't all that much – it was a non-stayers' year.'

He is satisfied that Call Boy, 4-1 favourite when he beat Hot Night and Shian Mor in 1927, was the best of his three Derby winners. Call Boy made virtually all the running and Elliott confirms that he always favoured the forcing style of riding Epsom, the catch-me-if-you-can tactics made popular by the successes of Steve Donoghue. 'Mind you, it was a different course in those days. It was bare, and almost always hard, with scarcely a blade of grass instead of the thick covering you have now. And Tattenham Corner was far more of a corner, not the curve it has become, so I'm sure our way of riding the Derby was right. Even now, if you have a horse that can go the pace, it is madness not to lie up in touch with the leaders most of the way. The majority of horses in the race are above the ordinary, so where's the sense in giving them lengths of a start?'

Elliott showed characteristic daring in leading from the gate on Nimbus in 1949, because there had been widespread doubts about the Guineas winner's ability to stay the extra half-mile. If the colt had cracked, the same critics who were throwing bouquets in the jockey's direction after the race would have been swinging cleavers. 'But I was sure he'd get the distance,' says Elliott, 'and if you aren't willing to back your own judgment when you get out there you shouldn't get up on the horse. As we went to the line, those were three spent horses, Nimbus, Amour Drake and Swallow Tail, but there could be nothing gamer than mine and he had his head in the right place at the finish.'

His voice subsides, the picture of that perfect June Saturday a quarter of a century ago begins to fade and we are back in the cool flat in London. And somehow the realisation of where this man has been, and where he is now, creates a poignant sense of dislocation. After retiring from the saddle, he trained successfully for a time for Marcel Boussac in France but there was a parting as the great equine dynasty identified with the house of Boussac went into decline. 'Beautiful-looking horses were still coming up every year but the engines weren't there.' There was another brief training period at Newmarket and then a severance from the game that is (unless TV is seen as providing an electronic umbilical cord) just about total.

He seems contented enough. He still has the companionship of his wife, does a lot of reading and enjoys the company of friends when they drop in. Yet, though it may be both presumptuous and sentimental to say so, a small weight is placed upon the heart by the thought of Charlie Elliott, who thrilled thousands of race crowds around the world, who knew so well the scent of the paddocks of Ascot, Chantilly, and Epsom, looking out in his latter years on Edgware Road tube station.

Pacemaker, June 1976

Requiem for a Champion

THE TARPAULIN THEY threw over the remains of Lanzarote on Thursday afternoon was a winding-sheet for our enjoyment of this year's Cheltenham Festival. Pleasure in the greatest of jumping race meetings died along with the best horse in the Gold Cup.

English attitudes to animals are often mawkish enough to turn the stomach but the emotional reaction to the freak accident that killed Lanzarote was robustly sincere, one that had to be shared by all who believe that great racehorses have a higher status than bingo cards. There was an unforced nobility about him that conveyed itself even to those of us who knew him only through his public appearances, something about his bearing and the carriage of his fine head, a blending of strength and good-natured placidity that tended to make respect and affection come in a single flood.

To see the brave light in his eye snuffed out so abruptly, champion turned to carcass in one slithering stride, was an experience to make the raucous human turmoil at Cheltenham, the betting and drinking and guessing and lying, all the marvellous nonsense that eddies through the place every March, seem for once like an intrusive side-show. There was an emptiness that couldn't be measured by the hand in your pocket.

Twenty-four hours later, as a thin and muted crowd of racegoers toyed unaggressively with the problems of a moderate card at Lingfield, John Francome, who had got up on Lanzarote before the Gold Cup with no more pessimism than Angelo Dundee feels when he slaps Ali on the shoulder at the first bell, still wore an expression of shocked remoteness. 'I feel bloody lousy,' he said at the door of the weighing room. 'I don't even want to go outside.' It was 25 minutes after the second race, a novice steeplechase in which he had given a smooth and promising introduction to

Clandestine from Richard Head's stable, and he had not found the inclination to change out of the blue and white hoops of the six-year-old's owner. He was preoccupied with things past. His young face is brightly, almost warily intelligent but now the steady eyes under the long lashes were clouded with thoughts that were far away from the hard bench we sat on.

'We had jumped that ninth fence and gone a stride or so away from it when Lanzarote's back legs went from under him,' he said quietly. 'He crumpled on his near hind and I knew straightaway when I looked at it that it was broken just above the hock. It was twisted up, not grotesquely but bad enough to let me know how serious it was. At moments like that you don't have to be a veterinary expert to realise the worst has happened. I waited with him till the vet came. All I could do was try to soothe him, hold his head down and keep him from trying to get up. Then the vet arrived and shot him, put him out of his misery.'

There was a heavy residue of misery among the humans who had worked intimately with Lanzarote. As he was carted from the scene of his death (near the fence that would have been the fourth from home on the second and last circuit in the Gold Cup) to a triangular space by the side of the course that is normally used for parking the ground staff's tractor, the sense of what had been lost reached achingly into everyone who had ever admired the horse. But it must have felt like a disembowelling knife to such as his owner, Lord Howard de Walden, to Fred Winter, the inspired trainer for whom the fatality was the latest in a series of disasters visited upon him by this race, and Harry Foster, the veteran stable lad who has cared for Lanzarote since the brown gelding went to Winter's yard at Lambourn. 'It's upset me more than enough but it's probably worse for the guvnor,' said Francome. 'He was bound to think a lot of a horse that had done so much for him and he obviously felt all the closer because he rode Lanzarote quite often in work at home. But most of all I feel sorry for Harry Foster. Harry's getting on a bit now, he's nearly 60, and you can imagine what an important part of his life that horse had become.'

It is not difficult. A stable lad accepts that his job will have more to do with hard work on raw mornings than afternoons of triumph at the racecourse, and to be given charge of an animal like Lanzarote is a small miracle that warms and brightens the whole of his existence. It was a permanent cold that settled on Harry Foster as his nine-year-old hero and friend was put away on that wet hill at Cheltenham. Lanzarote had won 19 hurdle races, including the 1974 Champion on that same course, and his three victories over fences had indicated that he could easily go on to dominate the tougher game and increase considerably his winning stakes total of £61,000. Foster had shared in a highly personal way in all those successes and the tears he shed on Thursday were not so much justified as inevitable.

There were other sad stories at Cheltenham, especially in a Gold Cup that saw the favourite, Bannow Rambler, and the formidable Fort Devon prematurely removed from the action and then, between its last two jumps, produced savage misfortune for another representative of quality, Summerville, who broke down dreadfully when the prize was at his mercy and will never race again. But much the saddest episode was the demise of Lanzarote. 'There's no point in talking or writing about it,' John Francome declared with sudden, understandable bitterness at Lingfield. 'It's all irrelevant. The old horse is dead and that's it.'

The pain, however, will stay alive in him for a long time, no matter how many winners he adds to the two he rode on Friday. Nor will Fred Winter be easily consoled. After his previous ill-luck with Pendil and Bula (who was, for bad measure, severely injured on Tuesday of last week) and this most recent nightmare, Winter must feel that fate has booby-trapped the Gold Cup course against him.

'If I were Fred I'd drive out of this place and never come back,' said a fellow trainer on Thursday night. Of course Winter will be back. Timidity is no more part of his nature than it was of Lanzarote's.

The Observer, 20 March 1977

Costly Day for Pigeon Fancier

THE SENIOR STEWARD in the sky has developed a grudge against Cheltenham. In 1975 part of the Festival was washed away, forcing the Irish to set up the biggest card schools outside Las Vegas, and last year the Tuesday programme was the victim of a genuine tempest. This was the year of the blizzard. Dog-sled teams could not have raced on Thursday, so the Gold Cup and several other great races were lost.

The loss was made more painful because we knew about it so early. In the Queen's Hotel the celebration of Monksfield's victory in the Champion Hurdle was still short of its crescendo when the snow began to batter on the windows. Dessie McDonogh, who trained the little horse to become the first winner that had come out of his yard since May 1977, was drinking Coca-Cola in the jostling din and trying to explain how optimism had survived that long drought. He is an unaffected young man who deserves more luck than he has known. 'I told Dr Michael Mangan, who owns Monksfield, that we had prepared him right for this one,' said McDonogh. 'He's a beautiful, brave little fella, the kind that gives back twice as much as you can ever put into him in training, a horse that will never let them beat him as long as he has enough left to make a race.

'Those were good animals against him, Night Nurse and Sea Pigeon, but I knew a mile out that we had them done. He was never off the bridle. He was in charge and I knew they would have to come and get him and that they weren't up to that. They were never going to get anything for nothing. Did you see him in the paddock? He looked better than anything. He was preening himself, glancing about him, waiting for the action, waiting to see what had the nerve to try to beat him. He had a coat on him that would have done credit to a Derby winner. I'm not making a case for myself but it is nice to prove that if the material is right you can put them on the racecourse ready to run. That little horse cost 760 guineas when I bought him. He didn't look cheap today, did he?'

Monksfield appeared very expensive indeed to Pat Muldoon, the friendly and charming Scotsman who owns Sea Pigeon, a horse that may well be, as someone suggested, the best hurdler never to win the Champion. Watching the big race with Muldoon and his two young sons, who had taken time off from Dunblane High School in Perthshire to be excited witnesses, was a poignant experience. The boys, Stephen and Leslie, were made doubly committed by standing next to Jonjo O'Neill, one of the very best National Hunt jockeys now riding and the man who was prevented by injury from helping their father's contender. 'Jonjo not only rides for me – he's a friend,' Muldoon said as the field sidled and pranced in front of the tapes. 'I hope he is proved right by what happens here. He could have ridden Night Nurse but he chose mine and just about every national newspaper has told him he is wrong. What they don't know is that he is acting out of loyalty as much as judgment. I told him that if Night Nurse was a stone better than mine he should ride the old champion but obviously I knew that there was no such difference, so I wasn't surprised when Jonjo said he would ride Sea Pigeon. We are a bit closer than an owner and a jockey might be. He'll hardly make a move without phoning me and I'm very grateful for that relationship.

'I have been unbelievably lucky in this game. I have been an owner for only seven years and I have had 75 winners in that time. My living comes out of the wholesale wine and spirit trade, not out of horses, so I can afford to regard it as a hobby. All my bills are paid through Weatherbys and I have never had to send them a penny since I started – my prize money has covered everything. Maybe that sort of luck makes it easier for me to enjoy the game, to treat the people I am involved with the way I'd like to be treated. When Sea Pigeon ran in the Chester Cup last Flat season, Lester phoned me early on to say he would like the ride. Now, Lester Piggott is the best jockey that ever lived as far as I'm concerned and I was thrilled that he wanted to sit on anything of mine, but I had to be fair to young Mark Birch, who does the horse in the Easterby stable and was his regular rider on the Flat. So I told Lester, with all the right apologies, that I'd have to let young Mark get up at Chester. The lad was really moved. "I can't tell you how much this means," he said. "Don't worry, I'll win for you."

'I went for a real touch and Mark didn't let me down. Afterwards, I gave him a grand on top of his 10 per cent and I think it meant a lot to him. He came here to Cheltenham today to watch Sea Pigeon and I think that says quite a lot about our connection. We're almost like a family, the people I have got to know in racing. My young boy is a very good show jumper and he goes down and stays with the Easterbys at times. They're nice family people and they help to increase the enjoyment I get out of racing. When I buy a horse I don't expect a return on my money but I expect the horse to pay for itself. I am prepared to pay a few quid for my hobby but I don't want it to be a hole in the ground that is swallowing up wages.'

Pat Muldoon's hobby might have seemed a little cheaper if Sea Pigeon had got to Monksfield (and perhaps with the assistance of the incomparable Jonjo it might have happened) but he is the kind of man who would take some pleasure in the thought that Dessie McDonogh and Dr Mangan had cause for a party.

The Observer, 19 March 1978

Sea Pigeon did win the Champion Hurdle with Jonjo in the saddle in 1980 but when the horse repeated the feat in 1981 the great Irishman was injured and a great Englishman, John Francome, had the ride.

The Saga of Red Rum

Since this piece was written (for a non-British magazine, incidentally), changes to the fences have diluted the uniqueness of the Grand National and some people now regard it as simply a very tough long-distance handicap. The Adelphi parties I describe are just memories.

SOMEONE, PERHAPS a heretical jockey, has said that if Torquemada had designed a racecourse, it would have been Aintree. It is true that the Inquisitor-General of steeplechasing submits men and horses to just about every interrogative ordeal short of piranha fish in the water jumps, but in justification the Liverpool track can claim that, invariably, it elicits true witness. Horse and rider tell the truth about themselves out on the bleak four-and-a-half-mile circuit of the Grand National, whose extreme distance, cruelly varied obstacles, and 500 yards of exhausting run-in make it the toughest race in the equestrian world.

The National, unlike the great Flat races, such as the Epsom or Kentucky Derby, or even another jumping classic such as the Cheltenham Gold Cup, has little of the pageant about it. Run in a raw northern landscape, usually at a raw time of year (when England's harsh March is yielding to tentative April), it is an occasion of red faces and virile voices and nerves stretched to brittleness. The tensions are emphasised rather than concealed by the ferocity of the party spirit that pervades Liverpool for two or three nights before the event. The main lounge of the Adelphi Hotel in the middle of the city – a vast, anachronistic oblong that looks as if it might have been salvaged from the Titanic – is an uproar of carousal in which a man could be shell-shocked by the champagne corks. Often some of the jockeys who will ride in the big one are to be found in the midst of the wildness, singing Irish songs or having toboggan races down a staircase on tin trays. But now and again on the Friday night before the fateful Saturday, a face will cloud over, as if its owner had heard the creak of an approaching iceberg.

These are brave men – the kind who accept crashing falls and desperate injuries as natural punctuation in their working lives, who sometimes need so many metal bolts and pins to hold their shattered bones together that they joke about bequeathing their remains to the local scrapyard – but as they await the start of the National, misgivings mingle with the thrill of anticipation. The fear is not so much of being killed or maimed (although the National might do either) as of being found wanting. For Aintree, on that early spring afternoon, separates the strong, the enduring, and, above all, the brave from the rest. In short, those four miles 856 yards and 30 jumps create heroes of a dimension seldom encountered in sport. The Grand National has been doing that since it was first run in 1839, but it is the good fortune of those of us who are around now to find ourselves contemporary with the greatest National hero of all, the 12-year-old bay gelding named Red Rum. Before Red Rum came along, six horses had been double winners of the race, and from Peter Simple (1849 and 1853) to Reynoldstown (1935 and 1936), they were all exceptional. But by the time he took his unique third victory on 2 April 1977, Red Rum had shown himself superior to any of them in coping with the frightening problems of Aintree. He won at his first attempt in 1973, did it again in 1974, ran second in 1975 and 1976, and then, unbelievably in an event that breaks hearts as readily as limbs, he came back to win again last year. It is a five-season record that has no equivalent in the past and is never likely to find even an echo in the future.

There were enough sentimental tears to make an extra water hazard when the old horse leaped the final fence on his own last April, leaving behind 41 rivals in various stages of disarray, and galloped up the straight into history. Even the ranks of the bookmakers could scarce forbear to cheer, although the 25-length victory gave them one of their costliest days of the year. They always have to dig deep when Rummy wins, for in animal-loving Britain no animal has ever been loved like this one. His hold on the affections of the nation utterly transcends racing. Schoolboys and grandmothers, turf aficionados and once-a-year 50-pence punters cherish him for reasons more compelling than his brilliance. They love him because he is a classic hero figure, because he rose from the harshest of working-class backgrounds and travelled the stoniest of roads to stardom, and because he made it on his ability, his smartness, his resilience, and most of all, on the burning purity of his spirit. 'At first glance, he doesn't look anything out of the ordinary,' says Peter O'Sullevan, the leading race commentator on British television and one of the country's genuine authorities on the sport. 'Of course, he obviously carries a hell of a lot more power than he did when he ran on the Flat as a two-year-old and three-year-old. He was a skinny little bugger then. But his conformation is still nothing very striking. He certainly doesn't have the formidable outline of the great steeplechasers of the past. Yet I'm sure you wouldn't pass him by, because you would notice his head. That head suggests the truth about him. It is full of intelligence and an awareness of his own worth. He has a look that says the Red Army couldn't intimidate him.'

The self-possession O'Sullevan indentifies has saved Red Rum from being overwhelmed by the celebrity that has engulfed him since his third National win. Throughout last summer he was making more personal appearances than most pop stars, opening shops and supermarkets, pubs and flower shows, formally switching on the autumn illuminations on the seafront at Blackpool, which is just along the road from his home stables at Southport in Lancashire. He was an honoured guest at the Horse of the Year Show in London and clumped around a hotel in the capital to enliven a promotional dinner. One hotel and two pubs have taken his name, and, since a major distillery was thinking of attaching it to one of the firm's products, no one was at all surprised when Red Rum's connections decided to transform him into a limited company with a view to swelling the £150,000 that represents the comparatively meagre reward for his prodigious exploits on the racecourse.

Even in the Flat season, it is rare for fewer than 50 fan letters a day to reach him at the least likely stables in England. Rummy's home is Donald ('Ginger') McCain's neat little cobbled yard set behind a used-car showroom on a busy street in Southport, a fashionable resort town within half an hour's ride of the Aintree course. Beryl McCain, the trainer's dark and handsome wife, handles the flood of requests for photographs, shoes, hairs from the champion's tail, and dutifully files the scores of poems he inspires.

The quality of the verse suggests that every surviving descendant of William McGonagall is a steeplechasing enthusiast, but Beryl is understandably taken with the sincerity of the eulogies and thinks one day they may make a book.

There are, too, serious inquiries from the cognoscenti, who want to know what special techniques enable McCain, a former taxi driver who freely admits that he was a minor league trainer until Red Rum arrived, to send the old warrior out like a lion each spring. Many of the experts still cannot accept the validity of a routine that sees the horse walk through the town each working morning, over a level crossing on a railway and between lines of lively traffic, to the beach – to be exercised on the sands. Sand galloping is generally held to be wearing and hazardous, but McCain removes most of the disadvantages by harrowing a strip for his horses, clearing away any dangerous debris and ensuring that the surface is not the hard, damp, and ungiving mass it would otherwise be. For Red Rum, who was afflicted half-a-dozen years back with chronic pedal ostitis, a bone disease of the foot that is usually incurable, that stretch of Lancashire beach may have been the only possible path to greatness. The Scottish vet who treated him when he went lame, and looked as if he would be a cripple for life, thinks the sea has done much to wash away his troubles. 'Sea water is a great thing for horses,' he says. 'It cools them off after exercise and stimulates the circulation.' Red Rum's spirit, too, appears to be invigorated by the wide spaces of the shore and the wild company of the sea when he goes about his training in the wintry dawns. It seems now, indeed, that everything that went before in his life conspired to bring him into the peculiar corner of the racing world ruled over by Ginger McCain, just as all the outrageous vicissitudes of his career on the racecourse might be seen in retrospect as leading him inexorably towards Aintree and immortality. But the old lad himself must have had little time to ruminate on destiny as he was buffeted from one hard time to another on the way up.

Red Rum began with the fairly basic drawback of having a mad mother. Mared, the dam who foaled him at the Rossenarra Stud in County Kilkenny at 6 p.m. on 3 May 1965, was such an uncontrollable hysteric in her racing days that her owner recalls her 'turning black with sweat and white with froth everywhere'. At Galway, on the day of her solitary victory in ten starts, she had to have a bucket of water thrown over her before she went into the paddock to saddle up. And Martyn McEnery, Red Rum's breeder, remembers that 'Mared was the same foaling as she was racing – all smoke and steam. It is just unbelievable that Red Rum could go on racing for so long without showing any signs of that temperament of his mother's.' Four times in the years ahead, Red Rum was to change hands in a public market, available on the first two occasions to anyone with the price of a modest second-hand car. His sire, Quorum, was fast, and the bay colt (or gelding, as he became in his yearling autumn, when he was castrated to defuse an incipient obstreperousness) was expected to make a sprint handicapper. But though he won twice and dead-heated once during two seasons on the Flat, it was not until he turned to the jumping game that he showed himself remarkable, and not until he reached McCain and the nearby arena of Aintree that he emerged as something incredible. By that time he had experienced four trainers and a score of jockeys, including Lester Piggott, and had grown accustomed to working hard for his living.

Donald McCain held a trainer's permit for 13 years before he had his first winner in a cheap steeplechase – at Liverpool, of course – early in 1965. But, despite the poverty of his resources, his flair for conditioning jumpers had become conspicuous by the time he found himself bidding for Red Rum seven years later. He was able to pay £6,000, four times more than he had ever previously given for a horse, on the authority of Mr Noel Le Mare, an aged millionaire who had made the improbable transition from passenger in McCain's taxi to patron of his racing stable. Le Mare's distant ancestors were persecuted Huguenots in France, and the family's tendency to suffer for religion was maintained when his father, a missionary in India, became a New Theologian and, in the son's words, 'got the sack'. Noel, who started working life on the decks of trawlers, removed the threat of redundancy from his existence by launching his own construction company. The family stake in it was worth £5,000,000 when it eventually went public.

Le Mare's one obvious link with McCain is an obsessive belief in the virtue of perseverance, and when they found they shared a longing to be identified with a Grand National winner, the tycoon and the used-car salesman became partners for life. That may have seemed a limited term when Red Rum was bought, for the new owner was already in his mid-eighties, but when his ninetieth birthday passed in September 1977, he was showing no signs of curtailing his vigorous interventions. McCain both admires and likes Le Mare, just as practically everyone in racing who knows him both admires and likes McCain. The trainer is a large, open-faced man with a strong crop of short, coppery hair that invites his friends to call him Ginger. His demeanour is almost always friendly to the point of generosity, but in rare moments, especially if he suspects he is being taken for less than he is, a glacial sternness comes over his features and only the resolute hang around to debate.

McCain was born and raised within a few hundred yards of his present stables, but in his early days his only connection with horses was that his grandfather drove two for a firm of provision merchants. They fascinated him from the beginning, however, and after an abortive effort to put up with the tedium of factory work, he attached himself to professional stables until a combination of difficulties with weight and a more specific problem involving a girl steered him back to his home area and the taxi business. His re-entry into racing was with one broken-down animal that cost £25. But after his marriage, his resolution carried him on to the former brewer's yard behind the car showroom in Upper Aughton Road and ultimately to Red Rum, who now occupies the box nearest to the street because he likes to be placed to follow whatever action is going on around him.

The extreme alertness that comes naturally to Red Rum is clearly one of the secrets of his mastery at Aintree. He has had distinguished successes on the easier 'park' courses around England, but his willingness to rouse himself for such limited challenges diminishes as he grows older. It takes the daunting fences of Liverpool to transform him into the most extraordinary of his kind. The most notorious of those fences loom like Gothic cathedrals in the nightmares of anxious jockeys. There are 16 of them on the Grand National course, and all, except the last open ditch (The Chair) and the water jump, are taken twice. Their unique construction – thorn dressed with fir – makes them so solid that any horse that hits one really hard is likely to go down as if shot. Not only are most of them taller than normal fences (eight of them are five feet) but there is a pronounced drop on the landing side in many cases, and the open ditches are alarmingly wide. Most riders consider that the worst obstacles on the course are the third, a six-foot open ditch and a five-foot fence; Becher's Brook, which is five feet six inches wide, with a fence four feet ten inches high; the Canal Turn, a five-foot jump almost on a tight left-handed bend; and The Chair – another six-foot ditch with a fence that is, at five feet two inches, the tallest on the course. None of these monsters has ever even ruffled Red Rum.

The richest irony in the whole story of the great steeplechaser's conquest of Aintree is that his first National win was essentially unpopular. He achieved it by three-quarters of a length at the expense of the big Australian horse Crisp, who, carrying top weight and giving Red Rum 23lbs, produced the most electrifyingly swift and fearless display of jumping the race has ever known. Crisp had never seen Liverpool until that Saturday in 1973, but from the third jump on the first circuit, that upright cliff of an open ditch, which he flicked over as if it were a footstool, he was clear and he never allowed anything else to get near him until his magnificent front-running began dramatically to drain his strength from the last fence. Even then, though he was beginning to sway like a punch-drunk fighter, Crisp would have lasted out to victory if he had not been opposed by another great horse. As it was, both he and Red Rum broke the Grand National record by the astonishing margin of 19 seconds, or about 200 yards, and just how marvellous the Australian's effort had been was demonstrated the following year when Red Rum, himself promoted to top weight, won in a canter from a chaser of the highest class, L'Escargot. In 1975, L'Escargot took revenge, but by finishing a brave second while giving his conqueror 11lbs, Red Rum convinced many people that he was indeed the supreme Aintree hero of all time, and any remaining doubters were converted the following year, when he was again the runner-up. What happened last April had the effect of lifting him on to a plane apart from all the thousands of horses that have contested the 133 Nationals run so far. When he came up the straight towards the line, head characteristically high, he found himself galloping into a narrowing corridor of delirious humanity. No other British racehorse, not even the royal winner of a Classic in the old days of Empire, ever received such a tumultuously affectionate reception.

'The crowd was spilling on to the track at the finish, converging to make a kind of tunnel of faces and deafening noise,' remembers Tommy Stack, who was on Red Rum's back when that bit of history was made. 'My one fear was that I would fall off, or that some other freak disaster would happen to us. But the old horse loved it all. He seemed to know the cheers were for him and to reckon he deserved them.' Stack, with a restraint that is almost treasonable in an Irishman, drank orange squash afterwards while a start was made on celebrations that were to roar and eddy across north-west England for days. But his joy over winning his first National was profound enough. Before the 1976 running, Stack had replaced Brian Fletcher, Red Rum's partner on the first three forays, just as Billy Beardwood had replaced his fellow Liverpudlian, Billy Ellison, as the stable lad looking after the phenomenon at home in Upper Aughton Road. 'He's a bloody marvel,' says the Irish jockey of the horse that has brought him the climactic experiences of an outstanding career. 'He's so intelligent, always looking for open spaces, always alert to loose horses and other dangers. He really does love the challenge of Aintree and jumps like a cat round there. Liverpool stirs him to show his true worth, and he just breaks the hearts of most of the opposition.'

'I think,' says Ginger McCain with a smile, 'that our fellow loves Aintree so much because when he's jumping those bloody huge fences like Becher's or The Chair, he's so long in the air that he gets a lovely rest. But, really, he is something different from any other horse. He's a total professional, like an old fighter who's been through it all and knows every move in the ring. His courage is bottomless and he never loses his verve. People say he should be retired to a life of leisure now, and obviously he deserves it, but when you look at him it's hard to believe that is what he'd want. He's still as full of himself as a two-year-old and has lost none of his appetite for training or racing. Barring accidents between now and the day, they'll have to shoot him to keep him from getting into the shake-up again in the 1978 National.' McCain struck a bet of £750 each way at 20-1 whenever the betting opened and is convinced he has an excellent wager.

Billy Beardwood, the stable lad, has invested too, encouraged by the nice coup he had last season. But the sincerity is unmistakable when he tells you that his real rewards from working with Red go beyond the financial. Between grooming strokes in the stable, Billy kids around, making fake lunges at his friend, and the horse responds by leaping around as playfully as a spaniel pup, 'If I'm ever too slow and he catches me by accident, he actually apologises,' says Billy. 'He snuggles into me and makes a strange bleating noise to say he's sorry. Everybody in the yard is potty about him. He loves Polo mints, and they're forever feeding him with them. He's certainly the best thing that's ever happened to me. I can't think of him as a horse. I think of him as another human being. I'll tell you, I've learned more from him than I've ever learned from any human being. Looking after him and riding him at exercise is an education. He sets some example to all of us.'

There is one shadow over Red Rum's preparations for his attempt on an outrageous fourth win in the National. Tommy Stack, at the time of writing, lies in a hospital, in traction with a shattered pelvis, his body at the kind of angle that makes eating food about as enjoyable as pushing a car uphill. 'At least I'm not going to have trouble with my weight,' he says, demonstrating again the spirited optimism that is essential to the men who ride jumping horses for a living. He manages to laugh at the bizarre nature of the accident that put him on his back for long, painful weeks. It did not happen in the hurly-burly of a race but in the paddock at Hexham, an obscure outpost of racing near Hadrian's Wall. An unrated hurdler Stack was going to ride reared up and came over backwards on top of him to crush the pelvis. 'When a horse rolls on you in a race, his momentum usually takes him off your body again pretty quickly, but what happened at Hexham was a lot worse. The whole dead weight of the animal settled on top of me, and I knew I had a really bad one. But I could wiggle my toes, so I could be sure that I hadn't broken the spinal cord, and that was a consolation.'

The severity of Stack's injuries would have dissuaded most men from ever going near anything less predictable than a rocking horse, but he never had any thought of giving up riding. Instead, he worked on the assumption that he would be back in action in January and fully fit to take the mount on Red Rum at Aintree. 'Nothing heals you quicker than having a horse like that waiting for you,' he says.

There is, too, the cheering knowledge that old Red has proved himself a safer conveyance than an invalid carriage.

Quest, March/April 1978

Horse Sense of a Champion

Willie Carson was already special when this appeared in 1978, but he was about to prove himself even more remarkable by winning the Derby in 1979 and 1980. He won it again in 1989 and 1994 and is still a seemingly ageless wonder out on the track.

FOR A LAD who once lived in a prefab in Stirling, Willie Carson runs into some strange accidents these days. He turned up for lunch on Thursday with his left ankle in plaster and explained, when pressed, that he had done the damage out hunting with the Quorn. 'I cannoned into another horse and my foot was turned right back,' he said. 'It was my second day hunting after the Flat, so I didn't take long to get into trouble. I thought it was just a bad sprain and I carried on and finished, or just about finished, the day's hunting. Hot and cold, I thought, that will be enough. Then next day it was unbearable. So I went up to London, that was on Tuesday, and saw the specialists who always look after my injuries. They detected that it was a chip on the fibia so maybe my plans about going to Hong Kong will have to be adjusted.'

Talk of adjustment brings to the surface the paradox in Carson's nature. He is the kind of man who can euphemise fanaticism as common sense, who can disguise obsession as the only sensible way to behave. 'Most people go on holiday to escape from their problems. I forget my problems when I go to work. You've read about trouble among jockeys lately, about Greville Starkey getting a bit worked up. I think that is natural in a place, in a life where there is tension, where pride and money are at stake, but I am fortunate in relation to these problems. I am loud at home and quiet on the racecourse. People are different on the racecourse. Maybe I enjoy racing so much because I find it is a place where I can shut out everything else, just concentrate on the job.'

That concentration, and the talent that justifies it, brought Carson 182 winners in the Flat season that has just finished and made him champion jockey in two previous years, 1972 and 1973. Thursday was his 36th birthday and the thought of how well his life is going readily dispelled any depression his injury carried with it. His face fits his body: small with regular features and so alert that you worry about your next remark. And when he talks about his attitudes there is the sense of noises from a familiar place, from the peculiar terrain that champions inhabit.

He tells of the childhood fights he had when boys from the junior school lifted the secondary boy up by the throat and were appalled to find his fists in their ribs and faces. 'I'd be taken to the class to account for what had happened,' he says. 'The teacher would look at me and then at the boy I was supposed to have been vicious with, and she would compare the sizes of us and give him a rollicking. It was embarrassing in a way, but I didn't mind too much.'

Combativeness shows through constantly in how he rides but he resents the suggestion that forcefulness is the essence of his abilities. 'They say I am all push, kick, wallop, they say I have no tact,' he tells you rather bitterly. 'I think I have as much tact as anybody. I don't hit horses much at all. I analyse horses, try to work out what goes on in their minds. Sometimes a horse has a feeling for the man who is riding it, the right vibes. You can learn about some of them by accident or even by mistake. A horse can be left at the start and suddenly you realise that one likes to be ridden from the back, or you can be giving an animal an easy and you discover that he runs a lot better when he is treated gently than he does if he is asked a lot of hard questions. Maybe the next time out you force him and he does nothing. But my own feeling about my riding is that I am not Scobie Breasley, not the man who is best at making horses enjoy themselves coming from the back. Unless I am on a horse that I know well, that I know to have a specialised way of running, I want to be there or thereabouts. If there is a pattern to my riding it is to be up with the leaders most of the way and you will often find that when people think I am stuffed I am able to come again and do the business at the line.

'As long as the horse will give, I will keep going. If the horse really packs in then there is no point in carrying on. Understanding horses is, for me, a matter of feel and experience. I've got to use the old word instinct. Speed is quite mysterious. If you ride a horse across a big open field you may have a certain sense of speed but it is not easy to relate that to the sense of speed you have when you ride the same horse at the same pace in a confined space or with other animals. The same applies to judging when horses are right and when they have gone wrong. I believe that I have the ability to diagnose trouble in the animals I ride by listening to their breathing, observing their actions and so on. I misinterpret the signs sometimes but I think I have a sense of when they are well and when they are not.'

Carson declares rather than admits that he sees most, perhaps 90 per cent of the horses he rides as machines that help him to make an excellent living. But some have a particular emotional significance. Obviously Dibidale, who would have won the Oaks if her saddle had not slipped somewhere before Tattenham Corner, is one of them, but the cast includes some less likely names. Red Johnnie is one. 'He was always a character,' says Carson, and then simplifies by adding that Red Johnnie was 'nuts'. The horse is, he says, 'the kind of old fella who would have you off. When he felt like it he was awkward. When he thinks he is better than the rest, he is a star, he'll hack in. But when he thinks he is going to be upstaged he gets out of the way. Maybe that makes him a bully but I fancied him. We got on well together.'

Perhaps the horse he got on with best of all was the stayer Parnell. He is especially pleased that Boldboy ran like a dream under him after a lot of foolish people made up their minds that Carson's force would not coax the maximum out of such a track-wise old player. But Parnell remains the favourite. 'He looked like a nonentity. He was very light in build, big ears, small body. But everything about him worked. He was like a Formula One racing car – nothing fancy, all business. I enjoyed riding him.'

When Willie Carson has that reaction to an animal, the punters often share his enjoyment.

The Observer, 11 November 1978

The Bid for Greatness

GREAT HORSE RACES refuse to be undramatic. If the form-book argues predictability, there is almost always a sub-plot to put a hectic stutter in the pulse. Most times the secondary theme is straightforward Dick Francis but at Louisville last weekend, when they had the 105th running of one of the greatest races of all, the Kentucky Derby, Mr Dickens seemed to take a hand.

There was certainly something nineteenth-century about the hard times suffered by Ron Franklin before he went to the starting gate at Churchill Downs on Spectacular Bid, the 3-5 favourite in this year's Run for the Roses. Franklin is now slightly less than a year short of his twentieth birthday but he still looks as adolescent, pimply and vulnerable as he did when he dropped out of school as a 16-year-old and took off from the family home in Dundalk, Maryland, at a speed that scarcely represented a round of applause for the quality of life there. He turned up at Pimlico racetrack in Baltimore and a trainer named Grover G. (but called Buddy) Delp took him in first as a horsewalker and a dung-shoveller, shortly afterwards on a basis that was more like father and son. Buddy's paternal affection for the boy was not stifled by the discovery that young Ron had a knack of encouraging the Delp stable's thorough-breds to get to the winning line before others with whom they had been asked to keep company. Since Delp is a master horseman who expects to collect rather more than a million dollars in prize money annually, the two soon had a good thing going and it was no stunning surprise when Franklin finished last season as America's leading apprentice with 262 winners. It was natural enough, too, that he should form a partnership with the brilliant new star that had emerged in his guardian-guvnor's barn, Spectacular Bid, a grey colt by Bold Bidder (by Bold Ruler) who had shown clear hints of greatness as a two-year-old and quickly became the dominating presence this season in the East Coast three-year-old races that are the traditional preparation for the American Triple Crown of Kentucky Derby, Preakness and Belmont Stakes.

In the early days of this racing year it would definitely have seemed that Ron Franklin had found happiness too easily to give him any chance of qualifying as a Dickens hero. Rescued from the threatening streets of Baltimore, given a warm home with the Delps in Laurel, Maryland, and exciting, rewarding work around Pimlico and the other big racetracks, he was in danger of jumping from the first to the last chapter and skipping all those intervening vicissitudes. Then came the Florida Derby and a series of blunders by Franklin so crass and so thoroughly recorded by television that they precipitated criticism of such persistence and hostility it might have made Nixon wince. Where previously there had been barbed murmurs about the jockey's alleged tendency to think at trundling pace, about the rawness of his technique and especially his clumsiness with the whip, in short a generalised and fairly muted suggestion that he was outclassed by Spectacular Bid, now there was a clamorous denunciation. And at first Buddy Delp appeared to be leading it. The trainer had betrayed misgivings about Franklin's competence last October by displacing the boy for a couple of races in favour of the experienced and often deadly Panamanian, Jorge Velasquez.

But Delp, who had been snubbed earlier by a foolish agent when he tried to secure Steve Cauthen as the rider to stay with Spectacular Bid through his championship season, abruptly decided that he had made his point. Franklin was swung back up on the Bid, as they like to call him, and the colt continued to give successive groups of opponents a receding view of his muscular rump. So everything was a lot better than bearable for Ronnie Franklin until 6 March at Gulfstream Park, where he rode the Florida Derby. The last and worst of his erratic manoeuvres took him along the rail into what could have been a death trap for his chances. 'He was just lucky that it was Jeffrey Fell, a really clean rider, who was on his outside,' one of the most informed watchers in the press box was saying at Churchill Downs as we waited for the big one last Saturday. 'Jeffrey closed the gap early, so the kid had nowhere to go. He had to check his horse, then move all the way round the outside to win. If it had been one of the hard men, like Angel Cordero, he would have waited until Franklin came alongside and then shut the door on him. They would still be picking splinters out of Spectacular Bid now.'

If the Bid – after taking the Birmingham-by-way-of-Beachy Head route to the lead and sailing home by four and a half lengths – came out of the Florida Derby unscathed, his rider did not. Before Franklin was back in the unsaddling area he was being violently berated by Delp, a balding, bulky man who has the unusual ability to invest a round, bespectacled face with a look of granite hardness. Idiot was the recurring noun in his comments and the adjectives were enough to make a police horse shy. 'Shoemaker is just a phone call away,' he told his jockey, invoking the intimidating name of America's Lester Piggott.

'Those Spics ganged up on me,' was the best Franklin could offer in extenuation. The Latins he had in mind were Angel Cordero, a Puerto Rican, and Jorge Velasquez. As Sunday afternoon wore on towards the late post-time of the Derby there was speculation about whether Cordero on Screen King would be intent on making the younger man pay for those remarks. Velasquez didn't have a ride but his fellow Panamanian Laffit Pincay would be on General Assembly and available to liaise with Angel if they felt that anything more positive than a few colourful Spanish reproofs was required. Franklin by then was at least reassured that he had the confidence of Delp and Spectacular Bid's owners, the Meyerhoff family of Easton, Maryland. The Meyerhoffs had always been generous towards Ronnie but the Dickensian twists of the story had become more worrying than ever when Buddy Delp, his benefactor, had indicated that the smartest thing about the lad was that he knew he wasn't smart. Stressing his own belief that you don't have to be top of Mensa's Free Handicap to ride horses well, the trainer added archly: 'If you ever call up the White House no four-foot-ten person is gonna pick up the phone and say hello.' The statement seemed offensive and ill-judged on two counts: firstly, it is impossible to argue convincingly that there is a connection between physical shortness and mental limitations and, secondly, if there was a connection one or two of the men who have occupied the White House could have walked under footstools to get to the telephone.

Explanations of how Delp came to make that crack while discussing a boy for whom he clearly has a deep affection usually

resolved themselves into an acceptance that the trainer is a volatile
man afflicted with hyperbole of the emotions and the assertion that
'he kicks Ronnie's ass for the boy's own good'. Some were not so
generous to Buddy. Walking through the pale 7 a.m. sunshine
towards the last light exercise sessions at Churchill Downs on the
morning of race day, it was necessary to ask for directions to
Spectacular Bid's quarters in Barn 41. The young man who assisted
went on to offer the hope that the Bid would be beaten. 'I got
nothin' against the horse,' he said. 'That's a real good horse. And I
got nothin' against Ronnie. He's not a quality rider but he's a nice
kid and I wish him well. But the trainer . . . Jesus, you couldn't fit his
head into a five-gallon bucket.' Buddy Delp was not unaware of
such views or the basis for them. 'If bullshit was electricity,' he said
as the Derby approached, 'I'd be a powerhouse.'

Buddy continued to be bullish right through to the off. Ten
three-year-olds were going to be lining up at the gate, all carrying
nine stone, but he was struggling to admit that it could be
described as even a two-horse race. He was, he confessed, giving a
squeak to the California champion, Flying Paster, only because he
did not want to geld the Derby of all its excitement in advance. All
right, so Flying Paster had won nine of his previous 10 starts, but
that was out on the West Coast where the living was easy. Now,
Delp reminded us, Paster was meeting Spectacular Bid, not merely
the winner of all five of his contests at three, but quite simply the
best racehorse ever to look through a bridle.

An extraordinary television preview on the eve of the Derby
gave visitors hungry for direct evidence the uncut tapes of all the
major races relating to the Classic and when the programme was
over old Buddy's optimism didn't come across as too outrageous.
Sitting alone in a hotel room, a British interloper found the hair
rising on the back of his neck as the screen was filled with the
stirring image of Flying Paster devouring opponents and the
home stretch to take the Hollywood Derby by 10 clear lengths on
14 April. But then it was the Bid's turn and the thrill was still
deeper. Film of a succession of his victories showed the grey to be
a magnificent thoroughbred, in action a giant of his kind. He was
seen to have great speed and the wide range of gears that gives
almost limitless manoeuvrability and once in command of a race,
usually by the beginning of the straight, it was obviously his habit
to gallop so powerfully ahead that the others scarcely ever

managed to put in a blow. He was something to behold and those recorded demonstrations of his talent implanted the thought that on Saturday 5 May he would be just about unbeatable.

One man who did not think that way was Dr J.A. Mohamed of San Antonio, Texas, who came to the late conclusion that his maiden colt Great Redeemer could win the Derby and spent $7,500 making Redeemer a last-minute addition to the field. Dr Mohamed, who is a diagnostic radiologist, had obviously seen something in his horse that was invisible to the trainer, Jim James, because Mr James resigned five minutes after the entry was made. No one except the owner, a Trinidadian Muslim turned born-again Christian, could find the heart to blame the trainer, since Great Redeemer's six straight failures on the racecourse amounted to the sort of form that should be printed on the side of a glue bottle. Still, it had to be assumed that some of the 128,000 who squeezed into Churchill Downs would support the doctor's lunacy with dollars. In the bars under the wooden stands at the Downs (a charming old country track dressed up for its one big day) the mint juleps were strong enough to undermine judgment and over in the infield stimulants of a less orthodox nature were helping thousands of young people to create the illusion that Woodstock had come to the races, so a few wagers on Great Redeemer were inevitable. But when the total invested on him rose beyond $50,000 there were rumours that the place had been invaded by religious fanatics. If so, they were surely the kind who would have been shouting for another round of drinks in Jonestown, Guyana. The biggest certainty of the afternoon was that the Redeemer would finish last and he duly did, fully 25 lengths behind the ninth horse. He almost ran over two photographers who were already on the course to greet the winner on his way back but, as a local reporter said, Great Redeemer was going so slowly that he wouldn't have hurt them.

Mohamed's folly was virtually forgotten by most of us as the field moved to the start. So, too, were Elizabeth Taylor and all the other self-advertising celebrities in the stands. The focus of our minds and our feelings tightened on Spectacular Bid and the silent figure in blue and black silks on the grey colt's back. Would all the hard words prove justified? Would a boy's incompetence get a great horse beaten? The questions dried the throat and brought a sharpness of anxiety that had nothing to do with money pushed through the betting windows.

We needn't have worried. Ron Franklin and the horse he loves hardly needed to break sweat to annihilate the opposition. They came out a shade slowly but Franklin remained cool and steered Spectacular Bid smoothly up through the field. Seventh going past the stands for the first time, they were sixth at the half-mile, fourth at three-quarters, second at a mile and sweetly in the lead soon after entering the stretch. There was a slight bump with Flying Paster going into the final turn but it was as negligible as the small cuts both horses brought back to their barns. Paster, who ran terribly to be fifth at the end of the mile and a quarter, was reported to have required infra-red treatment during the week. He may need heart and leg transplants if he is to challenge seriously in the Preakness that is now imminent on Spectacular Bid's home ground at Pimlico next Saturday. General Assembly, a handsome son of Secretariat, ran the winner closest in the Derby but, as Delp said, fighting to within two-and-three-quarter lengths may have squeezed General Assembly dry. So the Preakness seems there for the taking, and the Belmont too. But speculation about going on to switch from American dirt to French grass for the Prix de l'Arc de Triomphe is premature.

After the Derby, Ron Franklin, wearing the smile that only the vindicated know, said that all he had to do to persuade Spectacular Bid to devastate his field was talk to him nicely. He had 'tweeped' a bit to get the horse moving and then given him the word: 'Let's go, Big Daddy.' Hours later, he was still talking gently into the horse's ear in the darkness of the stall at Barn 41. Outside, Buddy Delp was more audible. 'Ronnie is not just the right rider for Spectacular Bid. He suits all horses. He's young and he makes mistakes but he is a natural. His secret is that they don't tire under him. It's been Shoemaker's secret through his career. With Ronnie the hands and the body-weight go with the horse, stride by stride, and the animal doesn't tire. It's a hell of a gift.'

The gifted boy was still murmuring. Perhaps he is not the best jockey in the world but last weekend he was the happiest, and he deserved to be.

The Observer, 13 May 1979

The Fat Man Shouting the Odds

Racing is magical everywhere, even when the eardrums are being battered by heresies delivered in a New York accent.

HE LOOKS, TALKS and dresses like someone who might earn his wages at a hole in the road with a pneumatic drill in his hands. What John Campo does for a living is train thoroughbred racehorses, and possessing clothes that could have been looted from a jumble sale by a blind man, and a verbal style that has less to do with the Ivy League than the New York race trains, has not prevented him from being the best man at the job in the United States this season.

To Campo that means being the best anywhere, because he views foreign trainers and especially the famous names of European racing as an alien, inferior breed. 'I don't think too much of them,' was his first muttered comment when the subject was raised in the small brick-built office alongside his barn in the backstretch training area at Belmont Park last week. The muted tone was not long sustained. 'Them guys got it easy,' he said. 'Give them 100 or 150 fancy-bred horses and they might do some good. They race just six or seven months a year and when they come over here you can't find their horses. They got a lot of bullshit about them.'

All of this seemed too much to leave unchallenged, even if it came from a man who took charge of the three-year-old Pleasant Colony in the middle of March this year – and by 16 May had sent the tall son of His Majesty out to win a rich stakes race and two legs of the American Triple Crown: the Kentucky Derby and the Preakness. The best way to bring Mr Campo up short was obviously to mention a few immortals, starting with Vincent

O'Brien, a trainer who won the Grand National three years in a row and has gone on to take the Derby five times, the Prix de l'Arc de Triomphe three times, the Washington International and so on.

There was, of course, always the risk of a little riposte about Storm Bird and the sufferings of those punters who were pulled on to the punch at Longchamp last weekend but, apparently, Campo is no more engrossed by racing news from Europe than he was by Voyager's dispatches from the round course at Saturn, so he did not go in for such niceties. His response to the case for the Old World horsemen was a touch more dramatic. He sprang out of his chair (not an easy feat for someone whose 18-stone bulk has a standing elevation of only 5ft 7in) and began to tear off the light blue windcheater with the Dunes, Las Vegas, insignia. He likes to go to the casino in the desert for his holidays but for the moment it seemed to be his visitor who was gambling dangerously. There was a sudden longing to be arguing technicalities with Henry Cecil or Dick Hern or even facing the ire of Ryan Price. John Campo is an Italian off the streets of New York and when he exercises his talent for staccato vituperation a hundred movies come to mind.

However, the removal of the jacket apparently meant nothing more than a loosening up of his debating method. Adjusting a baseball cap that might or might not have suited Sir Noel Murless, he said: 'I'd like to see any of those guys you talk about do what I did with Pleasant Colony – win the Wood Memorial on 18th April, the Derby on 2nd May, and the Preakness on 16th May. If they'd got him like I did on 13th March they'd have put that horse away for six months, put him on the shelf and then if he'd done something when he came back out they'd have told you what a smart move they'd made. And what age is Vincent O'Brien anyway? I'm 43. You know that? Forty-three. And what I've done hasn't been with all them fancy-bred horses he's workin' with. He wouldn't win three races a year with the kinda crows I got out in most of the stalls in that barn. I tell ya, you got some bullshit guys in Europe. I got two horses back from them clowns over there. One had a pulled stifle and they didn't know it. The other couldn't run worth three dollars. Give those characters some of these crows that can't walk, let 'em try to train these things.'

Campo's approach, which has fetched home $1,875,000 in prize money already this season, clearly reflects the belligerent practicality of his own nature. But he acquired more subtleties than

he readily claims during the years spent learning from several
American masters. He was brought up within sight of Aqueduct,
the second big New York track, a coarser, busier sister to Belmont,
and by the age of 15 he was being drawn towards racing. It was,
he says, the sort of fantasy world that appealed to a boy without
substantial education or family background.

Before he set out on the career that would make him the most
publicised trainer in America, a combative and successful extrovert
known throughout his business as the Fat Man, Campo served six-
and-a-half years with Eddie Neloy, who was an extrovert's
extrovert. Neloy worked, played, bet and brawled like two men,
often choosing cops as adversaries in his younger fighting days. He
was also a genius at putting horses on the track in unbeatable
shape, notably the memorable Buckpasser, Gun Bow and
Stupendous. Campo talks about Buckpasser with a hint of awe – as
well he might about a horse who won 16 in a row in the best of
company – but he says the greatest he ever saw was Kelso, the
incredible gelding who was America's Horse of the Year five
seasons running.

That verdict is understandable but his capacity for idiosyn-
cratic, some would say outlandish criteria (Vincent O'Brien is after
all rather good at his job) was emphasised again when he said he
had doubts about rating Secretariat too highly because he didn't
know if the Triple Crown winner of 1973 'beat any good
racehorses'. The statement sat uncomfortably with the memory
that just a few hundred yards from where we were talking,
Secretariat completed his Classic series by finishing 31 lengths in
front of his field in the Belmont Stakes, setting an astonishing
record for a mile-and-a-half and offering a performance that many
veteran horsemen considered the finest they have ever seen.

'Time don't mean nothin',' said Campo. 'It's the quality of the
opposition you beat that tells you what sort of horse you got.' Yet,
in common with all other American trainers, he pays plenty of
attention to the stop-watch when preparing his animals. To be fair,
he appears to pay attention to everything, waddling purposefully
about his domain, overseeing the shoeing of a horse, checking on
a leg here, a mouth there, issuing crisp instructions on who should
ride what and how it should be ridden. He favours girls on the
staff because they are more conscientious but he has his quota of
the Hispanic stable lads who are so plentiful around the 2,000

thoroughbreds at Belmont and says the language is no trouble. He is rarely ambiguous about what he wants done. On the telephone to Louisiana the other day, before flying to be there with one of his stable's three acknowledged stars, Johnny Dancer (Pleasant Colony and Real Prize are the other two), he heard that the weather in the south was disturbingly hot and that his man had acquired a fan to cool their entry in the $500,000 super derby. 'Fan – what do you wanna get a fan for?' he demanded to know. 'Get it away from the sonofabitch. How's he doin', how's he doin'?'

The trainer himself wasn't doing too well last month when a female vet who worked with his horses was found dead in puzzling circumstances on a beach north of Chicago. New York papers speculated without foundation about a romantic involvement. He said at the time that his wife was embarrassed. 'But nothing can ruin me,' he added. Whatever anger Mrs Peggy Campo was showing around the barn area last week was directed at Jorge Velasquez, the generally impressive jockey who had failed to correct a miserably slow early pace in the $400,000 Marlboro Cup at Belmont a week ago and come home a well-beaten fourth on Pleasant Colony. 'If I had a gun, I'd shoot him,' she said with a sour smile.

But a downbeat mood does not last long around Johnny Campo. In a television commercial he does for Off-Track Betting in New York, he is seen cuddling a foal in a paddock and giving encouragement with the message: 'I think you're gonna make it, kid.' The kid from the rough streets around Aqueduct has made it into the highest reaches of American racing.

And remember, baby, that means the world. He may occasionally mistake the significance of the initials JC and a few of his opinions sweep across the borderline between the outrageous and the indefensible. But the Fat Man brings a big talent as well as a big body and a big ego to the old game.

The Observer, 27 September 1981

Mysterious Death of the Red Terror

WHEN AMERICAN NEWSPAPERS carried stories early in 1932 about the Red Terror from the Antipodes they were not panicking over an infiltration by Australian Marxists. They were celebrating the arrival from the other side of the Pacific of one of the most remarkable thoroughbreds seen anywhere this century. The phenomenon was an enormous chestnut gelding called Phar Lap who had already, at the age of five, won 36 of 50 races contested in Australia and taken his regular partner, Jim Pike, to 27 wins and two seconds from 30 starts in just two years. Phar Lap – the name is borrowed from an oriental language and translates loosely as 'lightning' – was the hero of a nation at a time when romance was no more of an epidemic on the streets of Sydney or Melbourne than elsewhere in the industrialised world. And he remains almost as much of a focus for national pride today as he was when his blistering speed on the home stretches of Flemington and Randwick (and finally, on the run-in at Agua Caliente near Tijuana, Mexico) lifted the spirits of millions battered by the Depression. No exhibit at the National Museum in Melbourne attracts more awed attention than the image of Phar Lap's majesty that has been preserved by filling his hide with a taxidermist's sculpture. His huge heart is on display at the Institute of Anatomy in Canberra and his skeleton is in a third museum across the Tasman Sea in New Zealand, where he was born. Given the scattering of relics, the spell he casts is bound to be a little diffuse these days but he is still the people's champion.

His immortality is based on an astonishing mountain of achievements on the racecourse. Geldings, since they cannot transmit their quality to future generations and are therefore only as good as their last payday, are frequently overworked during their racing careers. Phar Lap was scarcely given time to draw breath between assignments and yet his constitution was so magnificent and his appetite for the game so exceptional that he just kept on winning. In the 14 days after taking the 1930 Melbourne Cup (the country's premier race) he went to post four times for four victories. That unbelievable surge included a week in which he collected £12,429 in prize money, a sum put into perspective by the fact that the Aga Khan's Blenheim earned only £10,036 for finishing ahead of 16 others in the Epsom Derby that year. It is perhaps just as relevant to the legend that Phar Lap (by Night Raid out of Entreaty, though there has been speculation over the right of the unprepossessing English stallion Night Raid to be accepted as the true sire of so outstanding a horse) cost the pittance of £168 as a yearling at Trentham in New Zealand and seemed overpriced at that when he reached the Sydney docks. At the end of a rough crossing, he was such a gaunt, ugly immigrant that there was some doubt about whether he was worth training and his first four races did nothing to dispel the misgivings.

Yet, having won an obscure juvenile maiden on his fifth outing, he was soon to develop into a great red god of a racehorse whose tremendous stride so regularly overwhelmed the opposition that he was eventually forced to concede crippling amounts of weight every time he was saddled up for action. The increasing severity of the handicapper and a pronounced decline in prize money as the economic recession laid siege to Australian racing (the Melbourne Cup of 1931 offered £5,200, its lowest figure for 24 years) combined to make thoughts of a foreign expedition natural enough, at least to one of his joint owners, Dave Davis, who was American by origin. The other owner, Harry Telford – who had been middle-aged and what is called, almost officially in those parts, 'a battling trainer' when he picked the heavily disguised prodigy from the Trentham catalogue and whose training of the champion had made him financially comfortable as well as famous – instinctively opposed the idea of going to the US and then travelling a mile or two over the border to the Tijuana Valley for the Agua Caliente Handicap, a race promoted with a lot of showbusiness swagger and an advertised first prize of $100,000.

Telford's reluctance was not supported by sufficiently persuasive arguments, and that proved to be a tragedy. Phar Lap, although nursing a cracked hoof, came from last to first with his old paralysing burst to break yet another track record and claim a purse that had diminished spectacularly between the writing of the publicity material and the writing of the cheque. The date was 20 March 1932, and within 16 days, while the sports page superlatives and the talk of Hollywood film deals and celebrity tours still swirled around his name, Phar Lap was dead. He had been taken to a horse ranch 25 miles from San Francisco, and there on 5 April he collapsed in his stall and died, leaving a mystery that has resisted all attempts to unravel it over half a century.

Some medical evidence suggested that a desperate attack of colic had killed him but many Australians were ready to believe that he had been poisoned by American race gangs, while some of his hosts were convinced that the feed brought over the Pacific by his handlers had gone wrong and done the damage. Still another theory was that he had eaten grass which had been sprayed with a weed killer, an explanation made more credible by a post mortem report that said the lining of the stomach was badly perforated as if by an irritant poison.

In the US as well as Australia and New Zealand, Phar Lap's baffling demise brought bigger headlines and longer, more solemn elegies – written in the papers and delivered over the airwaves – than the death of many a king would evoke. One American radio station called for a minute's silence and the *New York Sun* published a tribute in verse. It was pretty bad verse (like Robert Service in his selling plater's mood) but the old flyer probably took an indulgent view up in the 'Pasture ever green' to which the poet had consigned him. At least the reference in the first stanza to 'the big stout-hearted Phar Lap' was a long way from being an overstatement. The pump that drove Big Red to his 37 victories weighs fourteen pounds and in the Canberra Museum it creates a dramatic comparison with the six-pound heart of an army remount.

The Observer, 10 July 1983

A Good Thing for Outsiders

A WEEKEND IN Paris for the Prix de l'Arc de Triomphe always leaves some of us guiltily harbouring the presumptuous thought that national treasures can be given to the wrong nations. There has never been any inclination in this quarter to deny that the seventh Earl of Elgin's appropriation of those Parthenon marbles was more than slightly larcenous but moral objections might be convincingly answered if the English could devise a means of shifting the Arc, lock, stock and Bois de Boulogne, to the middle of Sussex.

The French treat the most important race in Europe so casually that if the British and Irish didn't turn up in droves the great event would be held in an atmosphere more in keeping with a rural gymkhana. Claims that the invasion force numbered 8,000 this year are hard to check but Longchamp was certainly no place last Sunday to practise your comprehension of Parisian accents. Admittedly, the locals are entitled to regard our attitude to big race days as a little crude. They would obviously have no desire to see the Bois de Boulogne polluted with the sort of vast and frequently Hogarthian throng that converges on Epsom Downs for the Derby. But if their response to the Arc is sophistication they can keep it – the affectation that is, not the horse race.

Perhaps our best policy on this side of the Channel would be to stop complaining about the French failure to appreciate the wonder of the first Sunday in October on one of the most beautiful racecourses in the world and just quietly continue to plunder its pleasures for ourselves. Why should we lament the fact that the most attractive grandstands in Europe are not bulging with punters, that the course is indeed rarely asked to take more than half the 80,000 it is designed to accommodate? If the Arc did draw the crowds that it should, most of those who turned up would have a choice between taking a vow of abstinence from betting for the day or risking a nervous breakdown from the frustrations of queuing at Pari-mutuel windows where the handling of custom is so slow that I found myself assailed once more last Sunday by the old fantasy that these grilles are manned by disabled veterans of Dien Bien Phu. If they weren't disabled to start with, a few were in danger of acquiring that excuse before the show was over, if the belligerent mutterings of two Americans stranded in one scarcely diminishing queue were anything to go by. When you are accustomed to making your wagers at Belmont or Aqueduct, where the lines melt away as swiftly as the illusions that cause them to form, Longchamp sometimes gives the impression of having been infiltrated by Gamblers Anonymous.

It goes without saying that if there was a conspiracy to protect romantics from the consequences of their imaginative interpretations of the form book, it wasn't quite thorough enough to extend to this victim. Occasionally the race to get on before the horses jumped out of the stalls almost went to a photo-finish but invariably I made it. And invariably I cunningly spared myself the need to do any extra queuing at the pay-out window. Still, even for someone who contrived to neglect both Habibti and Royal Heroine and then had to endure the sight of that other marvellous filly, Sun Princess, being out-galloped in the last furlong of the Arc on ground that was far more helpful to her conqueror, All Along, Longchamp remained the most enchanting of torture chambers.

Looking out from those handsome stands, lavishly garlanded on the day with tens of thousands of geraniums, towards the most unlikely and captivating vistas to be encountered within 20 minutes of the centre of any great city, it was hard to worry about donating a few francs to the enemy, even to the bureaucratic enemy behind the machine. Admittedly, as the Eiffel Tower emerged ever more clearly from the mist on an afternoon that began with a suspicion of rain but was dominated subsequently by the stunning clarity of the autumnal light, the odd sufferer may have speculated briefly about how high a man would have to climb to be sure that the jump would cancel all future bets. But such musings couldn't thrive against the thought that, once the traffic had eased, it would be only a short and pleasant drive to Montmartre, where they have specialised for a long time in applying balms to wounded spirits. In the past, the eating and drinking establishments around the Place du Tertre have made more bearable the pain of real body blows such as the defeat in 1970 of the great Nijinsky. Sassafras, who beat him by a head, had won the French Derby and was no scrubber but the victory seemed a sacrilege on that October afternoon a dozen years ago. The sickness in the stomach felt by myself and a Scottish punting ally had hardly anything to do with the fact that Lester Piggott and the magnificent athlete from Vincent O'Brien's stable were carrying everything we had taken into the track, including a couple of coins that had tried to roll under the hotel room carpet. The spectacle of Nijinsky faltering in the final 150 yards when Lester brought him level for the surge that had so often annihilated the opposition, and then veering to his left as the whip was used in a last effort to give his career the climax it deserved, is something burned into the minds of many of us who were there. Nothing in all the runnings of the Arc since it was first won by the Newmarket contender Comrade from a small field of 13 runners in 1920 can have contained a more essential sadness.

A further defeat by the considerably inferior Lorenzaccio in the Champion Stakes 13 days after the loss in Paris confirmed that Nijinsky, who had been seriously ill before becoming the first horse since Bahram in 1935 to win the English Triple Crown, was clearly drained of much of his brilliance before going for the Arc, and to run as well as he did was no doubt remarkable in the circumstances. But his failure that day is no less painful a memory for being readily explained.

However, the Arc has left far more thrilling images than bleak recollections over the years: moments like that provided by Sea Bird II, one of the best horses of this and probably of any century, when he pulverised a good field to finish six lengths in front of an outstanding rival, Reliance, and 11 lengths in front of the third, Diatome; by the successive wins in 1955 and 1956 of an animal entirely comparable with Sea Bird II, the astonishing Italian champion Ribot, who never lost a race in his life; or by the wonderful bursts that brought Vaguely Noble and Mill Reef home as emphatic winners in their years. Mill Reef was trained in England, which is so much of a distinction for visitors in the Arc (Migoli and Rheingold are the only two others sent out from here since the war) that the confidence rife within our particular assault squad might have struck anyone with a respect for the past as bordering on the eccentric. Yet it wasn't hopelessly irrational. Time Charter and Sun Princess had the form to justify optimism, plus the fundamental advantage of their sex in a contest that has been a benefit for fillies in recent seasons.

Of course, the Irish and the French had impressive fillies, too, in Stanerra and All Along, and there was late and reliable word that Vincent O'Brien was sufficiently sanguine about Salmon Leap to have had a bet on the colt, a procedure that is not at all habitual with the most inspired trainer of the modern era. There was also news that Salmon Leap, who can be damagingly nervous when he goes to work, had spent two of the most tranquil days of his life in preparation for the Arc. My informant's version of how this relaxation was achieved may have been tinged with hyperbole but it worked on me. 'He's had a bag over his head, cotton-wool in his ears, everything they can think of to con him into staying calm,' my man assured me. 'He thinks he's still in Ireland.' I remembered drinking with some Irish friends at Cheltenham when we weren't too sure where we were. But that had more to do with Bollinger in the brain cells than cotton-wool in the ears.

Anyway, the thought of a few quid of mine riding along with a considered investment by Vincent O'Brien had plenty of appeal and Salmon Leap became my second choice. The questionable honour of carrying my principal bet (the equivalent, detractors would say, of being ridden by a Sumo wrestler) went to Sun Princess. I expected her to reverse the King George VI and Queen Elizabeth Stakes running with Time Charter. How she dramatically vindicated that belief, but still found All Along her superior on the fast ground, is now history. Fortunately, as recorded in the Ladbrokes ledgers, it's not the most calamitous sort of history, since Willie Carson's splendid driving kept Sun Princess battling through to claim second place. Neither Willie nor Pat Eddery, who found Salmon Leap flying from the back of the field in the straight to finish better than anything in fifth, would begrudge 22-year-old Walter Swinburn another moment of glory to set alongside those that Shergar and Shareef Dancer have brought to a career extraordinarily begun.

Even Lester Piggott, the first of at least four men who declined the ride on All Along before it was offered to Swinburn, may have managed a wry smile. It would be very wry, but Lester has found Longchamp a magical place in the past and will do so again. So, barring accidents, will a few thousand more of us.

The Observer, 9 October 1983

The Daddy of Them All

WHEN AN AIRPORT is called Blue Grass Field and its baggage-area is looked down upon by a large coloured portrait of a Derby winner, the arriving passenger is entitled to the double assumption that he is in Kentucky and that if he isn't interested in the thorough-bred he had better keep his heretical prejudice to himself. Such caution was particularly advisable during this past week, when – just a few white-railed paddocks removed from the runway – some of the most extraordinary horse trading in the history of the world was being conducted. The November Breeding Stock Sales at Keeneland, about eight miles outside the old settlers' town of Lexington, may not have thrown up prices to compare with the 10.2 million dollars paid by Sheikh Mohammed Bin Rashid al Maktoum for a bay son of Northern Dancer at the Keeneland Selected Yearling Sales in July but they created some astonishing world records of their own. They emphasised, too, that the beget, begat and begotten game goes on booming more dramatically than any other business around and that the balance of power within it continues to shift steadily from the United States back to the old horseracing heartlands of Europe. And, almost inevitably, they supplied further proof that, in an industry which depends finally on the potency of great animals, where the best commodity to have in the bank is the right sperm, the supreme Big Daddy of the current era is Northern Dancer.

It is hardly coincidental that Producer, the seven-year-old who changed hands for $5,250,000 shortly before midnight last Tuesday to become the most expensive brood mare ever sold, is in foal to Northern Dancer or that Two Rings, who held the record for a day because of the $4,500,000 she fetched on Monday, is pregnant by Nijinsky, a brilliant son of Northern Dancer who has inherited his father's capacity for doing what comes naturally to wonderful effect. Nor was it fortuitous that Robert Sangster and his less publicised but no less formidable Irish associates dominated the consortium that bought Producer. They pride themselves in having some of the best Dancer blood available without resort to the old fellow's loins.

No one could be surprised when the leaders of the substantial Coolmore commando that invaded Keeneland, Vincent O'Brien, Sangster and the dynamic 35-year-old John Magnier, an impressive mixture of ruthless intuitiveness and calculating perceptions of whom it has been said that the softest thing about him is his teeth, were anxiously distracted by reports that Golden Fleece, Nijinsky's most distinguished offspring, had developed a colic at home in Ireland late last Sunday night. Golden Fleece, who was the fastest Epsom Derby winner for nearly half a century when he slaughtered his field in 1982 and is said to be insured at Lloyds for a sum within shouting distance of $40 million, is one of the foundations of their efforts to establish a true dynasty at their studs. The reports made it difficult for them to give their full attention to the Keeneland catalogue, whose several volumes are as thick as telephone directories and frequently give rise to numbers as unnerving as the dialling codes for Uzbekistan.

Some of the transactions at Keeneland in the not too distant past have been unlikely enough to encourage fantasies in a romantic interloper. A colt bought at the September Yearling Sales rather more than a decade ago for $1,200, which would hardly have paid for a decent drinks party in Lexington even then, went on to win two legs of the 1971 American Triple Crown (the Kentucky Derby and the Preakness Stakes) as Canonero II. Action at the four sales held regularly at Keeneland racecourse each year has intensified out of all recognition since Canonero II was a youngster (total business for 1969 was $26,079,000 while the figure for 1982 was $316,854,800 and another rise is safely predicted this year) and nothing has contributed more significantly to the transformation than an aggressive influx of money from this side of the Atlantic. Robert Sangster reckons that when he first started making shopping trips to Lexington about a dozen years ago the Europeans were responsible for about only 1 per cent of the buying, whereas now their involvement – if we include, as we must, agents representing the bottomless reservoir of Arab money

– is often as high as 60 per cent, especially when yearlings are on the market. 'You can look for perhaps 45 of the best 50 yearlings on offer at any of the biggest American sales to come to Europe, which is one of the main reasons why we have the strongest racing in the world today in terms of quality,' Sangster said last week. 'The terrible draining effect that occurred immediately after the Second World War when the aristocratic and Establishment families that controlled British racing sold so much of their best blood abroad, and especially to the US, is being thoroughly reversed. And everything achieved by the new determination to keep powerful male lines in Europe is being reinforced by what you are seeing here at this breeding stock sale, where we've been securing some of the finest mares alive.'

The magnificent seven-year-old Producer certainly seemed to belong in that category. Apart from having been a tremendous performer on the racecourse at the highest level in France and Ireland, her breeding is faultless as far back as Coolmore research could trace it, and she looks like a goddess. Even Vincent O'Brien, who knows just about as much as a man can know about what constitutes greatness in a thoroughbred, was thrilled as he watched her walked round in front of him, a dark bay with beautiful, almost wine-coloured streaks in her mane and tail. The great trainer was dressed as for the gallops in a blue, bulkily insulated jacket but, as ever, he had the appearance of a small, dignified country doctor as he peered over his half-moon glasses and sought to simplify his criteria for identifying an outstanding mare. 'It's like looking at a lady,' he said. 'She should be pretty, with a fine head and good, large, honest eye, nothing small or mean about it. Her conformation must be exceptional and, of course, she should move well.' That Producer met all of these requirements was confirmed when she was led into the small circle of wood chips beneath the auctioneer's dais, to be scrutinised by the prospective buyers spread over the 900 cushioned seats that rise away from the ring to create the appropriate sense of a theatre. Bidding for her opened at $3 million and, with the auctioneer interrupting his usual urgent jabbering occasionally to elaborate on her virtues, it climbed swiftly. When the group operating on Vincent O'Brien's judgment (the most conspicuous but by no means the only members of the consortium were Sangster, Stavros Niarchos, and a Californian millionaire named Danny Schwartz) intervened, it was through bids discreetly communicated from outside the walls of the main ring and transmitted by an alert Keeneland official in a strategically placed glass cubicle. They were soon making the running but even in that company there was a rustle of astonishment when a new bidder joined the contest at $5 million. He turned out to be Nelson Bunker Hunt, the Texan who has in his time controlled enough silver to embarrass governments, but his interest was quickly blunted and with one last $50,000 lunge the Sangster assault force took the price to five and a quarter million and won the day – or the night, since it was then around 20 minutes to twelve.

Most of the congratulations afterwards were, predictably, concentrated on the Englishman, who has used his family's football pools fortune as the basis of the most genuinely global commitment in the bloodstock industry. He has horses in Britain, Ireland, France, the US, West Germany, Australia, New Zealand, South Africa and Venezuela, and when asked how many he owns, says he finds keeping track of the total as difficult as a stamp collector might. 'Naturally, I can tell you about the Penny Blacks,' he adds, before conceding that the overall figure must be close to 700.

Sangster is a personable and pleasant man of 47, who refuses to let the scope of his interests impose any undue strain on him, preferring to enjoy the fact that bloodstock is currently a more attractive commodity than sugar or cocoa, than even silver or gold. Whether in fairly vivid casual ensembles, or a blazer and tie for the Producer coup, he gave the impression of being relaxed and unashamedly in his element at Keeneland. There is substance in the misgivings many people in racing feel about his tycoon's approach to the game, and the extent to which it makes the protection of a champion horse's stud value far more important than flaunting its talent through a sustained career in racing. The huge discrepancy between stallion fees and prize money – especially in Britain, where purses are 'so poor it is embarrassing' – is the essence of a justification that cannot hope to convince everybody.

Perhaps the launching of an international Breeders' Cup series of races, in which the top studs will swell the prize money by chipping in the equivalent of the enormous fees charged for their stallions, will help to establish a more exciting connection between what happens on breeding farms and on the track. The first

Breeders' Cup day at Hollywood Park in California next November will feature seven races and, incredibly, the lowest purse will be at least $1 million. Maybe that, too, will be another case of the rich getting richer. But when did we mug punters expect anything else?

The Observer, 2 November 1983

It is a sad footnote to this story that Golden Fleece's illness was fatal.

The Kid Who Came and Conquered

TO UNDERSTAND WHERE Steve Cauthen is now it is necessary to appreciate the full implications of where he has been. There is a lot more than an ocean, a few years and a reshaping of habits between the inspired boy who forced Americans to accept that a jockey could be a sports star and the quiet, insistently self-possessed man who has recently confirmed himself as the champion rider of the oldest racing country in the world.

Long before he ever imagined kicking horses home on the eccentric terrain of Brighton and Salisbury, Epsom, Ascot and Nottingham, before he dreamed of leaving Lester and Joe and Willie and Pat trailing as he surges, 20 or 30 winners clear, to the jockeys' title for the Flat season of 1984, Cauthen was a success in the United States on a scale such as no other teenage sportsman had ever known. The British punters who watch him comfortably outstripping those legendary rivals, so readily coping with the idiosyncrasies of a form of racing bemusingly alien to the centralised consistency of the game he knew at home, are not obliged to acquaint themselves with a journey so beset with vicissitudes that John Bunyan might have balked at writing the script. He is only 24 years old but, as his friend and professional adviser Jimmy Lindley says, 'he started life early' and there is about him today that hard maturity occasionally encountered in those who have had to live with fame as a surrogate for adolescence. That substitution laid waste to the glorious talents of George Best, among others, but Cauthen – supported through the highs and lows by the firmness of the bond with his family – was never in danger of surrendering his own clear view of himself and his abilities.

Talking on a recent evening over the table of a small restaurant in Lambourn, a Berkshire village that has only dedication to the thoroughbred to offer as a connection with his origins in Walton, Kentucky, his politeness did not obscure a morale so tough that railway sleepers could be broken across it. He was, of course, the most spectacular prodigy in the history of the American Turf. His father, Ron Cauthen, came of a family whose association with horses went back beyond ancestors who served with the Confederate Army and whose own upbringing in Sweetwater, Texas, 200 miles west of Dallas, led him naturally to a life as a worker in racing (a 'race-tracker'), specifically to the trade of blacksmith, to employment with a trainer called Tommy Bischoff and soon to marriage with Tommy's sister, Myra.

Steve thinks he may have sat on a horse at the age of one, knows he could ride a pony by the time he was one of the non-competing three-year-olds at his first Kentucky Derby in 1963. Between that childish glimpse of the old ramshackle shrine of American racing and his own historic win as an 18-year-old on Affirmed in the Derby of 1978, 'The Kid' – as his nation came to know him – was encouraged to assume that the only way was up. In 1977 he rode more than 400 winners and surpassed all previous totals for prize money by accumulating over $6 million in purses. Along the way he took in a clutch of incidental records, such as being the first rider for a quarter of a century to win six races in succession on a New York track, and 1978 brought the kind of experience that might be denied the greatest of jockeys – triumph in the three Classics that make up the US Triple Crown. Winning the Kentucky Derby, the Preakness and the Belmont in one season would leave an unquenchable glow in any rider's life, even if it came about freakishly in a year of moderate colts, but Cauthen had the extra, incalculable satisfaction of doing it on an outstanding horse who had to overcome the same remarkable adversary in all three great races.

Alydar was a clear favourite to take the Kentucky Derby and many good judges stayed with him through the other two legs of the treble but the celebrated power of his challenges in the straight never did more than bring the best out of the brilliant and resolute partnership of Affirmed and The Kid. No one who saw that contest between Affirmed and Alydar come to its crescendo in the attractive and historically appropriate setting of Belmont is likely to forget the details. Many say it was quite simply the greatest horse race they have ever seen. 'Those are the moments that jockeys live for,' he says. The dark eyes remain steadily alert in the fine-featured, almost delicate face but as he speaks it is easy to believe that they are seeing again the most exciting images of his life. 'Affirmed and Alydar battled out the Derby and then the Preakness and then there was the final at Belmont and the pressure was really on. I can remember at the top of the stretch when Alydar was breathing down our neck and I could tell Affirmed was tired. He'd had two hard races and he was tired. I thought, "I don't know if we're gonna make it." The whole life sort of goes through your mind in one split second and you think, "Shit, if we don't do it now we're never gonna do it. I'll never have another chance to win the Triple Crown." I can remember I pulled that little bit more out, that little bit extra and the horse pulled out that little bit extra. I brought my whip through and hit him left-handed, which I'd never done before because I'd never needed to. He found that bit more and we got there. We outbattled the other horse. That is a moment in sports history. To me it's like Muhammed Ali beating Frazier . . . it was an event . . . and I was lucky to be a part of it.'

The slight boy who steered Affirmed back to the winner's circle at Belmont on that summer afternoon in 1978 did so to the kind of national acclaim Americans had never before poured upon a jockey. Others had earned considerable fame and money but their grip on the public imagination had not extended beyond the cognoscenti of the tracks. Cauthen had impressed the insiders early and often painfully – serious bettors so frequently saw their fancies caught near the line by the fluid vigour of his driving finishes that they came to talk of being 'Cauthenized' – but what was unique was the ease with which he persuaded the followers of mainstream American sports that a jockey could be a hero figure.

Suddenly he had the marketable celebrity that had been granted to great football players and baseball players, a few golfers and an Olympic athlete or two, but never previously to someone who went to work on horseback. He made television commercials for American Express, for orange juice and sugarless gum, he was in constant demand for chat shows, he appeared on the cover of *Time* magazine. For the country boy ill at ease in the clamour of New York it all made for an exhausting schedule. 'Celebrity wasn't ever what I wanted,' he says. 'My ambition was to ride 400 winners a year, to be a jockey.' But, of course, he knew that what was happening to him was success and, out on the track at least, he savoured it deeply. As the Triple Crown Year of 1978 matured he could not possibly foresee the miseries that were about to crowd in on him. They began with a fall at Saratoga, not the most alarming of a career that has seen its full share of physical mishaps but one that brought the particularly troublesome consequence of a fractured knee.

While he was still making his way back from that accident, and trying to counter the reluctance of trainers to believe that he was himself again, his principal employer, Laz Barrera, the trainer of Affirmed, moved his string to California for the winter campaign. What followed was an unmitigated nightmare for Cauthen, a run of 110 rides without a winner, the sort of sequence that could have broken him but whose main effect has been to increase his self-sufficiency, strengthen his capacity to live with the fickleness of other people's reactions to his talent.

Of all the factors that created his devastating drought, the rapid loss of faith by Barrera and other trainers strikes him as most relevant. Even when the bleak streak was ended it was on a horse that Barrera let him have only because Laffit Pincay was sick. 'I was in two minds whether I wanted to ride it or not . . . but I did and I won and Laz was cryin' and kissin' me. But I felt, you know, I wasn't too sure about it, the whole thing. That was one of the most hurtful things because I was a young kid at the time and I really felt people would support you more when things got rough. You can't rest on your laurels but it was less than six months before that I had won the Triple Crown for that whole team.'

The press, too, had been battering him over the head with the reputation they had helped to build and when Robert Sangster approached him (not for the first time) about riding in England, the beleaguered prodigy was so fed up, psychologically drained, so in need of a dramatic change that the deal was made in 1979.

The will that had carried him through the crisis in California has been required in Britain as well. Having made a magnificent start, winning five Group races and capturing the Two Thousand Guineas with Tap on Wood in the first few weeks, he suffered along with Barry Hills as that trainer's horses were cruelly affected for a couple of years by the virus. But the Brits had made him welcome and he guessed that there would be ample rewards for sticking it out. Sitting in that Lambourn restaurant, a composed, well-barbered young man in expensive casual clothes, he made it plain that he is happy with the decision. He appreciates the rhythm of life in our game, its variety and traditions, its largely countrified atmosphere. As a fairly tall jockey at 5 ft 5 ins, he likes being able to ride at 117lbs or above, compared with the 112lbs he had to make in the US, and particularly he likes the long winter holidays that American riders daren't contemplate.

He talks interestingly on just about every aspect of racing and the firm voice – with its strange mixture of anglicised pronunciations and words like 'befoah' as reminders of Kentucky – delivers opinions with the same confidence that expresses itself through his noticeably long, strong hands when he is in the saddle.

Of Cauthen's style while riding in New York it was once said that 'you could serve drinks on The Kid's back at the eighth pole and you wouldn't spill a drop before he hits the wire!'. Lately American riders like his brilliant 'buddy' Angel Cordero have teased him about 'sitting with your ass in the air like Lester Piggott' but Angel ruefully admitted after an embarrassment at Sandown that adjustment was essential over here. 'I have never tried to change my basic style since I have been here,' says Cauthen. 'There's no difference in the way I have my feet in the irons. I've simply adapted to make me feel comfortable. Because the pace is slow here you have to get your horses settled. If you are sitting up their necks they are pulling you. The best way to settle them is to get a nice long hold down their necks. You can't fight a horse but if you can outsmart him and get him to co-operate that's the way you are going to win the battle.

'So basically the reason English jockeys sit so high in the saddle is because the tracks are so much stiffer you have to save a lot more horse. If you went the pace that they go in America you'd be walking up the last furlong of the finishes over here. In a finish some of the English jockeys have got exactly as much style, they are just as low as the best of our guys in the States.'

Steve Cauthen's horses haven't done a lot of walking on English racecourses this season and the flood of winners isn't likely to diminish when he replaces Piggott as first jockey to Henry Cecil next year. He does not know how long he will go on riding more than 3,000 miles from home but says he likes being here so much that he may just stay forever. For any Briton who doesn't wear silks at the races, that is good news.

The Observer, 1984

Steve Cauthen is back in the US now and encountering him over there is always enjoyable and rewarding.

Mellor Jumps Back to His First Love

IF SOME OF the thousands who head west during the middle three days of this week soon find that their betting wagons are drawn up in a besieged circle at Cheltenham, it may help just to think of Stan Mellor.

There can, of course, be no guarantee that Mellor-trained horses will bring rescue in the manner of US Cavalry remounts. But if the need is for a little philosophical justification of the irrational enthusiasms that keep so many in thrall to National Hunt racing – of the romantic resilience that enables them to battle on cheerfully against the odds (even the twenty-fives and thirty-threes) – then Stan Mellor is very much the man to provide it.

He is a special witness because it has taken him more than 30 years of the closest and most dramatic involvement with the jumping game to appreciate fully how central and indispensable it is to his life. Three or four years ago the old seductive dream of gaining glory and a far richer living on the Flat started to woo him away from the rougher side of his trade. The change of emphasis at his lively, hard-working yard on the edge of Lambourn in Berkshire was by no means calamitous but the pattern of results told him where his strengths and his basic affections lay.

He sent out 18 winners on the Flat in 1981, 15 in 1982, 12 in 1983 and nine last year. That brought him up to an aggregate of 89 in the dozen seasons since he began training after retiring as a rider in 1972, a total that makes respectable comparison with the 400-odd victories he has accumulated with his jumpers in the same period. To a man as honest and practical as Mellor, however, the lesson was clear enough.

He has no intention of abandoning entirely his ambitions for the Flat and of the 45 animals now lodged at his Linkslade stables

15 are reckoned capable of earning their keep in races that don't
include obstacles (not surprisingly, half of those are dual-purpose
performers who will be expected to take the tough route home as
they grow older). But he would like his darkly attractive wife Elain,
easily the outstanding lady Flat race jockey in the country with
nearly 50 winners to her credit, to supervise the preparation of the
more aristocratic creatures in his charge while he concentrates on
the hurdlers and steeplechasers.

'I don't regret having a go at the Flat,' he said over a cup of tea
after his string had exercised on Thursday. 'In an odd sense it's
been like a holiday. It has refreshed me. But I found that I really was
much more of a jumping man. I've got a big place here and it
seemed that we'd utilise it a lot better with Flat horses. It turned out
that I was looking at all the worst of jumping and all the best of the
other game. When I switched it made me see all the marvellous
things about jumping that I had been blind to – the fact that when
you get right down to basics it's better sport. I've got many great
friends on the Flat but it's got to be said that, all in all, the jumping
people are more fun to be with.

'There's obviously the chance to make more money on the Flat.
There's no money in training jumpers because there's nothing to sell
at the end of the day. You don't get into stallions. Even the best
horses have to be more or less given away when they have finished
racing. All you can say for this game is that it's just a good life but I
have learned to regard that as rather a lot. I'm certainly enjoying it
more now than ever before and I've got Flat racing to thank for that.'

The declaration of happiness was convincingly endorsed by the
smile spreading across a face that is pleasant, intelligent and
amazingly free of conspicuous scar tissue considering the hideous
abuse it has had to absorb in some of its 47 years. His hair is grey
now but the light-blue eyes are unclouded by memories of physical
sufferings that were often spectacular even by the standards of
National Hunt jockeys.

The most desperate of all came in the first running of the
Schweppes Gold Trophy at Liverpool in 1963 when Eastern
Harvest jumped too fast at the second flight and went down,
leaving Mellor to be ground and buffeted under the hooves of 40
pursuing horses. His face was in such a mess that he might have
worried about having to take it home in a parcel. But the 10
fractures and the loss of six teeth (which could have weighed down

the spirit of a young man who was due to be married shortly afterwards) alarmed him less than the suspicion that his back might be broken. He could scarcely move at all while lying conscious on his hospital bed but during a heavily drugged sleep he rose and walked naked around the ward. Next morning he felt paralysed once more but when the story of the nude somnambulist came back to him relief swamped embarrassment and he never gave a thought to quitting his dangerous job.

Eastern Harvest's fall prevented him from being champion National Hunt jockey for the fourth season in succession but, although he never took the title again, his career scarcely went into decline. He was subsequently second in the championship five times (once beaten by only one winner) and immortality in his sport was assured in December 1971 when he became the first jump rider to kick in 1,000 winners, a feat which even now has been equalled only by the great John Francome.

When he sets his horse-boxes off on the short run to Cheltenham this week, Mellor will be recalling the nasty hiccup he experienced there as he made his last surge towards the 1,000th appearance in the winner's circle. On the concluding Saturday of the December meeting in 1971 he needed just one victory from six good rides, but when the banker went wrong in the first the afternoon degenerated into mild nightmare.

The Cheltenham Festival was never likely to be the scene of much plundering by Mellor in his riding days because at 5ft 4in and 8st 10lb – physical proportions he inherited from his timber merchant father, who was a professional bantamweight boxer in his time – he was a lightweight who was bound to attract a huge volume of rides and to be wearied by the strain as March came round. 'Had the Festival been earlier in the season I would have ridden a lot more winners and been more fond of it. Now I am a trainer I don't have those problems and I mean to get very, very fond of the place.'

The process has already been assisted in recent years by the achievements of such as Pollardstown and Saxon Farm (both took the Triumph Hurdle and Pollardstown was second in the Champion) and by Royal Mail's second in the Gold Cup. And it could be accelerated significantly on Wednesday by Ten of Spades, a big, imposing five-year-old bay gelding from Ireland who may tow home a strong field in the Sun Alliance Novices' Hurdle.

Stepping out of his box at Linkslade to be photographed last Thursday, Ten of Spades had the instantly recognisable presence of a horse who believes in himself. His trainer shudders slightly at the rumours, rife after an exciting success at Cheltenham, that 'he is the best thing to come out of Ireland since Arkle', but confirms that he is exceptionally promising. 'He is a good horse with a positive attitude about everything. He needs the two-and-a-half miles of the Sun Alliance and he's got courage. If they are going to beat him up the hill they'll have to fight.'

One asset he thinks he is sure he can rely on is the riding of his main jockeys, the stylish and widely admired Mark Perrett and the excellent 4lb claimer Gareth Charles-Jones. No one would ever confuse their work in the saddle with the almost dervish urgency of their guv'nor in his prime but they have been getting the job done with impressive frequency and the stable starts this week with more than 30 winners in the ledger.

Perrett and Charles-Jones will never find Mellor pressuring them with his own former greatness as a rider. Most of his stories about the old days are distinguished by wry self-deprecation: 'When I began to lose my bottle I wanted to get right on the outside away from the trouble but not long after I got chary Josh Gifford's bottle started to go, too, and he wanted the outside just as much. Not only was Josh a brilliant rider but he usually had better mounts than I had, so he kept getting out there and pushing me back into the pack. I've told the bugger about it since.'

In addition to seconds in the Cheltenham Gold Cup and the National, Mellor had many major and memorable wins, including a defeat of Arkle on Stalbridge Colonist and of Mill House on King's Nephew, but it is typical of him that he should talk at greater length about the time 'a wonderful ride' on The Fossa at Aintree came to an end with the shambles at the twenty-third fence which put the 100-1 Foinavon into the history books in 1967.

'We were about fifth when The Fossa was baulked and I was left sitting on top of the fence with nearly 40 other runners liable to land on me at any moment. I scrambled down and ran for my life. Next day there was a picture in the paper of me sprinting flat out and I thought I'd been rumbled. But the caption said: "Pile-up at the twenty-third – Stan Mellor runs after his mount". My mount was on the other side of the fence and he wasn't much in my thoughts right then.'

Stan Mellor's days of sitting on the fence over the conflicting appeals of Flat and National Hunt racing seem to be behind him. I for one hope that what lies in front of him, starting with Cheltenham this week, is all the success he and his family could want.

The Observer, 10 March 1985

The Master's Last Furlong?

If there seems to be rather a lot about Lester Piggott in these pages, I make no apology. This piece was a response to indications that he was ready to retire 10 years ago. He and we soon learned that he wasn't.

TWO OF THE great institutions of British sport will combine to quicken the heartbeat of the nation on Epsom Downs this Wednesday, and when the shouting has died away and the last of us to leave the old arena are walking through the litter to the car park, we are likely to feel that the Derby will never be quite the same again.

Obviously, even if Lester Piggott does decide to turn probability into fact by making this his final season as a jockey, that will not end his involvement with the most remarkable horse race in the world. He will switch without interruption to the training of thoroughbreds and, since he is sure to handle plenty of animals of Classic quality, he should continue to exert a pronounced influence on the dramas of the Derby. But once he stops reaching for the coloured silks something will go out of that early summer afternoon on the Downs, at least for those of us who are almost exactly contemporary with Lester and so have come to regard him as central and permanent in our sporting experience. The Derby will remain a wonder whoever has to quit its stage, but the loss of the greatest master of its peculiar riding problems cannot be negligible. For more than three decades The Long Fellow has been giving virtuoso performances on the notoriously difficult instrument of Epsom.

There is, of course, an exceptional longevity about the fame of outstanding riders in Flat racing. Piggott was only 12 when he brought The Chase in at Haydock in 1948 as his first winner on a racecourse. He will be 50 in November. Considering that his legend was already a sturdy growth by the time he rode the earliest of his nine Epsom Derby winners (Never Say Die in 1954), it is scarcely surprising if his name is now the most instantly identifiable and, in several senses, the most emotive in the recent mythology of this country's sport. It is celebrity shot through with many subtleties of feeling. There is an inevitable ambiguity about the public's attitudes to jockeys, since much of the reaction to their work originates in the pocket. Steve Donoghue, the great Derby specialist of 60 and more years ago, and Sir Gordon Richards, who thoroughly dominated the riders' championship from the late 1920s until 1953 (when he at last won his first Derby), both evoked deep affection but they were called a few fancy names in their time by punters in the stands or gathered round the street corner bookmakers who flourished before betting shops were legalised. Nevertheless, there was a simplicity about the population's relationship to Donoghue and Richards that does not apply to Piggott.

He has always been more remote from his admirers than either of those two inspired predecessors, with a capacity to distance himself from the throng only partially explained by the slight deafness and mild speech difficulty he has countered with increasing success since childhood. Clearly those disadvantages must have encouraged him to believe that, much of the time, two could be a crowd. But the self-containment which grew out of such early tendencies has become so powerful in his mature years as to leave no doubt that he was born with deep reserves of obsessive will.

So much has been written – quite understandably – about the relevance of his ancestry that it is perhaps enough now to say that his bloodlines brim with hard, competitive professional horsemen and horsewomen on both sides of the pedigree, people who made a big impact at the highest levels of racing. Piggott's own father, Keith, did not let the tradition down during his career as a leading National Hunt rider and if he did not win the Grand National in the saddle he gained compensation by training Ayala to take the supreme steeplechase for Teasy Weasy Raymond, the hairdresser. Lester says matter-of-factly – there are liable to be a few fainting cases whenever he uses any other style of speech – that his father taught him everything he learned about race-riding in his formative years. However, perhaps the most vital elements of such a man's talent are too mysterious to be either analysed or taught. Sir Noel Murless, one of an elite of superb trainers who have provided magnificently prepared horses for Piggott to ride to success in 29 English Classics, three runnings of the Prix de l'Arc de Triomphe, two Washington Internationals in the US and countless other memorable races, has more right than most to make the point: 'You can teach a jockey many things but there is something you cannot transmit. It is the feeling, the sensitivity of a natural jockey. It is a mystery which only the horse, the great jockey and God can really know about.'

When all attempts have been made to assess the importance of the principal elements of his highly individual technique (made unmistakable in the biggest field by the elevation of his bobbing rear end, which is hoisted into the air because he likes to stand up in short stirrup leathers and happens to be notably tall for his trade at 5 ft 7½ in), a satisfactory explanation of how effective he can be is indeed just about impossible without reference to the Senior Steward in the sky. It is almost superfluous to say he is a brilliant judge of pace, whether coming from behind or dictating the pattern of a race at the front, just as it is simplistic to point to the terrible driving urgency of his finishes.

Despite all the years of wasting that have enabled him to go on riding at around eight-and-a-half stone when he might be walking the street at a stone and a half more, his athletic body generates astonishing power but, patently, that phenomenon testifies to the even more profound strength of his spirit. Yet here, too, his character refuses to manifest itself in orthodox ways. His extreme determination, many would say ruthlessness, hints at a deep core of something close to violence in his nature but for the most part it remains hidden and controlled, a volcano trapped in an iceberg.

In the paddock at Epsom on Wednesday there will be jockeys whose insides, if we could see them, might look like one of those bubbling retorts in a Hollywood rendering of Frankenstein's laboratory but Piggott's expression may suggest that the business on hand is a selling plate at Windsor. The journalistic habit of comparing his face with a crumpled parchment may be an offensive exaggeration but his features are inclined to be a shade more enigmatic than the Dead Sea Scrolls. His unrivalled record of big-race victories on the English Turf shows that the horses usually get the message, one way or another. Sometimes it is an aggressively direct communication, as when he drove Roberto up the Epsom straight under the whip to snatch the 1972 Derby from Rheingold, an animal subsequently good enough to win the Arc de Triomphe in Piggott's hands. Piggott rode like a man possessed to win that Derby. However, Vincent O'Brien, for whom Roberto is one of a current total of six Derby winners, four of which were ridden by Piggott, reported that there wasn't a mark on his horse. We have to conclude that in his use of the cosh, as in everything else he does from the saddle, Lester is an artist. Certainly those tough two minutes and 36 seconds out on the left-handed, severely undulating mile-and-a-half of the Derby course didn't seem to do Roberto any lasting harm, since he went on to become the only horse ever to beat the wonderful Brigadier Gerard, in the Benson & Hedges Gold Cup at York, under the Panamanian Braulio Baeza.

The 1972 Derby stays in the mind as an interesting statement about basic aspects of Piggott's career and about the undiminished status of a race that has withstood all assaults on its uniqueness since it was first run in 1780. There was, for a start, more than a whiff of the controversy that has never been far from Piggott's name since he first arrived as a schoolboy to charge through the sensitivities of senior jockeys and stewards of the Jockey Club alike with a belligerent precocity that brought him serious punishments for reckless riding. As he grew older, made a marriage that forged a connection with yet another racing family and had two daughters, his commitment to winning – though undiluted – was less rawly expressed on the course. But his fellow jockeys did not enjoy any noticeable increase in peace of mind, for he soon took to improving his chances in major races by angling so insistently for the most fancied mounts that many who thought their riding engagements were secure often found themselves grounded. 'Jocked off' is the trade term but some of the victims adjusted it slightly.

It would be unfair to hold Piggott responsible for the decision to give him the ride on Roberto, which had been due to go to the distinguished Australian Bill Williamson. The advice of Vincent O'Brien persuaded the American owner, John Galbreath, that a fall suffered by Williamson 10 days before Epsom had created doubts about his fitness to handle a horse who could be less than co-operative. Still, Piggott hadn't exactly played hard to get and when Williamson proved his soundness on Derby day by beating two short-priced favourites ridden by the English genius, resentment over the Roberto episode was compounded. Yet, however many in the crowd disapproved of the way Piggott came to ride Roberto, most honest critics had to agree that no jockey ever born could have served the bay colt better on the day.

His was a contribution to swell the army of good judges who would put him on the shortest list of the greatest race-riders in history. Unequivocal declarations that he must be the best of all are profitless, since they can be neither validated nor conclusively refuted in a game that goes back through so many generations. The Australians, the French and especially the Americans (whose brilliant elf Willie Shoemaker has driven home more winners than anybody else who ever lived) would advance candidates for the impossible title. And there would be English support for long-dead giants such as Jem Robinson and Frank Buckle as well as clamour for Richards and Donoghue. But probably the most intriguing comparison of all is that of Piggott with Fred Archer. What draws them together in the imagination, across more than 100 years, is not merely the towering scale of their accomplishments but the sense of drama each in his entirely personal way brought to the Turf.

In Archer's case, the dramatic merged sickeningly with the tragic late in 1886. Depressed by an endless cycle of brutal wasting, his system blasted by crude purgatives and further lowered by a severe chill and what was diagnosed as typhoid fever, he rose from his sickbed, took a revolver from a pedestal and wrestled off the restraining hands of his distraught sister before shooting himself left-handed through the mouth. The bullet severed the spinal column and killed him instantly. He was only 29 years old but had been champion jockey for 13 straight seasons, exceeding 200 victories in eight of them. He had ridden the winners of 21 Classics, including five of the Derby. Even allowing for the vastly different conditions that prevailed in Victorian racing, the figures are stunning. Archer was a very different man from Piggott but they are linked by obsession and inspiration and it may be a photo-finish between them to decide who rates as the most electrifying presence English racing has seen.

Of course, the game must go on and find new heroes if Piggott does retire, and it is fortunate that a likely heir is at hand. In fact, Steve Cauthen, who began as an astounding prodigy in America, has already developed into the most comprehensively equipped jockey now operating on our racecourses. 'When I watch Steve I am seeing the young Lester all over again,' says Jimmy Lindley, who once battled out a lot of hard races with Piggott and remains active in the sport, with BBC paddock commentator as only one of his roles. 'By totally different means they get the last knockings out of a horse. For me, they're so superior to most merely mortal riders that there is an unmistakable aura, a kind of green light that surrounds everything they do. They never seem to have to wonder what their next move will be. Many people can play the piano but you only get a few who can fill the Albert Hall and only one who is the best in the world. Even the American press had to admit eventually how special Lester was.

'You know the story about how he held Sir Ivor up for a short, devastating run to win the Washington International in 1968 and the American racing writers hammered him as a bum who nearly got the good horse beat. When Lester went back the following year and won the International again on Karabas they suspected there might be more to him and came crowding around with their questions. "When did you think you had the race won, Lester – coming into the stretch or a bit earlier?" But Lester's memory is as good as his riding. "I thought I had it won three weeks ago," he said. "Now f—— off." Those fellas should have known better than to mess with him.'

Even when he is being generous with his time, as he has always been to this reporter, Piggott is not the easiest interview. There is a pared-down practicality about his utterances that doesn't lend itself to lyrical evocations of glorious deeds in the rainbow jacket. A shrug, a gesture of the strong hands and an answer a third as long as the question may be the standard rate of exchange. The impression is not that formulating answers is a problem, more that he is so accustomed to letting his actions speak for him that words sometimes seem to get in the way of true self-expression. He deploys them effectively enough when he wants to make one of his wry jokes or to jump on a suggestion he doesn't like. It was the latter response he gave in the unlikely privacy of the jockeys' medical room at Goodwood some days back when I asked if all the cracks about his alleged tightness with cash had, over the years, angered or amused him. For a moment he looked a little like Marvin Hagler before the first round with Thomas Hearns and, although all he delivered were a few expletives, the inquiry was adequately answered. He was not amused. One man who should know believes that the celebrated concern with accumulating money in large piles is a source of a strangely aesthetic pleasure, like an involved game of backgammon, and insists that Lester has been open-handed in helping many people out of genuine troubles.

It was legitimate to suspect that there might be need of the medical room's facilities at the mention of the special and extremely lucrative retainer arrangements Piggott enjoyed until lately with Henry Cecil, the Newmarket trainer, and the recent story in this newspaper connecting the great man with allegations about the passing of tips which have provoked a Jockey Club investigation. But although he was again blatantly unamused, he made his objections about *The Observer* story courteously and indicated with impressive fairness that it would not prevent him from discussing other subjects with me.

The most natural of all was obviously the Derby and on that he hit his stride. He could not provide confirmation that this would be his last appearance in the race. 'I said I'd decide in June and that's what I'll do,' he said. 'Retirement is the way I'm thinking at the moment.' No, he didn't think he'd ride any of the horses he trained, although it was permitted. 'I think you should do one thing or the other. Riding has always been a job of work to me. That's how I've looked upon it and when you've finished that's it. It's a job that's changed a hell of a lot even in the past 20 years. You've got to be a lot more careful about how you ride nowadays. You've got to read the Highway Code every day.

'Naturally, I'll miss some of the exciting experiences. Above all, I'll miss the Derby because it is the most exciting race of the lot. Even an Arc cannot match it. Last year the Derby was only about twentieth among the world's races in terms of value but you'd still give anything to win it. Of the nine horses that have won it for me, Nijinsky was the best on his day but the most thrilling of those races was The Minstrel's in 1977. That was just a tremendous race.'

The past week has seen much speculation about the identity of the horse that will give him his chance of a tenth Derby. But Piggott was, as usual, keeping the options open as long as possible. So were the millions of small punters who see Derby day as a time for siding with the most extraordinary and enduring performer in British sport.

The Observer, 2 June 1985

Lester was to prove even more enduring than we then realised, coming back after serving a jail sentence for tax evasion to ride with enough of his old brilliance to claim a Breeders' Cup victory on Royal Academy. It was 1995 before he let his riding licence lapse.

Rainbow over a Day
of Objections in France

MR DANIEL WILDENSTEIN, millionaire art dealer and connoisseur of resentments, has been exhibiting a beauty throughout the past week.

The most philosophical owners in racing might have been drained of benignity by the experience of watching a horse of theirs pass the post first in the Prix de l'Arc de Triomphe only to be disqualified and dropped into second place. When it happened to Mr Wildenstein, whose name would not be too easily located on anybody's all-time list of good losers, such an ordeal was likely to trigger the napalm-launcher which his nature seems to keep permanently on red alert. There could be little genuine surprise when the Société d'Encouragement, the French equivalent of the Jockey Club, confirmed on Thursday that he had lodged a formal appeal against the decision that prevented his brilliant and brave five-year-old Sagace from taking the Arc for the second year in succession at Longchamp last Sunday.

What is difficult to imagine is just how Wildenstein, his trainer Patrick Biancone and Sagace's 20-year-old rider Eric Legrix can hope to persuade the committee who will hear their appeal that the two hefty shoulder charges their champion inflicted on Rainbow Quest during the final, decisive phase of the great race were insufficient grounds for disqualification. The first of those bumps, delivered near the one-furlong marker as Pat Eddery's perfectly calculated challenge on Rainbow Quest was intensifying towards its thrilling crescendo, might have been enough to warrant the demotion of Sagace. When the camera filming the horses head-on as their desperate contest brought them hurtling to the line revealed that Sagace had veered away from the rail once more and collided quite forcefully with the English contender it seemed that the French case was one even Clarence Darrow wouldn't have wanted to argue.

Yet the redoubtable art dealer apparently does. Surely he can expect no joy. An oil painting may evoke different responses from different pairs of eyes but that patrol film allows for no such subjective interpretations. One look at it made thoroughly understandable the vehemence with which Eddery declared that he was bound to be given the race as he jumped off Rainbow Quest to register the objection that later drew a bombardment of insults and non-lethal missiles around his head. It would have been slightly more logical (though equally cruel) had the French crowd vented their disappointment on the immensely promising Legrix, for his failure to change his whip from his right to his left hand when the struggle was at its fiercest did nothing to discourage poor Sagace's violation of the rules.

At Longchamp last Sunday the barbs exchanged between members of the English contingent and their traditional sparring partners were generally less witty than the sallies of Henry V and the Dauphin but there was no doubting the commitment of pride and expectation the home side had made to Sagace and his trainer Biancone, a 33-year-old who was seeking a hat-trick of victories in the Arc after the successes of All Along in 1983 and Sagace himself last year. Sagace is clearly something of a marvel and might well have held on to win without the aid of transgressions. Patrick Biancone insists that he was unable to train the horse properly for a fortnight before the Arc because of a minor problem and that on the day Sagace was running on only three sound legs. 'If he'd been right he'd have won by ten lengths,' the trainer added, forgivably exaggerating the capacity of an animal he regards as a true hero.

Obviously it was the determination to reinforce this reputation that persuaded the Wildenstein-Biancone partnership to have three runners, or 20 per cent of the 15-horse field, in the race. The original strategy, it seems, involved letting Heraldiste make the pace for a mile or so, then having Balitou handle that job for perhaps two more furlongs before Sagace surged away to provide a triumphant climax. But the action didn't develop according to that script and when Balitou was prominent in the extreme roughness that suddenly enveloped the race before the entrance to the straight many spectators felt that teamwork was being taken to outrageous lengths.

Detailed examination of the film evidence convinced a lot of experts subsequently that Balitou wasn't quite the sinister influence he had first appeared to be, that in fact the horse's jockey had been mainly concerned with self-preservation as he found himself part of the chain reaction set off when Heraldiste was abruptly moved out to give Sagace first run along the rail in the straight. Still, whatever the theories on the precise origins of that roughhousing, what is undeniable is that the mayhem totally snuffed out the chances of Shernazar, the English-trained second favourite, and that in general the capers of Sagace's two stablemates didn't brighten the prospects of any of his rivals.

I must confess that my sympathy with the entirely admirable French star and all who had bet him to odds-on was submerged in the satisfaction of holding a little bunch of tickets identified with Rainbow Quest. The need of their cheering effect was not lessened by the sickening nuisance of having the car broken into in central Paris during Saturday night or the uneasiness felt in the company of so many who transport much that is unendearing about British society to Longchamp on Arc day. Between the package tour parties, whose more aggressive elements swill, bellow and jostle with as much grace and civility as an invasion force of football supporters, and the smaller but equally deadly concentrations of hoorays, being British can be a bit embarrassing in the Bois de Boulogne on the first Sunday in October. One of the self-appointed toffs was seen pleading – thank goodness, unsuccessfully – for a privileged ticket while carrying a bottle of champagne in his hat. The hat must have concluded that it had a better than usual class of tenant.

Unfortunately, when the French take revenge for all this nonsense it ravages the innocent along with the guilty. They do it principally through the murderous inefficiency with which they operate their pari-mutuel system of betting. My sufferings under that blight go back 15 years and more but last Sunday was a particular horror, since I was kept so long waiting in line for my Rainbow Quest winnings that Bella Colora, the day's nap, was home and hosed before my knuckles could whiten around the francs. Don't tell me I should have switched to a betting queue. By the time that move was advisable, it was too late, because the operators at those windows were equally hopeless. Even allowing for the language difficulties and the clumsy declaration of requirements that are so prevalent on this afternoon, it struck me that one of the scores of expert bet-takers who function at Belmont or Aqueduct in New York could have caused the whole body of customers at Longchamp to melt away in ten minutes.

This ridiculous mess has gone far beyond a joke. It is unforgivable to deny racegoers the facilities for losing their money swiftly and without fuss.

The Observer, 13 October 1985

Jonjo and the Run of a Lifetime

THE REST OF humanity had better be wary from now on of the 42,000 of us who were on Cheltenham racecourse last Thursday. We cannot begin to guarantee that our babblings of what we saw there will not be sufficiently relentless to clear bars, cause communication cords to be grabbed on trains or tempt fellow passengers on aeroplanes to head for the exit at 35,000 feet.

People who witness miracles, even small ones of the sporting kind, are liable to carry around forever afterwards a deadly parcel of reminiscence and anyone who wants to avoid my 1986 Gold Cup monologue should be ready with emergency measures whenever the names of Dawn Run, Jonjo O'Neill, Charmian Hill and Paddy Mullins are mentioned. In three decades of watching supreme performers in a wide range of contests, there have been few experiences that have precipitated a greater flood of excitement and pleasure than the sight of Jonjo and that incomparable mare battling out of what seemed the hopeless finality of third place at the last fence. Dawn Run galloped with unbreakable pride up the killing slope of Cheltenham's run-in to pass Forgive 'n' Forget and Wayward Lad and make history by becoming the first horse to add a Gold Cup to a Champion Hurdle victory. The melodrama belonged in the last reel of one those old Hollywood films in which someone like the young Roddy McDowall came from about two parishes back to land the big prize.

Jonjo, with no director to adjust the positions for him in the closing scene, and with a phenomenon under him who prefers to boss her rivals from the front, had never exposed himself to the slightest danger of having a lot of ground to make up. He had concentrated on setting a dominating, draining pace while coping patiently with the wearing company of Run and Skip, whose tough rider, Steve Smith-Eccles, was determined to maintain the nagging proximity that might have invited the blunders to be expected from an eight-year-old with only four previous outings over fences. In spite of making her task more difficult by dropping her hind legs in the water and suffering a noticeable loss of momentum and then committing a more significant error by clattering the fifth fence from home, Dawn Run had burned off Run and Skip by the second-last but the superb veteran Wayward Lad (on which O'Neill took third place in the Gold Cup of 1983) and last year's winner, Forgive 'n' Forget, were swiftly, ominously overhauling her. And to everyone in the stands it looked as if she and Jonjo had been fatally engulfed at the final jump.

When the talent and heart of this inspired Irish partnership proved otherwise, the explosion of euphoria was such that some of the hats sent spiralling into the air might have had heads in them for all the owners cared. No result, not even the three Gold Cup wins in a row by the greatest of steeplechasers, Arkle, ever stirred a more emotional response than greeted Dawn Run's success, which had the unsurprising additional distinction of clipping 1.9 seconds off the record time for the three miles two furlongs and 22 fences of the ultimate test of the jumping code's elite.

The stampeding crowds in the winner's enclosure could have been extremely dangerous but good nature just held the line against hysteria and nothing happened to taint the happiness that suffused the entire occasion as thoroughly as it did the glowing face of Mrs Hill, who looked closer to 40 than 67 as she accepted the trophy from an almost equally delighted Queen Mother. With Dawn Run a noble, steaming presence off to the side, it was quite a day for heroines. But no one was likely to forget the heroes, especially when Jonjo O'Neill, rider of a race of flawless control and purity, produced another stroke of inspiration by taking an affectionate grip on Tony Mullins – son of Dawn Run's trainer Paddy and her regular jockey until being dislodged in more ways than one at Cheltenham in her fourth steeplechase in January – before hoisting the younger man on to his shoulders and carrying him up to the presentation dais.

It was a spontaneous, marvellously unforced gesture, utterly characteristic of the little Cork man, whose bravery, resilience, warmth and generosity of spirit so perfectly represent the irresistible qualities of a game which, at its best, is one of the most natural and attractive metaphors for life that sport has to offer. Maybe the natures that inhabit it tend to be so appealing because they learn early (and go on relearning) how to live not only with losing but with losing painfully, sometimes in the intensive care unit.

Jonjo himself has come through experiences severe enough to have put a more ordinary man in a wheelchair, if not in a hole in the ground. He remembers the time when his right leg was so hideously broken that it was 'like a sack of gravel', so devastated that an extensive metal plate and screws had to be inserted to help bind the bones, but he has readily put such ordeals behind him. When I asked during a long telephone conversation late on Friday night if the leg still bothered him, I got the riposte I deserved. 'Don't you think it was working all right yesterday?' he asked. Everything, of course, had worked beautifully, which was not something he was entitled to assume after schooling Dawn Run at Gowran Park in Ireland in January. Her behaviour that day was nightmarishly bad and after enduring two circuits on which she backed off from some fences, dived to the left at others and generally conducted herself like an eccentric menace, Jonjo was as near to despair as he ever sinks.

'At the end of that I didn't think she should be running in the Gold Cup, let alone be favourite to win it,' he said. 'She did jump the last fence of that schooling run well but one out of about 14 isn't exactly encouraging. Then on the Thursday before Cheltenham I went over to school her again at Punchestown and this time Tony Mullins rode another horse round with me and Dawn Run did everything I asked her to do, which I didn't think was possible after Gowran Park. So that raised our hopes, though there had to be worries about how she would go about her work on the day. Still, when people say they could see that I was a lot more nervous than usual before the Gold Cup, that I was obviously feeling the extra pressure, I think I've got to correct that a little bit. There's no point in denying that I had to be aware of how important Thursday was for me and everybody connected with the mare, but the responsibility that brought is not the kind to weigh me down.

'The way I look at it, I love the old game, it's my flippin' hobby as well as my livin' and above all I love riding really good horses. Going out there with something exceptional underneath you and getting the job right together is the greatest satisfaction. It is far better to be on a good horse than a moderate one and the responsibility involved can never reduce the thrill of that for me. But whether it's a favourite or 100-1 shot I go out to try to get the job right. I'm riding to fit the horse as much as I want the horse to fit me.'

He never considered charging off into the distance as Dawn Run has done while murdering opponents in the past. Cheltenham's hills and stiff obstacles would, he knew, have made such tactics madness. So we were privileged to see the ride of a lifetime, a monument to patience, nerve, courage and technical brilliance, the mature masterwork of a great jockey. 'Halfway through the run to the last fence she seemed beat,' he said on Friday night. 'But I let her get her own feet and she jumped it well. She's a moody old devil, and neither me nor anyone else could get her to do something if she didn't want to. She wasn't absolutely knackered. She was taking a breather, saying, "I'm going fast enough here". After Wayward Lad went two or three lengths up he began to hang across in front of me towards the rails. I realised he was tired and stopping and so did she. So we both got stuck in together.'

They did, even more dramatically than when winning the Champion Hurdle in 1984. At the line Jonjo, he admits, 'went crackers', which left him about twice as sane as a reception party that nearly made him the first rider to have a leg broken in the winner's enclosure. Through it all the bright face under the clump of reddish hair never lost its expression of delirious bliss.

Some man. Some horse. Some day.

The Observer, 16 March 1986

Young Man goes West

This is a Grand National report, mainly ad-libbed to meet the deadline, then tidied up afterwards.

A HORSE WITH a horribly scarred body but a beautifully intact spirit formed a perfect partnership with the brilliance of the youngest jockey in the race yesterday to bring the 1986 Grand National to the kind of heart-warming climax even the biggest losers had to cheer.

Richard Dunwoody and West Tip had been leading and moving like winners when they fell at Becher's Brook on the second circuit last year but this time both were too inspired to permit even the most intimidating of Aintree's 30 fences to keep them from glory. As the historic contest entered its decisive final half mile they were travelling so smoothly that the outcome already seemed beyond doubt. Although West Tip pricked his ears and gave slight hints of being excessively relaxed after passing Young Driver as they came away from the last fence, there was never any real faltering in the run to the line and at the winning post the margin of victory was a fairly comfortable two lengths. The quality of the performance was clearly indicated by the fact that the third horse, Classified, was fully 20 lengths back.

This was a genuine Anglo-Irish triumph. Dunwoody is a 22-year-old prodigy who was born in Comber, Co Down, and transplanted to England at the age of nine, and West Tip followed a similar route from his breeding ground in Southern Ireland. They were steered towards yesterday's unforgettable success by the patient skills of 36-year-old Michael Oliver, a trainer who represents the accumulated wisdom of an English family that has long and distinguished associations with the racing game.

Almost before the roars that greeted West Tip's victory had subsided, Oliver was eulogising the talents of his young jockey. 'I think Richard Dunwoody is far and away the most talented rider in England today and I have thought as highly of him for the last three years – ever since I saw him win a hunter chase at Ludlow as a newcomer to the business. I could not believe how magnificently everything went for us today, how beautiful and without a trace of a blemish Richard's riding was.'

Yet in the midst of such tributes to the human hero of the day there had to be moving praise for the brave horse who had survived an extraordinary catalogue of mishaps to dominate the toughest race in the world. Twice West Tip was close to being a carcass long before he ever reached Aintree. He might easily have died when, as a young animal, he became dreadfully entangled with some wire in Ireland but he emerged with nothing worse than some desperate scars on his hind legs. Then on 21 September 1982, only 150 yards from Michael Oliver's stableyard in Droitwich, Worcestershire, West Tip had his nearside ripped open by metal hoops beneath the load-bed of a passing lorry and his life, let alone his competitive career, looked sure to be over. But again his spirit carried him through, enabling him to overcome the trauma of wounds that required about 80 stitches.

Yesterday at Aintree nothing against him in the field of 40 runners could hope to deny a contender of such exceptional ability and powerful character. Many had realised after his display in 1985 and two excellent recent runs, particularly a fine win at Newbury, that he might be the one to be on and West Tip started at 15-2 second favourite.

Apart from a minor moment at The Chair and touching Ten Cherries at the Canal Turn first time round, he created the minimum of anxiety and those who backed him found their confidence rising to a happy crescendo as the horses who were still factors in the race came over the Melling Road for the last time. 'From three out I felt I could win but I did not want to put him in front too early,' said Dunwoody. 'I don't think he had ever been going quite as well as he was last year. I was just nudging him along most of the way but once I sensed that The Tsarevich might be going a little too freely, and wouldn't last home as well as we would, I was very optimistic.'

One man who must have been burdened with a fair amount of

pessimism at that stage was Terry Ramsden, the millionaire commodities dealer who is one of the most substantial owners in British racing these days and undoubtedly its most spectacular punter. Mr Ramsden had wagered frightening sums on his recently purchased Mr Snugfit and the weight of his money had made last year's Grand National second the 13-2 favourite at the off here. But at one point Mr Snugfit was almost two furlongs behind (in part the penalty for a serious early blunder) and it was not until the battle was almost over that he began to come through tiring opponents. He did so to such purpose that he made it into fourth place at the finish, which was a highly relevant achievement considering that the monster bets of his owner were struck each way. Terry Ramsden may not need the Pickfords van which might have been called into action if Mr Snugfit had won, but his consolation prize would keep an ordinary family in comfort for a century or two.

Young Driver's accomplishment in finishing second is made all the more notable if we remember that even the light weight of 10 stone he had on his back was 8lbs more than he had in the long handicap. The third horse, Classified, was one of a handful who were always going quite impressively on the second circuit – Kilkilowen, The Tsarevich and Monamore were conspicuous in that category – but a number of the most fancied runners were out of contention early. Door Latch fell at the first, Corbiere, winner in 1983 and twice placed in the event, fell at the fourth and the 1985 winner, Last Suspect, pulled up at the 18th.

Greasepaint, in the frame three times running in the National, finished 10th and Hallo Dandy, who was successful two years ago, slogged in 12th. The non-finishers included the top weight from Czechoslovakia, Essex, who pulled up before the 15th, and at the end only 17 of the 40 who started out were still standing. Of the jockeys who completed the course, Phil Tuck offered the most memorable summing up of how he had fared: 'If there had been another mile to go Mr Snugfit would just about have won.'

Richard Dunwoody did not have to be amusing. Neither did he need a bonus but West Tip provided a nice one. The nine-year-old gelding was not only his 42nd winner of the season but his third of the Liverpool meeting and therefore gave him the Ritz trophy as the most successful rider over the three days.

It was unsurprising in a sport where comradeship is no mere matter of lip-service that he should remember with sympathy the sufferings of Eamonn Murphy, the Irishman who would have prevented Dunwoody from being the youngest jockey in the Grand National if he had not been left bruised and sickened by a nasty fall from Stray Shot in the first race.

The Observer, 6 April 1986

Dancing Fails in the Quick-step

CALIFORNIAN SUNSHINE COULD do nothing to prevent yesterday at Santa Anita from being a dark and miserable experience for British racing as Dancing Brave, widely acknowledged to be one of the very best horses to run in Europe since the Second World War, trailed in a weary and utterly defeated fourth, nearly seven lengths behind the winner of the $2 million contest that had been expected to provide him with a perfect farewell appearance before he went to stud.

The electrifying surge along the home straight that slaughtered a marvellous field in the Prix de l'Arc de Triomphe less than a month ago and had given Dancing Brave brilliant victories in all his previous races except the Epsom Derby (where he was a cruelly unlucky loser) never threatened to come. Pat Eddery, the successful partner in the Arc, seemed to have the British champion poised for that killing swoop as he turned to face the mere 330 yards of the Santa Anita run-in with the leader, Estrapade, well within reach. But when Eddery asked for overdrive there was instead a totally uncharacteristic one-paced response.

Ahead of them, a horse well known to European watchers, Theatrical, was spiritedly challenging Estrapade but suddenly neither of those two had much hope of keeping control of the finish as New York-based Manila was pulled off the rail by Jose Santos to come pounding along on the outside for his sixth successive victory on grass.

Afterwards Guy Harwood, the trainer of Dancing Brave, was generous in his praise of Manila, but he must have been reflecting that his own hitherto magnificent performer had to be far, far below his peak to come home well behind Theatrical, a competitor he would have expected to outclass while both were doing their business 6,000 miles from here. Perhaps, too, Harwood's mind went back to the misgivings he had over Dancing Brave's well-being a few days ago when the horse betrayed clear evidence of suffering considerably from the strains of a long and punishing season and the draining effect of the journey to California. People close to Harwood say that he was tempted at that time to withdraw Dancing Brave from the Breeders' Cup Turf race and was only reassured by a revival of vigour late in the week. That recovery was made to appear illusory out on the tightly turning mile and a half of this beautiful course yesterday. Eddery had only minor trouble until he came to the straight. Keeping Dancing Brave balanced had been difficult, however, and he was on the wrong leg when the time for challenging came. 'The horse raced well up to the turn, we were positioned to make our move and then he just didn't have it,' the jockey said. 'Horses like Theatrical, and Darara from France, couldn't beat him with a hammer in Europe. He's off to stud now and they can't take the Arc away from him.'

The disappointment of seeing Sonic Lady made favourite and then thoroughly beaten in the Breeders' Cup Mile was rendered more bearable for many Britons in the huge crowd when Last Tycoon, a three-year-old who had shown his quality by outpacing some of England's best sprinters on their own ground, stormed up the short straight under Yves St Martin to win by a head from the locally trained Palace Music. The odds of better than 35-1 available about Last Tycoon in this turf race represented blundering prejudice by the American form students, and the cheers of those visitors who took advantage might have been heard on the slopes of the San Gabriel mountains as the Irish-bred, French-trained bay went ahead just inside the one furlong marker. Sonic Lady had held the lead fleetingly after moving smartly in second position for Walter Swinburn through most of the mile, but when she faded she did so rapidly and was only seventh at the line.

Her eclipse was sad but not the saddest of the day.

The Observer, 2 November 1986

The Human Factor in Dessie's Glory

WHEN THE TALK is of Desert Orchid and the Grand National, David Elsworth could take the easy route to public approval. He could open his mouth and make the agreeable noises expected of the guardian of a sacred object. He could promise to keep the nation's equine sweetheart at a safe distance from Becher's, The Chair and all those other threatening monsters by the Mersey.

Instead he offers the honest reaction of a racehorse trainer. That is his job and, as we enter the Nineties, few men anywhere can claim to do it better. Elsworth loves and respects Desert Orchid and has a sense of personal gratitude towards him that hardly any among the millions who have made the great horse a folk hero are in a position to comprehend. Yet it is natural for Elsworth to think like a coach with a superlative athlete in his care and what might well be an eminently winnable event up ahead. The trainer is still a long way from making up his mind about whether it will be advisable to send Dessie towards the hazards of Aintree after attempting to take a second Gold Cup at Cheltenham in March. All that he has done so far is act on the truism that if you don't enter you cannot run.

Of course, the mere fact that he entertains the possibility of running is almost enough to bring a lynch mob pouring across the New Forest to the gates of his Hampshire stables. However, even such waves of popular emotion are unlikely to make this gregarious but thoroughly independent 50-year-old renege on his own perception of how Desert Orchid's class relates to the notorious demands of the National. 'The Grand National is a great spectacle, a great institution but, in spite of all the hype, it isn't in fact a very good race,' he said last week over the whisky he relishes when the main exertions of the day are behind him. 'It is a handicap that is often won by not particularly high-class horses. True, they've got to have something about them, to be game, jump and stay. But very few of the winners have real quality. Desert Orchid has that in abundance and obviously I feel he has the credentials to win the race, if given a fair weight – say 12 stone or perhaps a pound over as a gesture.'

In judging this analysis against the risks inseparable from the perilous marathon, it should be remembered that no other human being knows nearly as much about Desert Orchid as Elsworth does. It is an understanding based on something more than physical closeness over the years in which the legend has been forged. A day spent with him up on the downs near Fordingbridge last week strengthened the feeling that this is a trainer lavishly endowed with the mysterious gift for two-way communication with animals that the truly outstanding practitioners of his craft always seem to possess. As Desert Orchid has moved through an increasingly enthralling career (one whose hold on countless imaginations goes far beyond his status as the record money-winner in National Hunt, with 29 swashbuckling victories from 58 starts and a long list of triumphs in major races, culminating in that late surge to glory at Cheltenham 10 months ago) he has benefited immeasurably from having the ideal man in his corner.

So, too, have an extraordinary succession of other superbly prepared horses Elsworth has sent out to astonish the racing world since becoming a full-time trainer barely a dozen years back. His ability to establish himself so quickly and score so consistently over jumps and on the Flat – punctuating his spectacular rampage through the citadels of National Hunt with even more remarkable plundering of big prizes at Goodwood, York, Doncaster and, above all, Royal Ascot, where his eye for thriftily purchased potential has regularly neutralised the economic advantages of more fashionable rivals – is sufficient in itself to identify him as someone born to train.

Yet his origins give no hint of such a destiny. Born in Salisbury, he was raised by his farm-worker grandparents in a council house half-a-dozen miles from the Whitsbury stables he now rents, a splendid two-yard complex with 250 acres of priceless downland gallops that the late bookmaking giant William Hill set up for Gordon Richards's switch from riding to training. He readily admits to having not the remotest sense of vocation when he left his secondary modern school at 15. It was while using his ferrets on some of the rabbiting forays that any self-respecting country lad of the time was likely to find appealing (these days he regularly shoots duck in titled company) that he first came into contact with racehorses. 'It so happened that a bit of heathland that was alive with rabbits was owned by Alec Kilpatrick and he exercised his string there,' Elsworth told me. 'I was drawn to the horses, although I was so ignorant that I thought the guy on each animal's back was its trainer. Anyway, not having any other prospect of a job, I knocked on Alec's door and soon I was dashing back for my suitcase and my push-bike.

'That stable was an isolated place and there was no such thing as television, so there was a lot of tale-telling around the fire at night. Soon I was hooked and on the merry-go-round for life. I'm still romantic about racing. If you're not, you won't keep the enthusiasm, the zest for the job that is the absolute key to succeeding, whether you're a racehorse, a trainer or anything else. This is not a game for precise commercial projections. It's about dreams and working to make them happen.'

His dreams of making it as a jockey foundered but through his years with Kilpatrick and as assistant trainer to Col. Ricky Vallance he was sampling every conceivable aspect of stables work and learning all the time. Already he showed unbreakable confidence and no matter how lowly his station invariably felt 'I was the one really training the horses'. He says now that 'even bad experience ends up as good experience' but two or three serious brushes with authority (the most conspicuous when he was fined £17,500 in 1988 after administering steroids to Cavvies Clown) have made it hard to stick with that philosophy. He is vehement that in each instance there was no criminality and can be scathing about the confused handling of such matters by the racecourse security service.

Three years in the racing wilderness during the Seventies turned him briefly into a market trader but he was simply marking time before launching himself as a trainer. By the time he did, he reckoned he had acquired more accurate insights into human behaviour. 'If you're pitched overboard, there are always plenty of people ready to chuck you an anchor.' But his basic exuberance is unquenchable and once he was back in action it was his talent for inspiring people as well as horses that brought meteoric progress. There is an unmistakable camaraderie among his staff, from his secretary and business organiser Chris Hill, a sharp Mancunian in his mid-thirties who brims with energy and friendly warmth, to his assistant trainer David Townsend and head lad Rodney Boult, he of the magical work-rider's 'feel' that has done so much for Dessie, to the stable girl I saw eagerly sweeping out a yard with a plaster on her hand. All of them are buoyed by the certainty that the brilliant feats of the recent past – in which Dessie's exploits have not obscured other heroes like the National winner Rhyme 'n' Reason, Floyd, Combs Ditch, Robin Wonder, Ghofar and Barnbrook Again over jumps, Melindra, Mighty Fly, Mighty Flutter, Miss Silca Key, Naheez and Indian Ridge on the Flat and, of course, the wonderful Heighlin in both codes – will be a springboard to greater glory.

Elsworth was champion National Hunt trainer of 1987–88 mainly through dominating important races. He recognises the present title-holder, Martin Pipe, as an extraordinary man but is baffled by the motivation that 'makes him dash around to all those little tracks getting winners of egg and spoon races'. His own ambitions focus more and more on the Classics of Flat racing. In the well forward Dead Certain ('I believe her form made her the best filly in Europe last year') and the almost equally formidable In the Groove he has live contenders for the One Thousand Guineas and hopes the 50 two-year-olds that will fill most of his 87 boxes this Flat season may include something else to improve on his tally of a third in the Epsom as well as the French Derby and a second in the Irish equivalent.

Being with this contagiously optimistic man, watching his mischievous but attractively open face animated by the genuine joy he derives from his work, and from the three young children his strikingly personable wife Janie has given him, it is natural to wish him well. If there is such a thing as a magic touch with animals, I would bet that David Elsworth has it. I think he would too. 'I've only worked with dogs and horses,' he said with a smile as I was leaving. 'But did you see that story about the hippo that died as they tried to get it back into its trailer on the motorway? I think that could have been handled better, you know.'

The Observer, 21 January 1990

Desert Orchid never did run in the Grand National. It was an omission that probably suited the majority of his fans.

Jonjo Jumps Towards Some Better Breaks

WHATEVER POWER ALLOCATES the tough times in life should have learned by now that there is no point in trying to break Jonjo O'Neill.

Terrible injuries, the threatened amputation of a leg, cancer that looked like being terminal and the devastation of his marriage – trauma after desperate trauma has only served to prove that he is not the cracking kind. Enthusiasm for living still shines naturally in his green eyes and, not surprisingly, the glint intensifies when Cheltenham comes along.

Other trainers will head for the Cotswolds with far stronger raiding parties than the handful of hopeful contenders O'Neill will send on the long haul from his Ivy House stables 10 miles north of Penrith. But no one will be more happily stirred by the special excitements of the Festival, more alive to its electricity. 'There's magic in the place,' he says with a smile and a protracted shudder of pleasure. 'I loved riding there, loved the tremendous atmosphere and the feeling that it was National Hunt's biggest stage. Of course, it was a lucky place for me. I rode a good few winners there and with two Champion Hurdles and two Gold Cup victories among them I'm bound to have wonderful memories of Cheltenham. As a trainer, I'm serving my time, building up steadily since taking my licence in 1986. But I'd always want to be the best at anything I do, so it has to be my ambition to send out winners at the Festival. Just competing there gives me a terrific buzz.'

If, however, his zest for the dramas of the racecourse is undiminished, the vicissitudes inseparable from the trainer's lot are never likely to grind down someone whose 37 years have been so overloaded with more basic crises. The battering his body took from falls during his riding career (he reckons they cost him the equivalent of three full seasons between his arrival in Cumbria from his native Cork in 1972 and his retirement in 1986) was severe even by the harsh standards of his trade. He still has metal pins in both arms and it was not so long ago that he had plates and screws removed from his legs. 'When I was struggling with the cancer and not earning, the metal out of my legs got me a few bob as scrap,' he told me solemnly last week.

There was a time when the metal in his right leg was far from a joke. It was bolted into position when the lower bones were left resembling a sack of gravel by being scissored between a passing horse's forelegs after O'Neill took what he regarded as 'a right easy fall, like stepping off a bike' from the back of the collapsing Sinbad at Bangor. That was in October 1980 and his reaction was dictated by the fact that at Cheltenham in the following March he was due to ride Sea Pigeon in the Champion Hurdle and Night Nurse in the Gold Cup. He had won the 1980 Champion on Sea Pigeon, the hurdler he considers the classiest horse he ever rode, and expectations of a repeat were duly fulfilled – but with John Francome in the saddle. Nor was his eagerness to be on Night Nurse at all irrational. The former hero of two Champions ran second in the Gold Cup.

But by then O'Neill's premature return to the saddle to ride exercise had caused that eight-inch plate in his right leg to move, setting up an infection so prodigious that a finger pressed to the diseased flesh disappeared as if into putty. Soon a full-scale emergency developed and when he went to Switzerland for an operation he was obliged, before going under the anaesthetic, to sign a document giving the surgeons permission to cut the leg off if they thought that necessary. It was saved and, although O'Neill was forced to stay idle until December 1981, his comeback was characteristically aggressive. By 1984 he was claiming a second Champion Hurdle on Dawn Run, the Irish mare who was to complete his apotheosis as a Cheltenham legend two years later when coming from third at the last fence to grab the most dramatic of Gold Cup victories.

Like his previous Gold Cup winner, Alverton, Dawn Run was to end her days tragically in a racing fall but on that March afternoon in 1986 no one dreamt of what lay ahead of horse and rider. Last week he recaptured the wild emotions of the day for me by vividly recalling every yard of the fiercely galloped three-and-a-quarter miles. 'I can see every grasshopper in the grass,' he told me after an account as urgent and riveting as a live commentary.

Come the August of that year of 1986, Jonjo O'Neill had abruptly run out of reasons for celebration. Pains under his arms, a tendency to tiredness that demanded increasingly frequent stops for sleep on the drives back from race meetings and a general decline in his physical strength had warned him that something was profoundly wrong but he concealed the extent of his difficulties until the evidence became so blatant that specialist diagnosis was inevitable. At first there was a suspicion of glandular fever but the reality was cancer and as it spread down his spine the prognosis was bleak. Courage and optimism had brought him many of the 901 winners he rode as a professional but now, as he entered into an exhausting regime of chemotherapy and radium treatment, the opposition seemed too powerful to be out-gamed. 'It's a fair frightenin' old word that cancer,' he said in Penrith during a dinner conversation in which he was often strikingly eloquent about his experience. 'Sitting in the specialist's room waiting to hear the verdict on what I had was pretty terrible. It was as if you had been running free and now you were caged. Then during the treatment there were times when I just wanted to duck out, not go on with it. I wasn't the bravest man in the world, believe me. I had to drive down to Manchester for it and there were times when I was sweating so much my hands were slipping off the steering wheel. When I got to the hospital I always had a horrible taste in my mouth. There was no taste coming from the treatment. I think what I was tasting was fear.

'I was given a jab so that I could drive back without being sick on the way but the moment I was in the house I'd be over the basin throwing up and I'd be like that for maybe four days. You felt so low and so helpless with the children standing round patting you on the back and saying, "It's all right, daddy, you'll be all right." I couldn't avoid thinking it was all over for me.'

However, part of his uniqueness has always been the way warmth and impish charm and lovability mix in his nature with the steel it took to be twice champion jockey over the jumps. Both of these elements in him responded to the untiring care of his doctors and nurses and the intimate support of family and close friends. He says he has too many debts of gratitude to be listed but admits that the former jockey and fellow Irishman Ron Barry was a vital influence. 'Ron, who has been such a great friend for so long and lives nearby, would come over for a crack and we would talk about old times. Much of it would be about little, trivial things but I'd think, "Wait a minute, I want more of this. I want to be there for more good times next week, next year and the year after." So I suppose the old will power came into play and I fought on. It was a rough passage but I made it and I'm grateful.'

The further paralysing blow of a particularly hurtful disintegration of his marriage was the next ordeal he had to endure and, since it overlapped with his recovery from cancer, its toll is hard to exaggerate. It is astonishing that his totals of winners trained have climbed from two or three in the 1986–87 season, to 15 in 87–88, 29 in 88–89 and (up till Friday) 22 so far this season. Now that he and his former wife, Sheila, are on reasonable terms again, and he is spending as much time as he can with the three children he plainly adores (Louise, 10, Gillian, 7, and Tom, 5), the upward trend should continue. 'Bearing grudges does no one any good,' he acknowledges. 'You've got to kick on into the rest of your life. The marriage break-up is a bit like having a serious fall as a rider – once the bruising comes out it's not so bad.'

Most of the psychological bruising from the divorce is out now and he approaches the monitoring of his cure every three months without qualms. And he is more than happy to meet the frequent requests to boost the morale of other sufferers from the scourge. 'You should have some strength to spare after coming through that lot. In my own life, I feel nobody ever had a better education in how to cope with the disappointments and frustrations of a trainer's existence. Maybe that's why I honestly think I'm getting a bigger charge from what I'm doing than I did from riding.'

The charge will be intensified if any of the runners he and his excellent, highly motivated stable team are sending to Cheltenham – probably Vicario Di Bray (an enigmatic giant who beat Champion Hurdler Celtic Shot at Haydock last January), Raise an Argument, Dutch Call, Caney River, Maelkar, Instant Tan and Sayparee – can get to the line first. If just one of them were as brimming with true quality as the master of Ivy House's 48 fully occupied boxes, his first training success at the Festival would be guaranteed and a move towards more fashionable quarters farther south and more emphasis on the Flat might be imminent.

But that comparison asks a lot of any horse, or any human for that matter.

The Observer, 11 March 1990

Winning Rules of the Titanium Man

BARELY A YEAR ago Bart Cummings seemed about to watch the fruits of a lifetime's brilliance as a racehorse trainer being swept away under an avalanche of debts created by the failure of an extravagant scheme to syndicate young thoroughbreds. The only reason people could not accuse him of being on his knees was that his knees weren't strong enough to support him. They were in such a desperate state that they would soon have to be totally reconstructed in a Sydney operating theatre.

Looking at his ravaged legs and at the apparent absence of any future for him in their business, the smart mouths of Australian racing said that if he had been a horse he would have been shot. But, far from being put down, he has used the 1990 season to stride once again to the forefront of his profession, trampling records underfoot along the way. And last week as the two-mile Melbourne Cup – the event ardently mythologised here as 'the race that stops a nation' – went to him for an incredible eighth time, the downfall of James Bartholomew Cummings had to be dismissed as nothing but an ugly rumour. He still has liabilities of 10 million Australian dollars (£3,970,000) and his efforts to prove that he does not deserve the burden are likely to embroil him in a bitter court battle with the prominent accounting firms that devised the syndication project as a tax-effective operation involving clients who did not materialise. However, as we talked on the morning after Kingston Rule (a powerful chestnut son of perhaps the greatest chestnut of all time, Secretariat) had taken him three clear of the highest aggregate of Melbourne Cup victories achieved by any other trainer, he had the quiet but recognisable air of a man who believes that winning is his destiny.

In a hotel suite 30 floors above the city centre streets, he wore a neat shirt and tie but balanced the effect with a grey suede jerkin he might favour around the stable yard. 'I don't want to be called an entrepreneur,' he said at one point. 'I'm a horse trainer. I'll let the entrepreneurs do their own thing.' His manner is engagingly civil but the observations are often dry and laconic and have never lost the capacity to deflate that he demonstrated memorably to a health inspector a long time ago, while he was still training in his native Adelaide. 'I'm sorry, Mr Cummings, I'm going to have to close you down,' the inspector said. 'There are too many flies in this stable.'

Cummings fixed the man with the kind of cool look that remains frequently in evidence today. 'How many am I allowed to have?' he asked. The inspector retired in confusion.

That there are no flies on Cummings or his horses when major prizes are at stake was emphasised again last Thursday on the attractive acres of Flemington racecourse, beside the Maribyrnong River on the outskirts of Melbourne, when Kingston Rule's success in the Cup two days before was followed by Weekend Delight's smooth subjugation of her 16 rivals in the Argyle Diamond Victoria Oaks, the country's premier race for three-year-old fillies. With those two jackpots, Cummings made himself the outstanding figure at the Spring Carnival that is the climax of the antipodean racing season. He stole centre stage away from David Hayes, the 28-year-old who had outstripped even the training feats of his legendary father, Colin, by taking a world record total of six Group races in one afternoon on the first day of the meeting.

After her jockey, Jim Cassidy, had driven Weekend Delight home for an Oaks win that was his own fourth in five years, and the sixth of Cummings's career, the celebrations were punctuated by a tribute. 'Bart's a genius,' said Cassidy. 'Everything he touches turns to diamonds.' The men in wigs can expect to hear contrary testimony but if they were at the races (and in Australia that's not too improbable) they will know what Cassidy means. Had the jockey acted on his assessment of the master earlier in the week he could not have resisted Cummings's entreaties concerning the ride on Kingston Rule. By opting for Just a Dancer, which didn't look much like Nijinsky as it struggled in twelfth of the 24 runners on Tuesday, Cassidy handed the glory and 10 per cent of the $1.3 million first prize in the world's most remarkable handicap to 24-year-old Darren Beadman. But Cassidy wasn't alone in shutting his ears to genius. Over a late breakfast on Wednesday, Cummings had told this interviewer that Weekend Delight might not be a champion but had 'a real chance in the Oaks'. In admitting failure to grab at the casually tossed pearl, the only possible plea in mitigation is that a head awash with the alien intricacies of Australian training methods had scant attention left over for tips.

In fact, with hand on heart for a lot of the sceptical cronies back on the battlegrounds of the British Turf, it must be reported that my first Melbourne Cup experience has been so dominated by the horses and the horsemen that even the seductive distractions of one of the liveliest betting rings ever encountered have been largely ignored. As for the rich parade of human exotica that Cup day always presents – the women literally done up like Christmas trees, the Romans spilling Foster's over their togas, the executioner, complete with mask and axe, leading a girl by the hand with a vagueness that suggested he could not recall where he had left the block – none of it could impinge more than marginally on the compelling excitement stirred by the action out on the green but rock-hard ribbon of the Flemington track. Quite a few among the two dozen animals that made up the modern maximum field in the Cup finished badly jarred (as, in their own way, did a good proportion of the 93,000 spectators). Kingston Rule himself was heavily bandaged next morning on his off hind leg above the fetlock, where six stitches had been applied to a gash he suffered 700 metres out when struck into from behind. It's not an occasion for milksops, equine or human.

Predictably, Bart Cummings, with his new titanium knees, was moving conspicuously well around his hotel suite. His digestion was sound, too. While describing Kingston Rule's enormous appetite, the ability to shift 25lb of oats along with other grain, compared with the 18 to 20lb that would make a feed for an average racehorse, the trainer removed a large omelette and a hillock of chips just an hour before he was due at a lunch appointment with the five-year-old hero's owner-breeder, David Hains. Expenditure of nervous energy presumably keeps the Cummings weight from being unduly troublesome. But Kingston Rule's fitness, like that of practically all Australian stayers, is controlled by a schedule of activity which would flabbergast many racing professionals in Europe.

For a start, it is thoroughly commonplace to give Melbourne Cup contenders a stiff, competitive race on the Saturday prior to the Tuesday of the great contest. Kingston Rule was one of the many tuned up in that way this year. The details of his regimen, as conveyed to me by Cummings, did not read much like the gym log of Buster Douglas. After galloping into second place over the 2,500 metres (slightly more than a mile and a half) of The Dalgety, a $151,000 event at Flemington on Saturday, 3 November, he was out before breakfast on Sunday morning to trot a mile, canter a mile and a half and then have a three-minute swim. In the middle of the afternoon he had an hour's walk, with 15 minutes to pick thistles, grass and clover in some of the tranquil areas the racecourse affords on the tree-lined banks of the Maribyrnong. More remarkably, on Monday morning, less than 36 hours before the supreme challenge of his life, Kingston Rule did impressively serious work, averaging 15 seconds a furlong for a mile and a quarter but running the last three furlongs in 40 seconds. Then there was a two-minute swim, a walk and another alfresco snack.

At 5.45 a.m. on the day of the race the horse was given a gentle pipe-opener, ending with two furlongs in what the Australians call even time, which means 15 seconds per furlong. 'He didn't swim that morning because he didn't need it – he was fit,' Cummings explained, without risking contradiction. 'If he had been a bit gross I'd have had him gallop those last two furlongs in 27 seconds.' Even some of the locals were taken aback by that searching gallop on the Monday but the astonishing Cup triumphs of the man who ordered it, which began with Light Fingers in 1965 and have included producing both first and second on four occasions, tended to stifle criticism. They should have a similar effect in England, where a stayer being readied for a major race might do that last demanding work five days beforehand, having had its previous race at least three weeks in advance of the big day.

Vastly different factors are in play on opposite sides of the world but the success of the Cummings techniques, accomplished mainly with horses bred and ruggedly nurtured in New Zealand, could be seen as lending weight to Richard Baerlein's contention that too many of our trainers treat their charges as pets rather than athletes. 'We've been working pretty much to this pattern for 35 years,' said Cummings. 'In fact there wasn't much difference in my father's methods when Comic Court won the Cup for him under 9st 5lb in 1950, except that now scientific developments allow me to use a much more concentrated protein diet than the old-timers had.

The English approach would not get stayers fit enough to run two miles at the sustained pace you see here, averaging 12 to 13 seconds a furlong for the whole trip.'

In setting a new course record last Tuesday, Kingston Rule covered the official distance of 3,200 metres (about 20 yards short of two miles) in 3min 16.30sec, which breaks down into fairly murderous fractions. 'It's because of these exceptional demands that we'd always want a Cup horse to have clocked plenty of mileage in races during the 12 to 14 weeks before the race,' Cummings elaborated. 'An aggregate of 12,500 metres raced would be ideal for a colt with the right constitution, like Kingston Rule, and he had near enough that. He was ready in every way. I knew when young Beadman brought him off the fence to make his run in the straight, Kingston Rule would be able to drive all the way to the line. I knew we had the Cup again after a gap of eleven years.' The shrewd, rather pouchy face under the high waves of silver hair was lightened towards a smile by the memory of what he had seen in that moment, making it easy to detect the Irish blood that comes from both sides of his pedigree. Though he will be 63 in a few days, and his son Anthony has shown himself well capable of maintaining the dynastic tradition so prevalent in Australian racing, Bart Cummings looks like someone with a lot of winning to do.

But his interest in horses goes deeper than the most glamorous lodgers at his large stables in Sydney and Melbourne. He worries about the way the parking of cars on racecourse infields has wrought havoc with equine bones and ligaments by causing dangerous strips of artificial turf to be laid across the tracks. The switch to underground access for the traffic is happening too slowly, he complains, as is the banking of tracks for greater safety. 'Horses became the forgotten part of the industry in Australia in the Eighties,' he says. 'Let's hope the Nineties will belong to the horses.'

Whatever happens in the racing of the Nineties, the chances are that Bart Cummings, the stayers' stayer, will be in the thick of it.

The Observer, 11 November 1990

Proof that European training methods could work in the Melbourne Cup was brilliantly provided by Dermot Weld when he stunned Australia with Vintage Crop's easy victory in 1993.

The Man from Laredo

BETWEEN THE FRENCH Derby today and the Epsom original on Wednesday, a family who come from South Dakota by way of Laredo, Texas, may give European racing a serious reminder about the quality of horsemanship that can still come out of the west.

Late this afternoon Keith Asmussen will be temporarily immune to the glorious vistas of Chantilly as he focuses tensely on the partnership formed by his 29-year-old son Cash and a three-year-old colt called Suave Dancer. Since Keith bought Suave Dancer as a yearling at the Keeneland Sales and conditioned him in Texas before passing him to Henri Chalhoub, the owner whose colours he will carry in the Prix du Jockey Club, the Asmussens have a double stake in seeing Cash's high estimate of the animal's abilities justified over the 2,400 metres of France's premier Classic. The current and most remarkable representative of the family's riding talent (Keith was in the saddle professionally for several decades and the younger brother, Steve, rode briefly at the top level before rising weight steered him into a training career in the Mid West) talks lyrically about the exhilarating power, the capacity for dramatic acceleration, with which great thoroughbreds thrill the men on their backs. 'They give you that rush,' he says, creating a strong impression that something is being said about blood and adrenaline as well as the devouring of ground.

For those who want a visible rendering of the experience, he makes an enthusiastic promise: 'If Suave Dancer runs straight on Sunday, you'll see "rush".' The qualification in that statement is acknowledgment of the veering waywardness in the Longchamp straight which caused the son of Green Dancer to finish three-quarters of a length behind Cudas after starting at Pari-mutuel odds of 1-10 in the Prix Lupin three weeks ago. Cash Asmussen's belief that the form can be reversed today (and the impressive Pistolet Bleu beaten into the bargain) is based on hair-raisingly vivid memories of the Lupin.

'Maybe Suave Dancer's behaviour that day was a case of pilot error,' he said generously after putting one mount in the winner's enclosure and two others in the frame at Chantilly on Thursday. 'I wanted to give him an easy race at Longchamp and I ended up leaving him with too much to do. When I brought him out into the middle of the course and he found himself isolated he ran very green. He didn't just duck out. He started running across the track. I was desperately anxious not to hit him, so at first I tried talking to him and just showed him the whip in my left hand. But eventually I had to let him have a smack and what happened then was, you might say, pretty exciting. While he was swerving left, naturally I had full tension on the right rein and when he suddenly went to the right under the whip he dropped about a foot of slack and for me it was like a waterskier having the tow rope sheared. I managed to get my skinny little ass back in the saddle but we were puckered up for a while there.

'Once we were together again I went to work on him but he was still too green to run straight. People in the stands must have wondered why I was riding him out when he had been all over the place like that but the truth is that he was eating up Cudas every time he took a stride in the right direction. If he goes the orthodox route from A to B, Cudas, Pistolet Bleu or anything else will have a lot of trouble staying with him.'

A more pressing question on this side of the Channel is whether the rest of the Derby field will stay with Corrupt on Wednesday – or if the powerful bay by Lear Fan will prove able to charge clear as authoritatively as he did under Asmussen's skilful encouragement at Lingfield in his final rehearsal for the big day. Though Corrupt may not have treated him to the full wonder of 'the rush', the jockey was sufficiently delighted by his only acquaintance with the colt to be convinced that they have a realistic chance of winning the Derby in a year when a majority of the best judges rate the English and Irish three-year-olds appreciably inferior to the French. Above all, he was immensely heartened by the way the first contender for the old prize to come out of Neville Callaghan's unpretentious stable brought him down the awkward left-handed hill that is a major part of Lingfield's genuine resemblance to Epsom. 'I haven't ridden the course very often but that was certainly the first time I've ever got to the bottom of the hill with a drop of juice left in the tank, so I've got to feel good about it,' he said. 'Lingfield really is like Epsom but in the Derby the pressures are far greater. To have any chance you need to be going well halfway down into Tattenham Corner because most of the field are likely to run out of gas and if you are only moving moderately yourself it's tough to avoid the wrecks. The first time a French horse comes to the top of the hill at Lingfield or Epsom, he is going to think the earth has dropped from under him. The only occasion that horses here meet anything as steep as that is coming down the ramp out of the van.'

His rides in the Derby barely stretch to a handful (he was second on Blue Stag last year) but his testimony on its demands is validated by the liveliness of his mind and a persistently analytical approach to his job. With justification, he thinks of himself as a horseman rather than a jockey. 'Coming from my family, I don't think I could be anything else,' he declares, pointing out that his mother, Marilyn, was an active trainer of quarter-horses before she concentrated on helping with her husband's training centre. The Asmussen genes should make him a stayer, too. His great-grandfather, William Asmussen, who emigrated along with the great-great-grandfather from Denmark to Canada, then became a farmer in South Dakota, is still to the fore at 96. Keith, whose own father left farming for horses, transferred his career to Texas because of the climate when Cash was five.

By the time he was 16, Cash had graduated through quarter-horse racing to the role of prodigy around the major tracks of New York. The hunger to be associated with the best in his business later took him to California and from there he was wooed to France as an unusually mature 20-year-old to ride the Stavros Niarchos horses in Francois Boutin's yard. Subsequent moves allied him, notably, with Andre Fabre and with Vincent O'Brien for one season in 1987 – an episode that wasn't all roses but which he values as educative exposure to a great horseman. Now, though a European rather than a French jockey, he is re-established in Chantilly with arrangements to ride for the yards of John Hammond (trainer of Suave Dancer) and Robert Collet as well as the horses owned by Henri Chalhoub.

Sitting on a bench outside the weighing room of his local track on Thursday, after the crowds had ebbed away from what may be the jewel of all racecourses, he waved an arm affectionately at the green acres stretching towards the chateau and its lake. 'Could you imagine a better place to come to work?' he asked seriously. 'I don't think the Man above would listen to me if I complained about my life. I have no regrets about how things have worked out. How can I count myself anything but very lucky? I rode a thousand winners in America in a five-year span, earning approximately $20 million in purses, then came to Europe to become champion jockey of France five times (1985, '86, '88, '89, '90), ride some brilliant horses here and have a few Group One winners in England, Ireland and Italy. And all the time I have been paid to have an education in life that money couldn't buy.'

With his dark hair and eyes and the excellent teeth that show frequently in a wide smile, he has compelling good looks and his face is at its most animated as he extols the advantages for a professional rider of being based in France. Nearly all jockeys have to fight weight, he says – admitting that, at 5ft 6 in, 8st 5lb is as low as he wants to come – but in Britain the ordeal is compounded by the grind of constant, wearing travel and the proliferation of fixtures that makes it almost impossible to shape a schedule well in advance. With five splendid courses located around Paris and 30 days' racing each year at Deauville, the French jockeys are, he is sure, much better placed to be conscientious about their work while still finding time to enjoy civilised living. The Americans, of course, have it harder than any of the Europeans.

'With nine races a day, 365 days a year and weights five or six pounds lighter, it's a tough game over there,' he says, with the authority of someone who was twice leading jockey in New York. 'And because there are no contracts, guys don't have the privilege top jockeys have here, of being assured of the ride throughout the entire career of a good horse. Every time you are on a good animal in the States you are aware there will be 15 guys in the hat to ride him next time out. Some of those trainers are liable to change jockeys on the way to the starting gate. There is no encouragement for a rider to nurture a young horse, handle him tenderly and bring him along. There are plenty of terrific horsemen riding in America but they get few opportunities to show how exceptional they are in that sense.'

It is concern with horsemanship, with 'knowing what really makes horses tick and trying to master the art of communicating with them', that is the central fascination of Cash Asmussen's life. It will take him into breeding when he retires from race-riding and probably ensure that he spends a substantial part of the rest of his life in Europe, though the marriage that he admits may be imminent would be to a Texas girl. For the present, he is determined to make his horsemanship show in his handling of horses like Suave Dancer and Corrupt. 'The greatest challenge for me when I get on a horse is to form a true partnership. Communication is the essence. If you absorb their messages, they'll absorb yours. You need a sense of pace and rhythm in the saddle and I believe in being flexible in relation to the needs of the horse and doing things smoothly. I don't think you have to blow up a mountain to move the sonofabitch – you might be able to just pick it up and ease it over.'

He dismisses critics who regard him as ungainly. 'I like to be effective but I like to be a stylist, too. When I leave the game I want to have left a mark. When you see the films you are going to know it's me and you are going to know my horse is laying his body down to give me his best and that when he pulls up he is going to know he has done something.'

So what will Corrupt do? 'He is a big, strong, solid horse who will carry me all the way, will come down the hill and stay a mile-and-a-half, and his temperament will cope with the parade. He's not a horse that's grasping at stars. He won't win by 10 lengths. But as a Derby contender, he's in the ball park all right.'

He may end up in the winner's circle, if he pays proper attention to the man from Laredo.

The Observer, 2 June 1991

Suave Dancer won the French Derby and the Prix de l'Arc de Triomphe. But Corrupt was a bit-player at Epsom.

Epsom Hero Ungenerous to a Fault

JOCKEYS ARE PAID for kicking home winners, certainly not for the quality of their post-race press conferences. They have no obligation to produce either profundity or entertainment for the microphones and notebooks that cluster round them in the minutes following a famous victory.

So clearly it would be silly to lumber in with heavy complaints about the streak of offensiveness that ran through Alan Munro's handling of some fairly mundane inquiries after he and Generous had made a flawless partnership in the Derby last Wednesday. What he had done on the racetrack was always going to count for more than anything that came across on the soundtrack. Yet, when all of that had been acknowledged, it was undeniably sad to find such a gifted professional responding to the most triumphant moment of his short career by behaving so gracelessly as to suggest that if charm were weight he could ride lighter than the youngest entrant in a Pony Club gymkhana. His arrogant performance in a cramped room under the Epsom stands was a trivial aggravation for those subjected to it, more of a bore than a hardship. But it may have made a rather worrying point about the 24-year-old himself.

If he could hardly maintain basic civility after an experience that might have been expected to leave him brimming with goodwill towards every creature on the planet, if he could not be generous after Generous, he is in danger of denying himself a lot of warmth that people would be inclined to pour his way. That was what made Wednesday's episode regrettable – the fact that he chose to be difficult in circumstances where most of his questioners were mainly concerned with sharing in the pleasure of a dream beautifully realised. Being asked for his thoughts about Richard Quinn (whom he supplanted last month as contract jockey to the

Saudi prince Fahd Salman and, therefore, in the privileged alliance with Generous) may have upset him sufficiently to justify his brusque refusal to deal with 'an unfair question'. However, the cool blankness of that reaction was in marked contrast with the gracious 'no hard feelings' statement that came from Quinn later, and much in the rest of Munro's remarks had an unfortunately egocentric tone.

'That's my business' was the most characteristic utterance of his press conference and each time it was delivered with the dismissive crispness of a brief-case being snapped shut. His approach was hard to reconcile with the idea of the Derby as the people's race. (Admittedly, the proportion of corporate hospitality groups in the smallish crowd had already exposed that view as a dated, romantic delusion.) Munro could make a case for insisting that the terms of his contract with Fahd Salman were strictly his business, although the question he brushed aside appeared to be focused more on the duration of the arrangement (surely a matter of legitimate interest) than the financial details. The point at which he did undoubtedly go over the edge into discourteous awkwardness was after a reporter asked for hints of the kind of advice offered by Lester Piggott's father, Keith, when Munro understandably sought guidance from the Piggott family on the eve of the Derby. 'That's my business, thank you very much,' he said, adding a hilarious line to the effect that he did not wish his attitude to be mistaken for brashness. Subsequently he did enlighten us to the extent that the senior Piggott's counsel, aided by films of some of Lester's nine Derby victories, concentrated on how a rider should cope with the extreme peculiarities of Epsom and where he would want to be at various stages of the great race. Having got that off his chest, he didn't really look like a man haunted by the guilt of having betrayed a major secret. What he does look like these days is a young fellow of personable appearance and exceptional talent who has developed a pretty fancy opinion of himself. Cockiness is no crime, especially in a trade where undue reticence is a recipe for being left back among the also-rans, and it has obviously been a significant element in the compulsive drive that carried Munro to the winner's circle 95 times last season and gave him one of the supreme honours of racing on only his second ride in the Derby. But the Turf is one of the areas where the penalties of overdosing on self-approval are particularly severe.

'This game tames lions, as Alan Munro will learn,' said one informed and unprejudiced witness of the press conference. 'There he was today with the chance to have the world at his feet, to put everybody on his side, and what does he do? He causes some of us to wonder how much we'll be rooting for him in the future. If he's this way after one Derby, what would happen if he ever started to make a habit of winning Classics. They might have to widen the weighing room door. When a young jockey has abilities such as he has, everybody in the business wants to feel good about his achievements. But Alan could make it a lot easier to be a fan.'

It is possible, of course, that Munro's admiration for Lester Piggott – who admires him in return – has persuaded him that there is no harm in seeking to emulate the abrasive independence that has always come naturally to the ageing master. But Lester's interview manner, like his riding style, is an unrepeatable original. His defective hearing and slightly impaired speech made remoteness a refuge at an early age and he was already identifiable as something unique before he was out of his teens. Soon he was established as part of the furniture of the nation's life, its favourite sporting gunfighter and, occasionally, its favourite mischievous grouch. With his face lined like a map of hard roads travelled, his capacity for pulverising put-downs and the inspired audacity of his jockeyship, he became one of the most magical presences in sport over the last 50 years – a figure who, for the inhabitants of this country at least, had an aura of excitement comparable with that surrounding a Pele or a Nicklaus (Muhammad Ali, the most charismatic sportsman in history, must always be left out of such ratings).

Even as he brought Hokusai in a distant seventh on Wednesday, the Long Fellow drew the eyes of a few devotees in the stands away from the streaming flaxen mane of Generous up ahead, reminding us once more that adopting him as a model would be the most hopelessly quixotic of exercises. There is scarcely a trace of emulation of Piggott in Alan Munro's riding technique. His method owes infinitely more to his several spells in American racing, featuring as it does a low, streamlined crouch close to the horse's neck. (His transatlantic journeys may have influenced his accent, too, for it is not easy to guess that he was born in York.)

But he has much of the single-minded ambition of the older

man and it helped him to return with his vigour utterly undiminished after a fall at Redcar last October which was so terrifying at the moment of impact that some who were watching thought he would be lucky to live, let alone ride again. He had an almost miraculous escape but was still so badly concussed that he required three months out of the saddle, so what he has accomplished since coming back is movingly remarkable.

Now there is the prospect of further glory in the company of Generous, whose ability to quicken so decisively off the demanding pace set by Mystiko in the Derby confirmed everything the winner's impressive trainer, Paul Cole, had read into the superb work the chestnut son of Caerleon had been putting in on the home gallops. If the new champion goes on to meet the French Derby winner Suave Dancer in the Irish Derby, the public can hold its breath for a real horse race.

Generous will gain much from the skills of Alan Munro. Equally, the jockey might benefit from reflecting on the reality that one glorious mile-and-a-half does not make a career. The trip to greatness is a bit longer and has even more ups and downs than Epsom.

The Observer, 9 June 1991

Warm Prospects for Wintertime

THERE WAS A hint of rawness to come in the weather of the Hardy country at breakfast time on Thursday, with a blustery wind that carried flurries of stinging rain. But on the long hill that rises from the village of Whitcombe, outside Dorchester, to a crest overlooking Weymouth Bay and Portland Bill, anyone with a weakness for the running horse could find reassurance that winter will bring its compensations. Toby Balding, the latest occupant of Whitcombe Manor Racing Stables, was exercising his string and as they pounded in single file up the testing incline of the main all-weather gallop a watching visitor had the warming thrill of being passed in rapid succession by Beech Road, Morley Street, Forest Sun and Cool Ground. If asked to name four horses whose talents and targets might encapsulate the excitements of the burgeoning National Hunt season, it would be hard to suggest a better yankee.

Morley Street, as the reigning Champion Hurdler who recently returned from Maryland after contemptuously dominating the Breeders' Cup Steeplechase for the second year in a row, must be seen as the star. The others, however, could be challenging his billing over the next few months.

Beech Road's inexorable galloping made a mockery of a 50-1 starting price in the Champion of 1989, and any suspicions of a fluke win were crushed the following month when he stormed ahead of another distinguished field in the Sandeman Aintree Hurdle. His steeplechasing career is about to get properly under way and, in the view of his trainer, prospects of fulfilling considerable promise could only be improved by a trivial tumble he had at a schooling fence in midweek. 'We managed to wrestle him to the ground but that will do him good, since he was starting to be a bit flippant, thinking he was stronger than the fences,' said Balding.

'He just stood off a bit far and touched the top of the last one he was going over. We schooled him twice more immediately afterwards and he was fine. Landing on the floor would teach him a little respect. Beech Road is a converted lunatic. He was very wild when we first got him. But lately he was beginning to go too much the other way, giving the impression that he felt it would be nice to leave the work to his friends.' Coming to Dorset had, Balding added, sharpened the attitude of an old campaigner who had become blasé around his former stables at Fyfield, in Hampshire, where 'he knew every blade of grass'.

The six-year-old Forest Sun is a hurdler already so impressive that his trainer felt impelled to remark, as the chestnut gelding strode smoothly past on Thursday morning, that it 'wouldn't be a surprise if he proved to be as good as Morley Street'. If Forest Sun's abilities will almost automatically define his objectives, there may be a continuing debate about the programme that should be mapped out for Cool Ground, though the argument seems sure to be heavily influenced by the strong beliefs concerning his profession Balding has accumulated in the 35 years since he first took out a trainer's licence before his 21st birthday. Cool Ground was fourth in last season's Cheltenham Gold Cup and his owner, Peter Bolton – who also happens to be the proprietor of the lavishly equipped Whitcombe complex and the man with whom Balding has signed a two-year contract that challenges him to establish the place as one of England's outstanding training centres – favours another tilt at the Festival's supreme prize in March. But 'the guv'nor', as Bolton is happy to call him, sees the Grand National as a nearly irresistible target for the big nine-year-old. 'According to a strict reading of the form book, Cool Ground is perhaps the fifth best 'chaser in England and that doesn't win you the Gold Cup,' said Balding. 'For him to have a good chance, it would have to come up really heavy at Cheltenham. It's not that he absolutely needs the mud but it helps him by slowing down the others.'

Confirming the visible evidence that Cool Ground has grown bigger and stronger, and reporting that he will go again for the Welsh National, which he won last December, Balding insists it should then be on towards Aintree. 'I think he is made for it. He is a superb jumper with enough toe to hold a position and over the National distance he would not be troubled by any going other than firm.' Such testimony cannot be readily ignored when it comes from someone who has sent out two winners of the ultimate steeplechase, even if he declines to claim kudos for the more recent of those successes, Little Polveir, who was bought just two months before his 1989 victory. There need be no such dilution of the credit for Highland Wedding's win exactly 20 years earlier. It represented a triumph of patient persuasion over the peculiarities of 'a right old pig' who specialised in being mulish when he was due to start an exercise gallop, waiting until Balding headed for him in the Land Rover and then taking off at speed 'so that I wouldn't see him work'. Yet Highland Wedding constantly carried the threat of doing something wonderful on a big day, what his mentor defines as 'the hope factor' at the heart of the racing professionals' love affair with their business. 'For a big, commonly bred horse he always showed speed and you felt it was worth spending so much of your time trying to seduce him into revealing his true capabilities.'

Balding himself, like his younger brother, Ian, whose career as a leading trainer of Flat horses has included the early glory of handling the magnificent Mill Reef, was uncommonly well bred to be skilled in such seductions. Their father, Gerald, was maybe the greatest English polo player of all time, a 10-goal master who, after returning home from the US to fight in the Second World War, was set up as a trainer at Weyhill by his American polo patron, Jock Whitney. Following the death of the father, the brothers were originally partners, with Ian showing memorable flair in the riding of many of their runners. Looking now at the substantially greater bulk of Toby, who at 6ft 2in is noticeably the taller of the two, it is surprising to learn that their minimum weights were once only two pounds apart, at 11st and 11st 2lb. 'But Ian has always been built like the Cambridge full-back he was, like a brick shithouse in other words,' says the elder sibling, who himself acknowledges a lifelong enthusiasm for sports beyond the Turf and concentrates these days on a tennis game noted more for its deviousness than its technique.

Toby Balding's connections with Fyfield ('I still have a presence there, like a wife') seem unlikely to be severed, in spite of Peter Bolton's attempts to convince him that he should settle in, long-term, at Whitcombe. Present plans embrace a return to Hampshire at the end of the two-year contract and the building of new stables on his recently extended acreage there. Everything might have been different had British Thoroughbred Racing and Breeding plc –

which Balding helped to set up as the first company formed in Britain to raise public money for racehorse ownership and which later bought his business 'lock, stock and barrel' and retained him as a salaried employee – not gone into liquidation. He suggests that the 5,000 investors in BTRB, whose aim was to make the fun of owning horses available comparatively cheaply, had a pretty good run in difficult economic conditions from the £1.2 million originally raised.

Balding has long had more than a narrow personal interest in the economic problems of racing, for he has been chairman of the jump racing section of the National Trainers' Federation 'for longer than I care to remember'. Throughout that time he has seen the industry's ills grow more acute. 'English racing's biggest problem is that our individuality, which is one of our great attractions, is also our downfall. Look at the number of tracks we try to support and the number of establishments like this that exist as separate entities. We have fought manfully for decades against having honest economic discussions but this recession has brought us hard up against the realities. I have approximately 70 horses here at Whitcombe at the moment, about 50 jumpers and 20 for the Flat, and that's as many as I want to handle. But, to be viable, this place needs at least 140 and it could easily accommodate three trainers, myself and two others.'

In the meantime, he ensures that the animals in his care gain maximum benefit from the wealth of facilities and services at Whitcombe. He particularly approves of the equine swimming pool but, as might be expected of such an energetic and outgoing personality, it is a human contribution that he appreciates most. Having an in-house vet, in the person of Brian Eagles, is an advantage happily compounded by Eagles's eager and expert interest in the actual training of the horses. Like Balding's daughter Serena, who is her father's secretary and personal assistant, and the assistant trainer, Jonathan Geake, the vet adds to the powerful sense of teamwork around the yard. It was Eagles who, as we found a hedge to shelter us from the gusty wind on Thursday, pointed out that the gallop being used rose by 165 feet in four furlongs, a gradient that made a half-mile climb as demanding as a mile-and-a-quarter on the level. 'If you push the horses' heartbeats beyond a rate of 200 per minute, you are conditioning them,' he said. 'A horse has a heart-rate of between 36 and 42 per minute standing in the stable and it goes up to about 225 at the climax of a race.'

Morley Street was one who apparently enjoyed having his pulse quickened. Though his feats over fences and the dramatic speed he has shown in Flat races have threatened to complicate his schedule in the past, this season he will have a single-minded preparation for the Champion Hurdle. 'He has a lot of quality and is a terrific athlete,' said Toby Balding, unashamedly admiring the chestnut seven-year-old. 'He might well have a future steeple-chasing on left-handed tracks, i.e. something called the Cheltenham Gold Cup.'

Ambition is epic down in Hardy country.

The Observer, 3 November 1991

Within five months, Toby Balding had to admit he was wrong. Cool Ground won the Cheltenham Gold Cup. Balding was not heartbroken.

A Bumper Day for the Irish

TEN MINUTES BEFORE six o'clock on Thursday evening, at a time when the gloaming may be closing in on the Cotswolds, the bleeding mass of Cheltenham punters will try to convince themselves that they have been given a new, if rather desperate remedy for their problems.

For the very first time the Festival will end with a Flat race for National Hunt horses, the kind of event (known as 'a bumper') that is traditionally regarded as the ultimate Getting-out Stakes at many Irish jumping meetings. The intensity associated with those contests, especially in the betting ring, is best conveyed by someone like Ted Walsh, who in his long reign as leading amateur rider in Ireland won more bumpers than the bookies care to remember but has vivid memories of a number of occasions when his fancied mounts failed to effect a grand rescue from penury. He recalls particularly how the layout of Leopardstown meant that jockeys bringing their horses back after the bumper, which is always the last race on the card (it is the seventh on Thursday), would have to pass through a hostile tide of the skint and embittered as they streamed towards the exits: 'If you had been beaten on an odds-on favourite, some of those fellas were ready to dig your mother up out of the grave and throw her at you.'

The one certainty about the Cheltenham bumper is that few Irishmen will be indifferent to its outcome. They are bringing a far more numerous and threatening force across the water than they have done for years and their prejudices will be well represented in the turnover of £60 million confidently expected from wagering over the three days of the meeting. If the animals they send out to negotiate obstacles do not reward their faith, redemption will be sought among the 25 who set off to gallop two miles on the Flat.

And it can be assumed here and now that one partnership of horse and rider will be burdened with the overwhelming bulk of Irish hopes. Tiananmen Square and Tim Hyde have only appeared in public twice but the remarkably handsome four-year-old bay and the University College Dublin veterinary student have made a big impression with their two victories, notably the second one at Fairyhouse, where they came home a distance clear of a field containing a handful of previous winners. 'He didn't beat those horses – he absolutely ate them,' said Ted Walsh. 'They went a good gallop, the time was good and they were running on a big fair track, so you have to be impressed when you remember that the winning margin must be over 30 lengths before it is defined as a distance. That was a slaughter.'

Tiananmen Square, who is owned by John Magnier, Vincent O'Brien's son-in-law and the man in charge of the famed Coolmore Stud, followed a pattern of development familiar among horses that make their names in bumpers. 'He wasn't good enough as a two-year-old or three-year-old and all of a sudden he came to hand around November-December time,' said Walsh. 'Then he went very quickly from being good to being very good to being special.'

Backers of Tiananmen Square could be forgiven for feeling a little concern about the inexperience of Tim Hyde in the saddle. As an amateur jockey who has not yet won 15 races, he still claims an allowance of 7lb. But, whereas normally he would be granted that assistance against fellow amateurs, the peculiar and controversial conditions of the Tote-sponsored Cheltenham bumper will allow professionals to compete, and young Hyde may reckon that half a stone isn't much of an edge when the likes of Peter Scudamore and Richard Dunwoody are lining up at the gate. However – though he is very much a part-time rider, unlike most prominent Irish amateurs, who are almost as committed as pros – he has a true horseman's background and plenty of experience of hunting and showjumping. His pedigree is outstanding, since his grandfather was an exceptional jockey whose rides included the great Prince Regent and his father, after a career as a professional rider, has established a profitable reputation as one of the most inspired judges of young horses now living. The older Hyde had memorable successes at Cheltenham in his riding days but no doubt one of his sharpest recollections of the place involves the moment when he and Kinloch Brae came down three fences out while leading in the Gold Cup of 1970. There are many who think it will take a fall on the Flat to beat his son and Tiananmen Square this week.

If they get the job done successfully, there will, insists Ted Walsh, be a depth of satisfaction that will stay with the veterinary student for the rest of his life. Walsh is 42 now and has made himself a significant voice on racing for Irish television and a newspaper journalist, in addition to running the small training and dealing stable inherited from his father. He still rides in bumpers and looks to have perhaps a handful of winners in a season (annual totals close to 50 weren't unknown in his prime) but has not gone over hurdles or fences since swinging himself off Attitude Adjuster after taking the Foxhunters Chase in 1986. He was champion Irish amateur 11 times but says his four victories at Cheltenham meant more than anything else.

Talking to Walsh on Friday was like having an early injection of the unique spirit of Cheltenham and of the uplifting liveliness, love of the horse and contagious humour the Irish bring to it. He remembered that he had rated the chances of Attitude Adjuster as negligible because he was a tough horse who had needed plenty of physical persuasion in gaining narrow wins on the way to the Festival engagement. The fact that in 1986 the English authorities were starting to clamp down seriously on free use of the whip seemed sure to be a problem.

With a view to adjusting Attitude Adjuster's attitude, his rider gave him a couple of blunt messages with the whip on the way to the start. 'I knew I wouldn't be able to do a lot with it during the race but I thought I'd better let him know in advance that I had it on me. As it happened, he was on song from the moment we jumped off and he won easily without any need for me to put pressure on him.

'It was funny afterwards when Peter O'Sullevan said some kind things on television about the restraint I had shown. Peter was praising Ted Walsh, the experienced Irish amateur, for demonstrating the correct approach to employment of the whip. But if the race had been run at home, I'd have cut rashers off him. I had absolutely dissected him at Thurles a fortnight before.'

Ted Walsh is the least sadistic of men but he has always understood how much the winning of horse races can mean to his countrymen. Tim Hyde will have the same awareness as he is hoisted up on Tiananmen Square.

The Observer, 8 March 1992

The Irish won that 'bumper' – but not with Tiananmen Square.

Hero on a Hill of Broken Dreams

NATURAL APTITUDE AND the lack of it shaped last Thursday's contest for the Cheltenham Gold Cup. Its most influential figures were a jumping horse who will never be at ease with his job in life and a jockey who rides as if born to the work. Carvill's Hill was dead last of the five finishers when he came up the rising ground to the winning line at a weary stagger after a series of exhausting errors that had broken his spirit and reduced his admirers' pre-race eulogies to a rubble of embarrassment. Adrian Maguire used the same stretch of turf in front of the stands to persuade even those who suffered as a result of his triumphant drive on Cool Ground that they were privileged to be watching a 20-year-old Irish prodigy capable of emerging before long as an undeniable master.

Maguire has such extraordinary balance and authority in the saddle, is so much a fortifying extension of the half-ton animals he partners, that some of the best judges in racing are already comparing his gifts with those of the greatest National Hunt riders of the past. In sad contrast, recent attempts to bracket Carvill's Hill with the supreme equine talents of steeplechasing, Golden Miller and Arkle, have been exposed as the creations of romantic and deluded imaginations. Any neutral with a feeling for the game was bound to be longing for the display of crushing superiority that would have put the giant bay among the legends, and a few of us were irrational enough to bet at cramped odds in the superstitious hope that declared faith might help him towards immortality. It is legitimate to replace that sentimental commitment with sympathy – for the severely discomfited horse and the outstanding trainer and rider associated with him. But what is certainly not legitimate is the widespread rumble of disapproval that has greeted the tactics with which Michael Bowlby and Golden Freeze utterly disrupted the always fragile rhythm and composure of Carvill's Hill. The suggestion that Jenny Pitman (who had a second, more fancied runner in Toby Tobias) should be disciplined by the Jockey Club for telling Bowlby to keep Golden Freeze aggravatingly close to the favourite at the front of the field, refusing to drop in behind or stride on ahead, is deeply unconvincing.

Far from condemning Mrs Pitman, we should perhaps be grateful to her for saving us from continuing belief in a lie. A lie is just what the race might have told us if Carvill's Hill had been granted absolute freedom to accommodate his own peculiarities, had been left to jump along at the front in comfortable isolation. Given such a luxury, the brilliant Peter Scudamore on the ten-year-old's back might well have minimised his flaws and brought him home a winner, perpetuating vast misjudgments of his abilities. In this space and in many other places there would have been an eagerness to celebrate him as a magnificent phenomenon and to let the thrill of victory smother memories of his wayward past. Comparisons with Arkle would have been epidemic. Now, instead, we must face a simpler truth: Carvill's Hill is a steeplechaser with the capacity to produce great performances but is not a truly great steeplechaser. Would Arkle have been done out of any of this three Gold Cups by a little awkward company? Just as the best footballers must rise above the spoiling attentions of cynical opponents, so the best horses should cope with everything short of direct physical interference. At least Carvill's Hill wasn't having his shins kicked, as Pele and George Best frequently did. The horse's inadequacies under pressure were betrayed on Thursday as early as the first fence, which he ploughed through with a frightening exhibition of self-destructive clumsiness that one expert defined as 'an absolutely ignorant jump'. Optimists tried to persuade themselves that the initial blunder would have a sobering effect but in fact Toby Balding, the trainer of Cool Ground, was justified in asserting that Carvill's Hill could be only a minor threat from that moment on. He made another terrible mistake at the ninth and there followed a sequence of ragged, hazardous jumps so draining that he was virtually pulled up two fences from the finish, leaving Adam Kondrat and The Fellow in the lead far sooner than they wanted to be and thus at the mercy of Maguire's characteristically furious challenge on the run-in.

Losing the Gold Cup by a short-head for the second successive season obviously inflicted more pain on The Fellow's desperately unlucky connections than was brought to young Maguire by the imposition of a four-day suspension (21-24 March) for excessive use of the whip. No one wants to see horses subjected to undue punishment but expecting the jockey to put down his whip, when he knew that using it could mean the difference between victory and defeat in his sport's most highly rated race, would have been as quixotic as imagining that Lester Piggott was going to stop drumming on Roberto's hide in the last furlong of the 1972 Derby. As his haul of winners for the season approaches 70, Maguire can reflect on a year as astonishingly successful as any jump rider of his age has ever enjoyed. His dizzying climb to his present position of having leading trainers clamouring for his services began when he rode Omerta to an easy win in the Kim Muir Chase at the Cheltenham Festival of 1991 and followed up quickly with success on the same mount in the Irish Grand National (he had been on crutches three days before the race, yet beat top professional Charlie Swan by the minimum margin in a hectic finish).

By the time he had turned pro himself and headed for England, his record as an amateur with the County Limerick trainer Michael Hourigan showed 17 winners on the track and 48 in point-to-point races. So informed observers of his career were sure he would do well on this side of the water but none could have foreseen the scale of the impact he has made since joining Toby Balding at his Whitcombe Manor stables in Dorset. The attention guaranteed by his strike-rate might have scattered the wits of a less level-headed young man but as fourth youngest member of a working-class family of nine in Kilmessan, County Meath, he had an upbringing that did not encourage dangerous vanities. Confident predictions of development towards genuine greatness owe almost as much to the soundness of his temperament as to the natural horsemanship that informs everything he does with a body handily proportioned (at 5ft 4in and about 9st 3lb) for riding jumpers. Maguire seems to improve nearly every horse he sits on and as early as last November one English trainer, John Ffitch-Heyes, was already sufficiently impressed to declare, rather provocatively: 'Martin Pipe is very foolish not to pay him a £50,000 retainer and have done with it.'

Pipe has been doing fairly well (the shattering disappointment of Carvill's Hill notwithstanding) through his alliance with Peter

Scudamore, whose wide range of gifts and superb professionalism have never been seen to better effect than on Minnehoma in a spell-binding Sun Alliance Chase last Wednesday, and scarcely needs advice about hiring arrangements. But he knows too much about the game to quarrel with the judgment implicit in Ffitch-Heyes's naughty remark. And there can be no doubt about how highly Scudamore rates Maguire. It was the counsel of the champion and of the other towering talent among National Hunt riders, Richard Dunwoody, that hardened their young rival's decision to come to England last year.

With Scudamore and Dunwoody setting a wonderful example, and a substantial group of excellent jockeys forever drawing the best out of those two masters, these are distinguished times for National Hunt jockeyship. A talent like Adrian Maguire's can only make the good times better.

The Observer, 15 March 1992

Cumani's Grand Obsession

FUNCTIONING IN HIS second language is never likely to reduce the force or clarity of Luca Cumani's opinions, least of all when the subject is the kind of horse race that created the first big gamble of the Flat season at Doncaster yesterday. Cumani is an Italian who can summon considerable eloquence in celebration of the English racing scene he has been brightening since the mid-Seventies but mention of handicaps, even those with the pedigree of the Lincoln, brings a hard directness to his words. 'I don't like handicaps,' he said in the office of his Bedford House stables at Newmarket on Thursday. 'I think they are a form of Communism. Ideally, I believe the best horse should always win a race. Handicaps are a denial of that principle. If you are beaten a head, giving seven pounds, you have the best horse but you haven't won. Handicaps constitute 50 per cent of races run in England but the only people that really love them are bookmakers. It's a fallacy that they suit punters. Bookies want them because they offer the biggest profit-margin.'

Such criticisms are given extra weight by Cumani's impressive record of success in the form of contest he condemns (two Cambridgeshires head a formidable list). 'I have no difficulty winning handicaps but I feel strongly that they are not a fair representation of what racing should be about. With handicaps, you are governed by another person's opinion of your horse. Once a trainer finds a horse is overrated there is a huge incentive to cheat. Cheating is not a particularly pleasant pastime and it is also expensive because you have to keep running a horse that has no prospect of winning. We would be better off in every sense with a system of conditions races from the bottom up – from sellers and claimers and auction races up through all levels to

Listed and Pattern races.'

These objections do nothing to weaken Cumani's conviction that a trainer of racehorses is more the master of his own destiny in England than in any other country. He recognises that men like himself, with individual yards and the use of such a wide range of gallops and canters at Newmarket, are blessed compared with their counterparts in places like the US or Italy, where trainers are crowded into stabling areas at racetracks and obliged to exercise their animals on the same dirt surface used for racing. 'The fundamental explanation of why we have so many good trainers in this country is that here it is a lovely job,' he said. 'Nowhere else in the world is it such an exciting and attractive occupation and you perform best when you are happy.'

Yet only a happy obsessive could be so upbeat in the face of the problems inflicted on Cumani by a serious recession and the loss of perhaps 40 well-bred horses from his care through the Aga Khan's decision in December 1990 to concentrate his racing interests in France. 'You do have to be obsessed, though you must be capable of maintaining a balance to avoid going round the bend. One characteristic that definitely links the leading trainers is a devouring appetite for knowledge. None of us will die knowing 10 per cent of what there is to know about the horse but we are always striving, trying to analyse our experiences for indications of how we can be more effective.'

What appeals to him particularly about the life is that someone with such commitment, and possessing the less easily defined capacity to establish a rapport with horses and a feel for each one's needs and precise abilities, can start with very little and go all the way to the top. In his case, the only riches at the start were in connections and credentials. His father, Sergio, had such a commanding stable in Milan that he was Italy's champion trainer 10 times before he died at 53. Luca, whose youthful self-control could keep his six-foot frame inside 10 stone (even with a couple of stones added he still presents a handsome, elegant figure), was an amateur Flat race rider good enough to be European champion in 1972. He came to England for the first time in that summer to take a two-month holiday job at John Winter's stable and in November 1973, as a 24-year-old, he became assistant to Henry Cecil. Acknowledging that he had earlier been taught 'the principles of life and the principles of training' by his father, Cumani says he learnt from Cecil all he needed to learn about the special practicalities of training horses in England – the nuances of placing animals in races, the demands of different tracks and all the other peculiarities of a world with which he had fallen in love. By October 1975, a mortgage and some help from his parents enabled him to buy Bedford House for £75,000. An English wife, Sara, and two children (Matthew and Francesca) came later.

His very first winner was in a Group race, and he had already saddled Konafa to be second in the One Thousand Guineas. Gaining places in Classics became something of a habit and the quality shown by Tolomeo in finishing a fast-closing second in the 1983 Two Thousand Guineas subsequently brought victory in the Arlington Million, reinforcing Cumani's view of the US as a legitimate hunting ground. Appropriately, to say the least, his first Classic winner anywhere was Old Country in the Italian Derby of 1982. The breakthrough in England was produced by the remarkable Commanche Run, whose 1984 St Leger success was followed by a brilliant four-year-old season. Still, Cumani felt the Derby was 'a race that other trainers won'. Then his initial batch of horses from the Aga Khan brought a handsome colt with exceptional presence and athletic movement. He was called Kahyasi and in 1988 he won both the Derby and Irish Derby (his trainer thinks he deserves more credit for the fact that his time at Epsom was the fastest since electronic clocking was introduced).

Ensconce gave Cumani another Classic with the Irish One Thousand of 1989, and 1990 was statistically his best year, with 108 winners and £1,314,646 in prize money, figures that do not include winners at Belmont and Aqueduct in New York and an Italian Group One race. The Bedford House horse population has dropped from around 185 to about 130, and it was not surprising that last season's aggregate of races won fell to 72, worth just over £1 million.

With his distaste for 'crystal-balling', Cumani is modest about the prospects of two of his charges quoted at 33-1 for the Derby, Masad and Bonny Scot. The most reliable promise of stirring deeds is represented by the four-year-old Second Set. After winning the Sussex Stakes last year, Second Set had the rest of his season flawed by illness but is flourishing again and should reaffirm his status as a top miler.

No one can question Luca Cumani's status as a top trainer.

The Observer, 22 March 1992

There was another exceptional achievement for Cumani in 1994 when Barathea won the Breeders' Cup Mile at Churchill Downs in Kentucky with a spectacular demonstration of class.

Old Ways get a Rough Ride

THERE IS MORE than an ocean between the rival concepts of racehorse management that flourish in Europe and North America. Conflicting interpretations of Arazi's failure in the Kentucky Derby last weekend showed yet again that this is no minor theoretical divergence. It is often characterised by the emotional intransigence and mutual self-righteousness of a generational argument, which it plainly resembles. Trainers on this side of the Atlantic tend to be convinced that centuries of experience have developed methods of preparing the thorough-bred for competitive action that are the most effective to be found anywhere. American racing, whose briefer history and special conditions have encouraged a harsher, more intensive empiricism, is full of people who are sure that much in the Old World approach is old hat, questionable practice protectively clothed in tradition.

When it comes to insularity, there is little to choose between the two attitudes but it is the US case that is usually put with more aggressive vehemence. Few horsemen over there will have any truck with the offensive hyperbole sprayed around by John Campo, a New York trainer who once told me on the Belmont backstretch that Vincent O'Brien in his prime would not have won three races a year 'with the kinda crows I got out in the stalls in that barn'. But the Arazi episode has reminded us that there are many quieter Americans who believe that the considerable weight of dollars hauled away from their tracks in recent seasons by horses from across the water would have been multiplied if the animals had not been under the control of a bunch of 'Eurowimps'. That was the term employed last week by one of the US's foremost racing writers, Andrew Beyer, of the Washington Post, in condemning the conservative instincts of those who plot the campaigns of our leading horses. Europeans, Beyer told readers of his syndicated column, 'seem obsessed with avoiding defeat. They habitually duck and dodge competition and retire their horses prematurely; when they run and lose, they respond with a litany of excuses.' Having pointed out that running eighth under Pat Valenzuela in a Kentucky Derby field of 18 represented the first bad race of Arazi's life, Beyer suggested the natural riposte would have been a challenge on Saturday in the second leg of the American Triple Crown, the Preakness at Pimlico, near Baltimore. There, he declared, the chestnut colt from France would have been likely to 'annihilate his rivals in the manner that was expected of him' at Churchill Downs.

As supporting evidence, he recalled the experiences of Hansel, who finished a dismal tenth as the Kentucky Derby favourite in 1991 and then proved himself a champion by winning the Preakness, and Snow Chief, 20 lengths adrift in the Derby of 1986 and a runaway victor at Pimlico. Beyer was unimpressed by the assertion from many respected European judges that the key to Arazi's Derby failure was a fundamental lack of stamina, a genetic inability to beat worthwhile opposition at Classic distances: 'Even if Valenzuela did take Arazi too far back and then moved too abruptly, and even if the colt's optimal distance is not one-and-a-half miles, I cannot believe that a more fit, more seasoned Arazi would not have won the Kentucky Derby . . . I cannot believe that the awesome running machine we saw last fall is congenitally incapable of running a final quarter-mile in 26.4 seconds and outfinishing the likes of Lil E. Tee.'

Those sentences embraced the principal elements of a debate to which Andrew Beyer was always certain to make an interesting contribution. The son of a professor of American history, he might have been heading for the academic life if, in his final year at Harvard, he had not made a dramatic choice about two very different kinds of examination facing him on a June day in 1966. One concerned Geoffrey Chaucer and the other was the Belmont Stakes. Beyer, having decided he knew more about the horses than about the 14th-century poet, curtailed his formal education and committed himself to the track. The core of his passion for the racing game is betting (his painstakingly calculated speed figures provide his country's punters with their most reliable guide to the merits of the animals they wager on) and he never seeks to make his writing brim with lyricism. But the sight of a great racehorse at the gallop undoubtedly thrills him and his views on Arazi reverberate with the conviction that a massive talent is being misused. His thick-lensed glasses may have steamed up as he bent his lean figure over the keyboard to wax increasingly indignant: 'If the Eurowimps follow their usual pattern, the discovery of a convenient career-ending injury may be imminent.' At that point, he seemed to have lost patience with forensic objectivity and started swinging for the crotch. Thus he found himself able to skip lightly over such crucial factors as Valenzuela's eccentric riding and the relevance of the knee surgery performed on Arazi after he dazzled the racing world with his supernatural surge in the Breeders' Cup Juvenile at Churchill Downs last November.

In fact, the jockey's handling of the colt – which involved dropping him in dead last as the field passed the winning post first time and then launching him on a spectacular, energy-draining charge on the wide outside up the backstretch to loom in a challenging position at the entrance to the home straight – struck most laymen and experts alike as suicidal folly. Ridden to exploit his devastating powers of sustained acceleration in the decisive phase of the race, Arazi might have overcome any stamina deficiencies well enough to win from an unmistakably moderate field. Valenzuela said after the defeat that he had not lost faith in Arazi as a phenomenon, but faith in Valenzuela as a partner must be more precarious.

The operation on the horse's knees presents a less straight-forward issue. However, leaving aside the comments of some informed observers who claim to have seen indications that Arazi was suffering more pain in the Kentucky Derby than could be explained by simple tiredness, it is easy to believe that the surgery harmed his chances by reducing the time available for his preparation. Francois Boutin's protestations on that score once the contest was over would, of course, have been received more sympathetically had he not insisted before the race that his contender was at a peak of readiness. Andrew Beyer was voicing the feelings of many Americans when he sought to pin most of the blame for the humbling of the marvel on what they saw as a presumptuously undemanding schedule mapped out for him on his way to the Kentucky Derby. 'If an American trainer took a horse to, say, the Epsom Derby, and declared that he was going to train the horse just as he would at home, we'd think he was a moron,' wrote Beyer. 'But when Boutin tried to defy all American precedent and prepare the horse in a typically French style, with a single, untaxing prep race, most people's doubts were quelled by the Europeans' habitual success in races here.'

A specific contribution to the quelling process was the fact that Arazi's historic gallop on Churchill Downs dirt in November followed two victories in the Breeders' Cup Mile by the Boutin-trained Miesque. The silver-haired presence moving among them in a cloud of Montecristo smoke was not someone the locals could take lightly. But they had never really believed that an easy race at Saint Cloud was sufficient to prepare a three-year-old to win their Derby and they were driving home the point last week, eagerly led by Beyer. 'The requisite methods of preparation for the Kentucky Derby bear little resemblance to any other race, here or abroad, because it is uniquely stressful for a horse,' he reminded his public, listing the strains of going 10 furlongs so early in the season, of competing in a field much larger than will usually be seen on the tight tracks of the US and the exposure of contestants to the noisy turmoil of a carnival atmosphere. 'That's why great American horsemen have always trained and raced their three-year-olds hard before the Derby: to imbue them with the necessary physical and mental toughness. We may now surmise that daily canters in the tranquillity of Chantilly don't accomplish the same purpose.'

Arazi happens to be trained at Lamorlaye but, everything considered, the converted academic is not guilty of a wild surmise.

The Observer, 10 May 1992

Hope for Brittain's Foreign Policy

EXERCISING HIS STRING of thoroughbreds before the birds have found their voices is not something Clive Brittain does simply because he likes being the first trainer out on Newmarket Heath each morning. 'Horses tend to work more honestly in the dark,' he assured me last week.

Talk of darkness was hyperbole, a currency in which Brittain has always been at home, but he has no doubt that the limited visibility immediately after dawn helps to concentrate the equine mind. 'Working at first light, you don't see the horses until they are less than a furlong from you, so they can't see far either,' he said. 'They don't find themselves facing a long, staring gallop, which a lot of them dislike so much that they would just switch off. Others, when they can see for a mile or so, run much too fast for their own good. Going out as early as we do, we cut down on those problems.' The explanation is a reminder that Brittain's methods, even when they strike other trainers as quirky, are usually rooted in convictions rationally drawn from experience. His self-belief, and the legendary confidence with which he surrounds just about every contender he sends to the races, will be considerably nourished in Paris this afternoon if User Friendly's hitherto invincible form is maintained in the Prix de l'Arc de Triomphe.

But whatever happens at Longchamp to the remarkable daughter of the Derby winner Slip Anchor, the haughtiest human denizens of the racing world can no longer justify the slightest trace of condescension towards the Wiltshire sausage-maker's son who took her there. That some who enjoyed a more cushioned entry into his profession can still affect to look down on him is a miracle of superciliousness. It is a phenomenon that irritates his admirers much more than it concerns Brittain, who has no need of verbal rebuttals when his record in 1992 alone is enough to inflict terminal embarrassment on the ranks of the patronising. 'That gives us eight Group One wins this season,' he was able to confirm quietly after Sayyedati galloped the acclaimed 'pocket rocket' Lyric Fantasy into total submission in the Cheveley Park Stakes at Newmarket on Wednesday. He did not have to point out that three of the eight were Classic victories by User Friendly, who took the English and Irish Oaks and the St Leger on her way to the Arc. It is more his style to put the smart mouths down neatly by mentioning that his training quarters are his own property, though the highest wage he ever earned in more than 20 years as a stable lad was £17 a week – 'and that was rated good pay'.

The wages could not be considered bad if weighed along with the richness of education he gained over the two decades by being close to the master of Warren Place, Noel Murless, the greatest English trainer of his era. A man of Brittain's bright alertness and ambition was unlikely to waste a minute of the time he spent as an involved witness of how Murless handled brilliant champions such as Crepello, St Paddy and Petite Etoile.

Memories of the Warren Place years are made fonder by the fact that it was there he wooed his wife, Maureen, who was his employer's secretary. They were married in 1957 but it was not until 1972 that Brittain (helped by astute ante-post betting on the Murless runners) had saved sufficient money to launch his training career. In the 20 years since, his most publicised characteristic has been a smiling but utterly stubborn refusal to accept other people's assessments of his horses. His insistence on challenging aristocratic opposition with apparently modest animals, his eagerness to have a tilt at the discouraging implications of breeding and form, has invited so much comparison with Don Quixote that it is intriguing to speculate how many readers of *The Sporting Life* and the *Racing Post* have been turned on to Cervantes.

It is safe to assume that rather more of them have been attracted to Brittain's banner. Ordinary punters don't have to be told that, whatever critics may say about his comparatively low strike rate, his optimism is often far from wild and his horses have a habit of winning at juicy prices. That was notably true of his first Classic winner. Julio Mariner took the 1978 St Leger at 28-1, and when the dazzling filly Pebbles (subsequently heroine of the Eclipse Stakes, the Champion Stakes and the Breeders' Cup Turf) came home three lengths clear in the 1983 One Thousand Guineas she was 8-1. Terimon, of course, did not have to win to bring a bonanza (when he was 500-1 second in Nashwan's Derby, Brittain was a vigorous each-way backer) and Bold Arrangement was an even more historic runner-up in the Kentucky Derby of 1986, a performance that could only sharpen his trainer's appetite for overseas adventures. Considering that Pebbles is one of only two British-trained horses to claim a Breeders' Cup jackpot and that Brittain's Jupiter Island is unique in having gone out from this country to lift the Japan Cup, his optimism obviously travels remarkably well.

This season, with a handful of foreign successes added to around 60 so far at home, is emphasising the point. However, it is not the statistical soundness of his achievements that makes Clive Brittain a presence to cherish in English racing and guarantees that countless thousands will be trying to will User Friendly over the Longchamp line ahead of the splendid Epsom and Irish Derby winners, Dr Devious and St Jovite, and the rest of her formidable rivals in the Bois de Boulogne. His appeal resides in what he is even more than what he has done. The amiable openness of his nature, and an enthusiasm for the horseman's life that remains dew-fresh at 58, make it unsurprising that more than a few of the staff he is forever praising could qualify for long-service medals. It was Jock Brown, his assistant trainer, who came to Brittain's mind when – during our conversation in his study, a small room as welcoming as the Labradors that lolled around the carpet – he offered a spectacular illustration of how reduced vision can help a racehorse. Failing to remember the name of the animal in the story, he said: 'Jock will know, Jock forgets nothing.'

Brittain himself has a fine memory for essentials, such as the fact that the horse in question, which turned out to have been called Swinging Tribe, was 'probably the biggest pig I have ever trained'. That opinion persuaded the trainer, on a day in August 1976, that the 8-1 or so being offered about Swinging Tribe in a mile race at Brighton should have been stretched to 80-1. But as he got up into the stands and saw the sea mist beginning to roll across the Brighton course, he remembered a foggy morning when he had sent this no-hoper up Long Hill at Newmarket as a lead horse to a really useful stablemate. When 'the pig' emerged from the fog at the end of the gallop with eight lengths to spare, the rider of the good horse reported that he 'just couldn't get near that bastard'.

Soon after the start at Brighton, the field were enveloped in thickening mist and when they reappeared Swinging Tribe, true to his own peculiar form line, was 15 lengths clear. It was not a triumph that Brittain could build on. Finding the going a horse requires is one thing. But even he is not so quixotic as to believe he will get a pea-souper whenever he needs it.

His face – with the long upper lip that folds back so readily into a smile and the eyes that become large and round when he is at his most enthusiastic – is as youthful as the lean body and both convey an impression of happy energy. Of course, he has known plenty of experiences calculated to lower his spirits, like the car crash that nearly killed him in the Seventies and, more recently, the failure of Mystiko to sustain in later races the surging power he showed in winning last year's Two Thousand Guineas. Mystiko's troubles seem to be entirely in his mind, endorsing Brittain's maxim that 'fitness is not all about galloping but also about getting your horse to the races mentally able to cope with it'. The grey son of Secreto had revealed a complicated temperament early in his life. But solo work in the patient hands of Michael Roberts (the thinking rider from South Africa who is about to take this season's jockeys' championship) had relaxed him so successfully that both Roberts and the trainer thought Mystiko could be made to settle in the Derby and overcome doubts about his ability to stay a mile-and-a-half. Brittain now acknowledges that Epsom on the most clamorous day of the year was not the occasion for testing their hypothesis. 'Up to the Guineas he was a super horse but at Epsom he became so upset in the parade ring that he had run three races before he got to the post. The ordeal probably shot his nerve. Since then, in our efforts to get him back to his true form, we have tried five different ways of training him. So far we can't get the balance right but I still don't accept that we have lost him altogether.'

Brittain appreciates the good fortune that has brought him, so soon after seeing his hopes of a first Derby disintegrate, to today's thrill of hoisting George Duffield on to the likely favourite in another of the world's great races. User Friendly, who never ran as a two-year-old, pleased him from the day she was sent to Carlburg by her owner, Bill Gredley, who had bred her at his Stetchworth Park Stud nearby. But it was her first race that told the trainer how good she might be. 'Sandown is notorious as a graveyard for horses that meet trouble in running, they've almost no chance of making up ground lost through interference, but she was stopped three times, and she still got up and won by a length-and-a-half. I turned to Bill Gredley and said, "We have a hell of a filly on our hands".'

Unbeatable is what she has been so far, and if she has a bigger fan than Brittain it can only be one of the two Gredley children, Timothy (6) and Pollyanna (5). 'When they come into the yard, User drops her head to be cuddled and they rub her neck,' says Brittain. 'She is a big filly but the children play with her as if she were a teddy bear.' User Friendly behaves well towards adults, too, but lays down limits. 'She never turns a hair in her work,' her mentor reports, 'but when she is coming close to a race she lets you know she is getting edgy and it's time to back off then. She won't stand for being fussed around too much.'

Perhaps her greatest asset on the track, Brittain suggests, is that she can quicken twice. 'Good horses will usually quicken and sustain the burst for half-a-furlong or a furlong or, in exceptional cases, two furlongs. But the vast majority have only one real change of gear, whereas she has two. She can accelerate to the front and then, if something comes at her, she can quicken away again. Given reasonable luck in running, she is definitely equipped to win the Arc. She has the high cruising speed needed, she can be settled quite easily, she has the pace to get in the race and the pace to get out of the race – by going clear of the others.'

That would be a sight to cheer the heart. And there would be the priceless bonus of the look on Clive Brittain's face.

The Observer, 4 October 1992

Sadly, we didn't see that look. User Friendly was beaten a neck by Subotica in the Arc.

Riding a Crest at the Festival

MARK DWYER AND his Cheltenham mounts deserve each other. There is quality to burn on both sides of the alliance. It was always predictable that Richard Dunwoody and Peter Scudamore, clear first and second in the contest for the jump jockeys' championship, would occupy the same positions in the betting on which rider will urge home most winners over the three days of the Festival. The combination of exceptional talent and a firm association with powerful stables assures both of an intimidating volume of good partners. But if the glory criterion is applied, if we try to identify the jockey who has the best hope of claiming a sliver of immortality in the Cotswolds, Dwyer is as well placed as any man who will be swung into the saddle at National Hunt's greatest meeting.

Adam Kondrat on The Fellow may have more obvious prospects of dominating the Gold Cup than Dwyer has on Jodami, and the bookmakers' prices on the Champion Hurdle suggest that Dunwoody on Flown or Scudamore (if he opts to ride Granville Again) has just as much right to optimism as the 29-year-old from County Meath can draw from teaming up with Coulton. However, considering the balanced strength of his hand in these supreme classics of hurdling and steeplechasing, it is simple fact that no one is a better bet to complete the historic double. The mere awareness of such a possibility might tighten like a ligature on a rider's nerves, especially when it occurs in the context of truly outstanding chances in at least three other races at the Festival. But Dwyer's nature seems well equipped to take the strain. His horsemanship, intelligence and capacity to analyse in advance the demands made on himself and the animals he sits on, and to assess objectively in retrospect how he and they have coped, are all remarkable. Almost equally important, perhaps, is the general strength and liveliness of his personality.

Close observation of him as he delivers his post-race report to a trainer, particularly to Jimmy FitzGerald, the fellow Irishman who first launched his career in England and remains his principal employer now that he is operating as a freelance, is sufficient to make it plain that this is not someone who could ever settle for being a competent adjunct to a four-legged athlete. The wiry figure – he is 5ft 10in and can do 10st 1lb readily – is quietly animated, intense at times, and maintains a flow of relevant information and interpretation. 'Owners get plenty for the riding fee when Mark is in the saddle,' one expert witness told me, 'but they get almost as much value again from what he has to say when he steps down.' He can also be rather interesting before a race, as he was last week when he told me that an odds-on favourite he was about to ride for FitzGerald at Sedgefield had a tendency to show alarming marks on his hide if given a hard look, let alone a few smacks with the whip. Since any trouble over excessive use of the whip could have endangered Dwyer's Gold Cup challenge, Polar Region's susceptibility to weals might have been a major complication. 'He has a lot more stamina than pace and I'm not convinced he can win without a few slaps but I don't want to take the slightest risk of being done, so it's a problem,' the jockey said with a rueful little smile as he headed towards the paddock.

Fortunately, the rest of the field were not impressively endowed with either stamina or pace and the favourite's backers had no reason to suspect the minor drama behind a smooth victory. But anybody who studied the video of the race carefully would see the Dwyer whip arm shape to impart direct encouragement and then check halfway through the action, settling for theatrical gestures that the most zealous animal rights activist could hardly have questioned. Dwyer smiles easily, with his blue eyes as well as his teeth, and these days he has no cause to ration the happy expressions. His mood was very different not so long ago. He suffered along with FitzGerald when, for nearly 18 months, a cruelly persistent virus prevented the horses in the yard at Malton, Yorkshire, from finding the zestful wellbeing normally induced by the spirited master of Norton Grange. At the start of this season, the rider, who is married and father of two young children, decided to terminate the stable's retainer on his services and go freelance. Thrilling vindication of that decision has come swiftly with coveted rides on the likes of Jodami (trained by Peter Beaumont) and Coulton (trained by Mick Easterby) but Dwyer clearly takes as much pleasure from the resurgence in FitzGerald's fortunes that sends their old double-act to Cheltenham with three of the most exciting contenders of the meeting in Sybillin, Trainglot and Aslan.

The trainer would obviously be happier if Dwyer were available for two more of his runners at Cheltenham, the outsiders Native Mission in the Champion Hurdle and Gold Options, in the Gold Cup. For his part, the jockey emphasises how relieved and delighted he is that his relationship with FitzGerald was never seriously damaged by the tensions inseparable from that bleak period of frustration ('Everyone did well to come through this patch in one piece'). He values the bond between them, one first forged when he arrived at the Malton yard in the autumn of 1982 and quickly strengthened by shared triumphs with the great steeplechaser Forgive 'n' Forget, winner of the Gold Cup in 1985 and an apparent certainty again in 1988 until a broken leg cost him his life. But Dwyer points out gently that he could hardly be expected to agonise over choosing the short-priced Coulton and Jodami in preference to Native Mission and Gold Options, whose combined odds soar beyond 5,000-1. He is famously capable of recognising much finer distinctions in equine merit. Though born (one of eight children) into a family with no racing background, he brings to his job a formidable range of innate gifts, from the ability to settle the most awkward horses to a beautifully controlled and unobtrusive style of race-riding. 'The only way to find out precisely how well Mark is going in a race would be to stop him and ask,' an awed admirer told me. The experience of riding 66 Flat winners as a teenager in Ireland helped to refine technique and judgment but the brightness of mind was always there.

'To be a proper jockey, you have to have a head to begin with,' he said. 'You've got to be able to distinguish what it is that each horse needs to make him run, when to be sympathetic and when to apply persuasion. Some want a short rein and some want a long rein. When you find out what they like, you have a good chance of getting them on your side. Fighting and pulling at them is hardly ever the answer. And I think it is part of my job to assess the abilities of the horses I am competing against as well as my own. I do my best to work out how good they might or might not be.'

On that basis, he had to be asked for a contribution to the

Cheltenham survival kit. 'The Fellow has an outstanding chance – you cannot question his right to be favourite in the Gold Cup,' said Dwyer, dealing with the biggest issue first. 'On the book, Jodami has to find 10lb on him, which is quite a bit. The ground looks like being in The Fellow's favour, whereas Jodami is the only one of my mounts that would appreciate rain. In fact, I'd like it to stay dry through the first two days and then piss down after the last race on Wednesday.

'As trainer, Francois Doumen is able to produce The Fellow just right on the day and, after being beaten a short-head in two Gold Cups, his price is justified. But I am still convinced I have a wonderful chance. Garrison Savannah and Cool Ground, when they beat The Fellow, were 6lb and 8lb below Jodami's rating now. He has beaten Run For Free and Chatam and I don't see why he shouldn't do it again at Cheltenham. Like Mr Beaumont, I couldn't be more delighted with his form at the moment. He is a marvellous horse, a real nice type of ride, with no vices. Touching wood, I'd say that the least of my worries would be Jodami's jumping. He's great at the game. The Beaumont family are naturally getting nervous as the Gold Cup draws near. But in my position, you have to forget the importance of the occasion and do your job.'

Discussing the Champion Hurdle, Dwyer stresses the significance of Dunwoody's choice of the fast-ground specialist Flown rather than Kribensis, Morley Street or the other attractive options offered. He also acknowledges the threat from the high-class Flat credentials of Ireland's Vintage Crop, though he believes the big field in the Champion will compound the disadvantages of Vintage Crop's inexperience. Nothing impresses him more than his own ally, Coulton. 'He looks to be an outstanding chaser in the making but the Champion would be a nice bonus. Coulton is a very big horse but travels so well that you can nearly put him anywhere in a race. He wouldn't have a great turn of foot but has a high cruising speed and could come with a long run, creeping his way smoothly through the field. He is a very fast jumper, which is useful to say the least.'

Such talk encouraged a flexing of the betting arm and when we moved on to the three main elements of Jimmy FitzGerald's challenge there was an impulse to lunge at the nearest bookmaker. Sybillin, a superbly quick, accurate jumper 'with loads of toe', deserves to be the shortest-priced favourite at the Festival in the

Arkle Trophy. Aslan, who specialises in taking extreme liberties with the opposition in the Flat races for National Hunt horses that are known as bumpers, may do further damage in the contest of that kind sponsored by Guinness on Wednesday. But on the same day there will be another candidate for glory and gratitude. Trainglot was talented enough on the Flat to run fourth in the Ascot Gold Cup and to land a tremendous gamble in the Cesarewitch. Dwyer is lyrical about his prowess over obstacles and how he might thrill all but his opponents at the Festival, especially if he goes for the Coral Cup Handicap Hurdle instead of taking up his alternative engagement in the Sun Alliance Novice Hurdle.

I have a feeling that Trainglot will have the heavy responsibility of preventing the wolf from bounding right through the door and having cubs upon the hearthrug.

The Observer, 14 March 1993

Mark Dwyer won the Gold Cup on Jodami. Coulton was not good enough in the Champion Hurdle but has since developed into a high-class steeple-chaser. The FitzGerald horses ran far below their form and were found to have been 'wrong', with a bad blood count. My own financial pulse was rather weak by the Thursday evening.

National Ends in Fiasco

Trying to make instant sense of the Grand National that never was made this one of my least pleasant memories of Aintree.

NEVER IN MORE than 150 years of producing sensational incident has the Grand National offered anything like the bewildering mixture of drama and farce that spread across Aintree yesterday and ended with the 1993 running of the world's most famous steeplechase being declared a void race. There could be no other decision from the stewards after a hopelessly confused reaction to the second of two false starts left all but nine of the 39 jockeys in the field galloping their mounts at the first fence in the belief that their sport's toughest test was officially under way.

One rider who was never going to travel far was Richard Dunwoody, who found the heavy starting tape winding itself so tightly round his neck that when the horses coming behind him trod on the streaming tape he was almost yanked from the saddle of Won't Be Gone Long. But while Dunwoody, the leading National Hunt jockey of this season, concentrated on avoiding strangulation, others raced on, totally unaware that behind them the starter, 64-year-old Captain Keith Fyffe Brown, was desperately waving his red flag to signify that their efforts were meaningless. When Brown flourished that flag with similar urgency a few minutes before, the first false start had been confirmed by the waving of another flag, that of his colleague, Ken Evans, stationed between the starting gate and the first fence. But this time – perhaps because the starter's recall flag remained furled as he raised it anxiously above his head, perhaps because another abortive beginning to the great steeplechase seemed so improbable – Evans failed to appreciate what was required of him and made no signal for the riders to pull up and go back.

Thus a fantasy race went pounding on over the punishing four-and-a-half miles and 30 fences that constitute the National, leaving only those lucky nine who had realised the truth (they included the one woman participant, Judy Davies on Formula One) to loiter in baffled frustration at the gate. People tried to shout word of what had occurred from the sidelines as the deluded competitors in the race that never was galloped by, and the extraordinary reality dawned on many of the jockeys at various points out on the course. But most of the messages were lost in the buffeting wind and rain and a substantial body of men and horses settled down to go all the way, obliging BBC commentators to record the flying leaps and the cruel falls while constantly reminding their audience that what they were seeing was a hectic charade.

By the time the leaders reached the notoriously threatening 15th obstacle, The Chair, they were confronted by a single cone in front of the jump and the figure of an official flourishing a flag. However, these riders knew that the prolonged delay they had endured in the miserable weather at the start had been caused by animal rights protesters and they guessed that another demonstration was creating complications at The Chair. In any case a single cone usually indicates that there is a specific, limited problem, such as an injured horse, on the other side of part of that fence and the sensible policy for those who wish to avoid disqualification is to skirt that section and jump further along. So The Chair was negotiated by those contenders who were going best and an anticlimax of historic proportions became inevitable.

It was all certain to end in tears and Jenny Pitman, the only woman trainer to win the National (with Corbiere in 1983), provided some of them after the least fancied of her three challengers, Esha Ness, had gone past the post first in the phantom contest. John White had driven Esha Ness up the long Aintree run-in to hold off three fellow Irishmen, Charlie Swan on Cahervillahow, Adrian Maguire on Romany King and Norman Williamson on The Committee. Those four men from across the water had suffered enough without finding that the turmoil of complaint and recrimination stirred by the most spectacular shambles any major sporting event has ever precipitated contained a peculiar insult to their native land.

When one of the emotional victims, John Upson, trainer of the heavily backed Zeta's Lad, sought to emphasise the failings of the Aintree system for signalling restarts he pointed out that things were done infinitely better in 'a backward little country like Ireland'.

Maybe it would be wrong to judge anyone too severely in yesterday's unprecedented circumstances. But many in the crowd were aggressively intent on conveying their anger to Captain Brown, for whom the whole episode was an agonising valediction as he stepped into retirement after being a Jockey Club starter since 1975. As he made his exit from the racecourse, escorted by police through loud boos and the threat of jostling, the sad captain may have taken a little comfort from the apportioning of blame implicit in a formal announcement by Rod Fabricius, the acting clerk of the course at Aintree: 'The first time the starter signalled the false start the recall flag was shown. The second time the starter signalled a false start the man with the red flag further down the course was in the correct position but he did not show the flag to the jockeys.'

The unavoidable conclusion is that the basic arrangements for the start of one of the world's great sports events seem to have been intolerably ramshackle. Peter Greenall, chairman of Aintree Racecourse, provided nothing to contradict that view in a long formal statement: 'A Jockey Club inquiry is taking place, so I cannot answer detailed questions about the affair. But I can say that discussions are in progress with the sponsors Martell, the Jockey Club and the BBC about possibilities of re-running the race although I must say I think there is only a small chance that such a complicated event can be restaged this year and cancelling the race completely for 1993 is the most obvious solution. I share the sadness of the trainers but at least we did not have a tragedy, a horse or rider badly hurt.

'Ken Evans is a Lancastrian in his late fifties who has operated with the recall flag at the last two Nationals before this one. The reason that the race was declared void under the relevant rule is because the recall flag was not shown. In both cases of the false start the strong winds blew the tape into the horses and on both occasions there was a horse's head over the tape. The tape is the sort that flicks up, not the kind that springs back out of the way. The whole procedure will be reviewed very thoroughly indeed. Ken Evans has been interviewed by the stewards. I thought the animal rights people had very little effect. What was more significant was that several of the horses were refusing to line up properly, which made the starter's job very difficult.'

John Upson was unlikely to be placated by that explanation. 'It wouldn't happen in a point-to-point race in Ireland,' he said. 'There a man would stand in the middle of the track with a white flag and you would either run him down or stop. I spent a year getting my horse ready for this day. I have sweated blood with him. I have come here today absolutely ready to run Zeta's Lad and this is what happens.'

Neither was Upson guaranteed to sympathise with the Chancellor of the Exchequer, who will lose about £6 million by the refunding of £75 million in ante-post wagers and bets struck on the day. Nor will the trainer be inclined to agree with Peter Greenall's parting words: 'Obviously this was a very regrettable incident but I don't think it will be detrimental to the race at all. When Oxford sank, it didn't hurt the Boat Race.'

The Observer, 4 April 1993

Saddled With Greatness

FATHERLAND HAS YET to establish a champion's credentials but he will be sent into action at Epsom on Wednesday from the most distinguished corner a Derby contender could ever have. In terms of years of experience, or just plain years, the bay colt's human support team easily outstrip all other trainer-jockey partnerships in the field. But long service is hardly what counts in the careers of 76-year-old Vincent O'Brien and 57-year-old Lester Piggott.

If thoroughbreds were inclined to brood on such matters, Fatherland might be overawed by the combined weight of achievement associated with the two men who will shape his challenge on the Surrey Downs. Their records in the Derby alone are breathtaking (Piggott has ridden nine winners, O'Brien has trained six and four of the successes have been shared) and they have so frequently dominated so many other great races that posterity is left with no option but to see them as the most legendary figures of their sport in the twentieth century. In O'Brien's case such categorisation may amount to serious under-statement. Given the range and volume of his accomplishments in both National Hunt and Flat racing during the 50 years since he saddled his first winner as a licensed trainer at Limerick Junction on 20 May 1943 (Oversway's prize money was £74), it is difficult to resist the argument that he has proved himself the greatest master of his craft in the entire history of racing.

There are endless statistics to back that claim. But perhaps it is enough to remind ourselves that the Cork man won three successive Cheltenham Gold Cups with Cottage Rake, and a fourth with Knock Hard, three successive Champion Hurdles with Hatton's Grace and three Grand Nationals in a row with three different horses (Early Mist, Royal Tan and Quare Times) before he began his unprecedented harvesting of the Flat's major honours. His total of Derby victories is still one short of the seven amassed by Robert Robson, John Porter and Fred Darling in earlier eras. O'Brien's Epsom wins are, however, set amid an extraordinary collection of further triumphs, including 10 victories in other English Classics, 27 in Irish Classics, one in the French Derby , three in the Prix de l'Arc de Triomphe, one in the Washington International and one in the Breeders' Cup Mile.

Yet even that list does not begin to convey the influence he has exerted on thoroughbred racing in recent decades. Any assessment of his impact would have to take account of his pre-eminent role in making the Northern Dancer bloodline a seemingly inexhaustible wellspring of brilliant performances in Classic races.

'I was so lucky to see Nijinsky as a yearling,' O'Brien told me last week, offering a characteristically modest over-simplification of the historic moment when – having gone to E.P. Taylor's Canadian stud to check on a Ribot colt and been disappointed by what he saw – he ran his uniquely perceptive eye over the other yearlings on show and picked out the son of Northern Dancer. In 1970 Nijinsky became the first winner of the English Triple Crown since Bahram 35 years before, and then went on to be an exceptional stallion.

That O'Brien is still sending significant ripples through the breeding industry is confirmed by the fact that six of the 17 Derby colts who stood their ground on Friday at the five-day declaration stage were sired by animals trained on the rich acres of his Ballydoyle Stables in Tipperary: Tenby (by Caerleon), Fatherland and Barathea (both by Sadler's Wells), Blues Traveller (Bluebird), Redenham (Sir Ivor) and Zind (Law Society). But it wasn't such proof of his relevance to this year's race that made the chance to visit him at Ballydoyle last week so attractive. The appeal was more basic. How often do any of us sit down with somebody who may well have been better at his chosen job than anyone else who ever lived? The bonus, of course, is the quiet, self-effacing warmth with which O'Brien tries to talk matter-of-factly about a career that must always, in the end, testify to something magical at the core of his gifts, a rapport with the racehorse too profound to be rationally explained. A minor but interesting aspect of the special relationship is the effortless facility he has for recognising horses as individuals even, as his wife Jacqueline points out, 'when they are little more than dots on the horizon'.

When his stables housed 70 or 80 thoroughbreds rather than the 10 lodged there now, he would identify each at a glance, and do the same with scores of others in the nearby studs with which he was involved. 'And yet,' said Jacqueline at dinner on Tuesday, 'Vincent often cannot tell you the markings of a horse. An animal might have two white feet and he wouldn't have noticed.'

'If you look at me,' said O'Brien with a smile in my direction, 'you know me without checking off my features and my colouring. You just know me. That's how I am with horses. It's not strange.' No stranger for him, perhaps, than being able to tell that a horse had the makings of a Derby winner before it had ever seen a racecourse. A striking example of that capacity emerged at the same dinner table a decade ago when Mike Dillon, of Ladbrokes, who has become a friend of the family, was being light-heartedly pressed by Mrs O'Brien to ease the cramped odds available about Assert, a three-year-old that would go out next day from the training stable of her son David to win the Irish Derby. 'Don't bother with Assert,' said Vincent. 'Get Mike to give you a price about that horse we have out in the yard for next year's Epsom Derby.'

A 100-1 bet was struck on 'that horse'. It was Caerleon and he made a commanding debut at the Curragh the following afternoon. Dillon had reason to be grateful a year later, in the summer of 1983, when a memorable thunderstorm so softened the going at Epsom that O'Brien decided the colt would not run there. They went instead to Chantilly and won the French Derby. Caerleon, who is by Nijinsky, was always a magnificent specimen of his breed. When Mrs O'Brien complained that she could never be sure which elements of a horse's conformation should impress her, Vincent said: 'If you want a really good-looking horse to keep in your head as a model against which you judge everything else, go and study Caerleon.' Later he would praise Royal Academy (another son of Nijinsky and one who brought early glory to Lester Piggott's comeback by winning the Breeders' Cup Mile at Belmont Park, New York, in 1990) as a similar paragon.

On the Derby prospects of Fatherland – who will run in the colours of an American, Robert Lewis, after Jacqueline O'Brien's midweek sale of 50 per cent of the horse – the jury of experts is still out. There is a persistent worry about stamina but at least recent rain has reduced the fear that a combination of firm ground and Epsom's undulations would be his undoing. O'Brien bred the horse from a mare he bought as an anniversary present for his wife and liked him from the start because he was a highly active foal and moved well. 'He's not a big horse, just 16 hands,' O'Brien said last week. 'You have to like his action. He is a very good mover, well balanced, a good goer. Obviously at Epsom he will have to be ridden to get the trip, will be held up to come late. We could hardly have anybody better than Lester for that job.'

The alliance with Piggott has been one of the most exciting themes of the trainer's campaigning on the Flat but its first triumphant phase ended less than cosily in 1980. There were several difficulties and one of them was the impression that Piggott's riding of the stable's horses at exercise was telling the jockey more than it was telling the trainer. O'Brien, who has never believed in conducting 'trials' on the gallops, was disturbed to see the great rider allow his exercise partners to pull ten lengths ahead of his mount and then pick them up steadily in a way that was highly informative about what he had underneath him. None of that prevented the master of Ballydoyle from being the strongest influence in encouraging Lester to return to the saddle in 1990, or diluted in the slightest his conviction that the Englishman is the supreme rider of Flat horses: 'He never gets over-excited and because he stays ice-cool he is able to think clearly and quickly at all times.' Since his comeback, the jockey has returned to exercise horses at Ballydoyle. 'But I only let him ride slow work,' said O'Brien with a smile.

The trainer himself is trying to work more gently than was his wont, in response to the pleas of doctors attending him in the immediate aftermath of an operation for an aneurism. Jacqueline O'Brien's support is, as ever, crucial and so is the closeness of his family of two sons and three daughters. The elder son, David, proved himself a consummate trainer by saddling a Derby winner in England, Ireland and France before he was 30, but found the pressures of the job were intolerably compounded by his own perfectionism and gave up training a couple of years beyond that birthday, in 1988. It is Charles, the second son, who is now committed to training and continuing the dynasty.

A hint of the talent that is bred in Charles's bones is contained in the story of the first real 'touch' Vincent O'Brien had on a racecourse. The year was 1941 and he was in his twenties and assisting his father Dan, a farmer who bred and trained horses for sport at the heart of the original steeplechasing country in County Cork, when an outbreak of foot-and-mouth disease cancelled the local point-to-point season and seemed to impose idleness on an interesting mare called White Squirrel. 'But I continued to ride her out and one morning I decided I would jump off in front of a couple of the decent Flat horses my father kept and see how well she went,' O'Brien recalled fondly. 'The answer was very well indeed, so I waited eight or nine days and tried her again to confirm there had been no fluke.'

Satisfied, he entered White Squirrel in a bumper (a Flat race for jumping horses) at Clonmel. 'But I didn't tell my father what I knew about her, because he would have told all his friends and that was no good to me. Once I was in the jockeys' room, changing to ride the horse, I sent a friend to tell my father what was going on and he had a tenner at 20-1. I had only £4 in the world and by the time it went on the price was 10-1. But White Squirrel came home readily enough in a field of 27, so I was happy and father won the most he had ever collected in his life. At first he was delighted. But when the details sank in he was furious at the thought that this brat had told him to have a bet on his own horse.'

In the 50-odd years since that day, few people have objected to being told when to bet by Vincent O'Brien.

The Observer, 30 May 1993

Raise a Glass to The Voice

SOMETHING HE SAID with his hand over the microphone emphasised Peter O'Sullevan's right to be known as the voice of racing. The words were pithy rather than eloquent: 'I'll have 10,000 to a thousand.' That was 12 months ago, he was talking in pounds sterling and the recipient of the message was a representative of the Coral bookmaking organisation who had stuck his head into the BBC commentary booth. The man was there to alert the nation to the fact that Montelado, a magnificent Irish six-year-old who had just made a procession of the first race at the 1993 Cheltenham Festival, could be backed for this year's Champion Hurdle.

O'Sullevan was never going to be a mere conduit for such information. He has a profound sense of responsibility towards the television public he serves but another side of his professionalism makes it anathema to let a value bet slip by. So the mike was muffled, the wager struck and the broadcast seamlessly resumed. Leg problems prevented Montelado from competing in Tuesday's Champion. But The Voice, though a fortnight into his 77th year, surprised no one when he descended on the Cotswolds impressively sound in wind and limb. It was all in the week's work for him to combine vibrant descriptions of the most intense three days in racing with a little elegant socialising and calculated betting skirmishes that swiftly recouped the Montelado grand and then put the account healthily in credit. He has been doing much the same for decades.

The credibility O'Sullevan enjoys with all serious racegoers, as well as with millions whose only experience of the track is by way of a TV screen, is reward for the width and depth of his involvement in the sport. And nothing does more to help him connect with the mass of racing's followers than his lifelong commitment to punting, his happy addiction to the small dramas created by horse-players when they suspend accepted reality in favour of a private if heightened version of it. As an Old Carthusian member of the Jockey Club who is welcome and at ease in the company of the Royals, he scarcely qualifies as an Everyman of the Turf. He has gained glory and profit on the Flat and over jumps by owning animals as exceptional as Be Friendly and Attivo. His rating as an adviser on matters equine is such that he is a crucial influence on the strategies of his friend the Marquesa de Moratalla, the Spanish noblewoman who owns Thursday's Gold Cup winner, The Fellow. P.J. O'Sullevan appears unlikely to have an empathetic relationship with the man in the Glasgow betting shop.

Yet in such places he is regarded almost as an intimate, certainly as somebody with whom beleaguered scufflers can have a rapport. His feel for the heartbeat of racing – the throb of excitement that does not communicate itself to everybody, but puts those it reaches permanently in thrall – permeates every word he utters on air. He does not have to refer to being a bettor. He is one, and that identity is as intrinsic as the rich but unfruity voice, the knowledgeable assessments and the unforced gift for vivid and well-rounded language.

It has been claimed that when The Fellow lost the Gold Cup by a short-head to Garrison Savannah three years ago, O'Sullevan's Francophile tendencies and his links with the Marquesa's stable, not to mention his investment at 50-1 of sums that could not be mistaken for bus fares, momentarily undermined his detachment and encouraged the error of suggesting that The Fellow had won in a photo-finish. Such talk seems wild, considering how often he has read big races involving his own horses without allowing triumph or disaster to have the minutest effect on tone or inflection, let alone judgment.

If a discernible warmth crept into O'Sullevan's voice as The Fellow galloped powerfully up the Cheltenham hill last week ahead of Jodami, we should not suspect that it had anything to do with the financial loyalty he had shown to his old ally (ante-post at 100-6). He was delighting in an overdue victory for a nine-year-old who was contesting the supreme championship of steeplechasing for the fourth time, and had twice missed the prize by the narrowest possible margin, and in the vindication of a rider, Adam Kondrat, whose competence had been cruelly called into question. In fact, O'Sullevan was in superb form throughout the three days, as this reluctant absentee from the Festival can testify. My injured leg obviously caused less grief than Montelado's, but presumably he thought less about what he was missing. My frustration might have been unbearable but for friends' dispatches from the front. Having The Voice bring the thrills of Cheltenham into the living-room through the television set was one thing. Having him elaborate on the day's excitements by phone was a marvellous bonus, especially when he was reporting on his regular visits to the box of J.P. McManus, the agreeable Irishman who has long been a matchless leviathan in the betting ring.

Last week, J.P.'s exploits stirred the customary swirl of myths and rumours, notably the tale that he had backed his seven-year-old Gimme Five to win £1 million in the last race on Tuesday afternoon. 'It's not even half-true,' the man himself insisted on Friday morning. He was speaking from his 400-acre farm between the towns of Limerick and Tipperary, having just driven the youngest of his three children to school, a homely chore for someone more often associated with coming down on bookies like a wolf on the fold. As usual, the realities of his betting were extraordinary enough without embellishment. He did have a major lunge at Gimme Five. It started when Stephen Little, in a single bet, laid him £250,000 to £30,000 – and there were other spectacular onslaughts. Gimme Five's sluggishness was expensive even by J.P.'s standards. But resilience is the essence of his nature and when Danoli, Ireland's banker of bankers in Wednesday's Sun Alliance Hurdle, lived up to the advance billing, the McManus bombardment included bets of £155,000 to £80,000 and £60,000 to £30,000. 'That put the wheel back on the bike,' he told me.

He was then poised to wreak havoc, as he sent his brother to seek 10-1 or better about his own contender, Time for a Run, in the Coral Handicap Hurdle. But sevens or eights was the best he was offered. Then, when the horse duly won, the starting price was announced as 11-1. 'If you don't get on an 11-1 winner of your own at Cheltenham, you reckon it's time to down tools and that's what I did,' he said. Charlie Swan kicked home another winner in his colours, Mucklemeg, in the 5.50 on Wednesday but McManus did not back her. He maintained the truce with the enemy throughout Thursday, making Danoli his last wager of the meeting. 'I finished a little ahead,' he confirmed.

And, along the way, he had poured some Haut-Brion for Peter O'Sullevan. Special men should drink special wine.

The Observer, 20 March 1994

A Jockey Worth Wooing

ANYONE TRYING TO find greatness in this year's Derby should look above rather than beneath the saddle. Among the men due to reach for the silks on Wednesday afternoon are a number whose names will resonate decades after those of the horses they will swing round Tattenham Corner have been buried in the obscurity of small print in record books.

Mention of Lester Piggott will, of course, stir exciting images as long as hoofbeats sound on turf, and Willie Carson, if a less towering legend, is certain of abiding status in the history of racing. Also set to be in action are the cream from a couple of younger generations of jockeys: Eddery, Asmussen, Swinburn and the embryonic master, Dettori. But no rider in the Derby will be more valued for the assistance he can guarantee the colt under him than Michael Joseph Kinane. That much could be deduced from the elaborate pitch made by Henry Cecil amid the pre-breakfast freshness of the Newmarket gallops last Wednesday as he sought to cajole Kinane into agreeing that King's Theatre should be his partner on the Surrey Downs. Much of the case had already been made by the contrast between the highly satisfactory work King's Theatre put in for the Irishman over 11 furlongs on the Limekilns and the earlier, comparatively sluggish endeavours of the principal rival for his attentions, Foyer, from Michael Stoute's yard. But Cecil was prepared to deviate from his usual languid ways in the interests of persuasion.

The great trainer turned ardent wooer as he bombarded the small, wryly smiling figure opposite with arguments designed to establish that the animal he had already ridden in three races (one win, two disappointments) would show significant improvement at Epsom. The son of Sadler's Wells would, the cultured voice insisted, relish the softer ground he now seemed sure to have on the big day and, crucially, had never been better in his life. Kinane's wide mouth merely lifted at the corners into a broader, more impish grin. Once he had discussed the issue with Sheikh Mohammed (owner of both King's Theatre and Foyer) and the Sheikh's racing manager, Anthony Stroud, the unsurprising decision was that he would indeed ride for Cecil. That outcome was scarcely charged with ill omens for Kinane. It was at Newmarket exercise on the equivalent morning a year ago that he first sat on Commander in Chief, the horse he subsequently brought home three-and-a-half lengths clear in the supreme Classic while Pat Eddery on Tenby, the Cecil stable's leading challenger and hot favourite for the race, laboured in with the stragglers.

When Commander in Chief carried Kinane into the winner's enclosure, Sheikh Mohammed's reactions could hardly be simple. He had tried unavailingly to negotiate first claim on the rider's services at the beginning of 1993. But the terms fell short of what was needed to lure Kinane away from existing arrangements based on a close, 10-years-long association with the brilliant Irish trainer Dermot Weld, a highly lucrative commitment to Hong Kong that takes him there annually for roughly six months between mid-October and early April, and the eagerness with which he is offered attractive jobs by top English stables while he is in Europe. The Sheikh's willingness to be perhaps the foremost supplier of such outside riding engagements, in spite of the polite rebuff he received last year, pays tribute to a reputation for extracting maximum effort from all kinds of horses on all kinds of courses around the world, and especially for delivering superb performances in the great races. Some respected judges suggest that Kinane, who will be 35 next month and is plainly at the height of his powers, is probably the most effective jockey currently active on any continent.

To justify the scope of such claims, they do not rely on his successes in Ireland and England (though his galvanising of Belmez to overcome Old Vic in the King George VI of 1990 was unforgettable) or even his haul of prizes on the far side of the Channel, which include an Italian Derby and the 1989 Arc on Carroll House. Nor do they dwell on the mountain of stakes he amasses in Hong Kong, where last winter's total was about £1.5 million. What does give remarkable weight to his international CV, and to that of his mentor Weld, is the unique achievement of having won the Belmont Stakes, third leg of the American Triple Crown, and in 1993 the Melbourne Cup, the national institution Australians had regarded as impregnable against foreign assault.

They should have known, from the extent of the Irish influence in their own country, that there had to be at least one exemption from that assumption. They should definitely have been wary when Weld and his contender, Vintage Crop, arrived among them with doleful tidings of how much dehydration and weight loss the six-year-old gelding had suffered on the 38-hour journey from Europe. And when Kinane joined the team shortly before the race, complete with a Hong Kong fan club intent on ravaging the Flemington betting ring, there was no excuse for complacency. Within minutes of meeting Kinane off the Dublin plane at Stansted last week, Chris Smith and I had no doubt that we were in the company of somebody formidable.

He is physically compact (5ft 4in, comfortable riding weight 8st 4lb) and it is not hard to believe that when his father Tommy, once a National Hunt jockey whose competitiveness could take on a pugilistic intensity, encouraged him to strip to the waist for sparring sessions with his three brothers, Michael showed a marked aptitude for boxing. But it is the impression of an inner, contained strength that comes across most forcefully. Though he is naturally amiable and the firm planes of his face melt readily into smiles, the large, deep-blue eyes under the thick blond eyebrows are alive with a challenging directness. Confronted by his alliance with Weld, a former vet in whom charm and articulacy mingle effortlessly with shrewdness, alert Aussies might have suspected they were about to be pulled on to the punch. In fact, that antipodean coup, which must rank as the most spectacular, perfectly executed act of international plunder racing has known, exemplifies the potency of Kinane's approach to his career. He draws nourishment for his far-flung sorties from a background so steeped in horsemanship that he was in the saddle before he could walk, and from a continuing closeness to his roots. He, his wife Catherine and their two daughters live on the Curragh, on a property that has 50 boxes and an equine pool serving the surrounding trainers. One of his brothers runs the pool business for him, another is an assistant to Weld, and the third works at his father's yard nearby.

But, far from being made insular by all that homeliness, he is stimulated by the abrupt switches to his other life. 'It is a bit of a jolt moving from the Curragh to a 24th-floor apartment in Hong Kong, but a change is as good as a rest,' he said. 'I thrive on the high of all the different environments my job takes me into.' Professional adaptability is no problem. His innate gifts are huge and they have been developed by the hard disciplines applied by his first trainer, Liam Browne, and later by Weld. He was three months short of 16 and still at school when his first ride became his first winner. 'It was over a mile-and-a-half at Leopardstown on a horse called Muscari that finished up a very good sprinter. I was told to hold on to him as long as I could and I did so until my arms gave out. When I had to let him go, he crept round the rails and got up to win. It was a victory for sheer ignorance.'

Neither lack of control nor ignorance is noticeable these days. His classically orthodox riding style is recognised as imparting as much urgent propulsion to a thoroughbred in a tight finish as any jockey in the world can produce. But his mental capacity means even more to Weld. 'Rating Michael as a rider, I'd say first and foremost he is intelligent,' the trainer told me. 'Of course, he is an excellent horseman with wonderful hands but his thinking and his patience are equally important. By patience I mean that if things do not suit him in a race, if he finds he is not in the position he wanted, he does not panic but waits for things to happen around him and picks the right moment to move.'

Just as they had done when Go and Go annihilated the 1990 Belmont field, both of them made all the right moves in Melbourne. Weld, not best pleased when Vintage Crop was installed 6-1 favourite well in advance of the Cup, stressed the gelding's difficulties and let the locals concentrate on his fellow invader, Drum Taps, dual winner of the Ascot Gold Cup. 'I wasn't going to play all my cards up front,' he recalled. 'But I was open and frank with the Australians afterwards.' Kinane smiled again at the memory. 'It was marvellous the way Dermot let the limelight shift to Drum Taps, who is more glamorous than my old fella. Vintage Crop is lean and mean. He was reported to have worked badly but then I found he had been ridden by the lad who minds him and who, with his own saddle, would have weighed about 11st. We beat Drum Taps five-and-a-half lengths in the Irish St Leger at levels and we were getting half a stone in Melbourne. I was only eighth or ninth when the front runners sprinted for home more than four furlongs out, but when I asked mine to go he jumped from under me and we strolled in by three lengths.'

Listening to him talk through races is nearly as thrilling as watching him ride them. King's Theatre may not be good enough to win this Derby but Michael Kinane certainly is.

The Sunday Times, 29 May 1994

King's Theatre, given a tremendous ride by Kinane, finished second to Erhaab in the Derby.

Barathea Swoops, Lochsong Swoons

WHEN ALL THE dramas and lurching fortunes of the 11th Breeders' Cup settle and clarify in the memory, the British who were at Churchill Downs in Kentucky will be left with two images that represent the full gamut of racing experience. Barathea's spell-binding victory in the Mile – a flawless declaration of quality that finally identified the four-year-old as the great horse his Newmarket trainer, Luca Cumani, always insisted this son of Sadler's Wells was – encapsulated the exhilaration that comes when the dreams that are the driving force of the sport are ideally realised. The earlier sight of Lochsong, the pride of Europe's short-distance specialists, labouring wearily in as a distant last behind 13 American rivals in the Breeders' Cup Sprint, exemplified the depth of pain the game that Phil Bull called a magnificent triviality is capable of inflicting.

All kinds of other emotional stories unfolded on America's most historic racetrack during the cool, breezy afternoon. There was the triumph in the Breeders' Cup Turf of Tikkanen, an animal trained in France by an Englishman but bred, owned and ridden by Americans, and the two wins (Flanders and Timber Country) that strengthened D. Wayne Lukas's position as the most successful trainer in Breeders' Cup history and confirmed his resurgence after a depressing lean spell in which he had gone through four years and 20 starters without scoring on the richest day in world racing. There were, too, the honourable second place gained by Henry Cecil's Eltish in the Juvenile, the fourths of Peter Chapple-Hyam's Erin Road in the Distaff and Paul Kelleway's Belle Genius in the Juvenile Fillies and, outstandingly, the fast-finishing second of France's Hatoof in the Turf.

But the intensity of feeling surrounding such results does not alter the reality that, for most of us from Britain, recollections of the occasion will crystallise into the moments when Barathea found glory and Lochsong stumbled through the worst ordeal of her life. She had travelled to Louisville as the queen of European sprinting and she finished with dirt on her face and lead in her legs. For some of us, the hurtful memory may last even longer than the happy one. All the huge disadvantages inherent in trying to beat North America's best sprinters on their own ground closed in on Lochsong and totally swamped the talent that has made her such an electrifying sight at Ascot and Longchamp. Frankie Dettori had slowed her almost to a walk, 20 lengths behind the decisive action, by the time Cherokee Run, the betting favourite, delivered a killing surge to head Soviet Problem near the line and claim the afternoon's first jackpot of $520,000. Almost immediately Ian Balding, the trainer of the beaten champion, was admitting that he would find the sadness just about unbearable if he had to accept this performance as the last note of Lochsong's remarkable career.

'Her owner, Jeff Smith, may give her another chance in the equivalent race next year at Belmont,' Balding said. 'This would be a terrible note to finish on. She has run stones below her best and that is heartbreaking. She simply has not run her race. Perhaps we did a little bit too much with her on Thursday (when Lochsong dazzled the Churchill Downs clockers by covering three furlongs of a training workout in 33.4 seconds) although that would not have been too much for her at home.'

Dettori, the brilliant young Italian who is sweeping to the jockeys' championship in Britain, could be optimistic after Lochsong coped reasonably with the showbiz preliminaries and arrived at the starting gate without betraying much evidence of the highly-strung behaviour that has ruined her chances in the past. She was spared the ordeal of parading along the full length of the grandstand, being permitted to move gently towards the stalls on the far side of the track in the company of a pony called Downstream. On board was Marilyn 'Fifi' Montavon, perhaps the most formidable female, human or equine, on the premises. Her dominating presence may have helped to persuade the temperamental visitor to be demure.

The six-year-old mare, a daughter of Song, is famous for breaking smartly and reaching full momentum in a matter of strides. But here, on perhaps the most taxing afternoon of her life, she came out of the gate moderately. 'She had been fine going to the gate,' the jockey said. 'And even after she broke slowly I did not have to be too worried because she soon got back into it and we didn't have any trouble laying up. Things turned bad for us when she couldn't change her lead leg going into the turn out of the back stretch and once she had to change legs again to come into the finishing straight she was gone. She was never comfortable on the turns, she didn't like the track.'

It was always certain that the unfamiliarity of her assignment would impose immense disadvantages on Lochsong. Instead of blazing up a straight course as she usually does, she was asked to deal with an elongated U-shaped track that involved negotiating two tight bends and there was always the danger that in battle conditions the lady would not be for turning.

She had, of course, the additional problems of racing on the dirt for the first time in her life and was faced with the strain on her stamina of an extended six furlongs when all her spectacular triumphs have been gained at five. In the circumstances, those who made her the most heavily backed of all the 13 British contenders at the Breeders' Cup were making a declaration of faith that had left logic in the cupboard.

The Sunday Times, 6 November 1994

Happy Swanning in His Own Pond

IT IS NO surprise that Charlie Swan seems to carry the form-book of Irish National Hunt racing around in his head. Why shouldn't he have encyclopaedic knowledge when he wrote so much of the encyclopaedia?

In 1994 Swan, who will be 27 on Friday, rode 123 winners in Ireland, surpassing by 14 the record for a calendar year that he set in 1993. The full significance of that figure will not register instantly with many people in Britain, where we have become accustomed to seeing Richard Dunwoody and Adrian Maguire zig-zagging about England, Scotland and Wales for 10 months of the year, riding six days a week and often taking in more than one meeting in a day, to drive their totals towards the 200 mark or even beyond it. For Ireland, where there are usually only two, at most three, jump fixtures a week in the winter (imposing a limit on the mounts offered that cannot be balanced by the tradition of mixing National Hunt and Flat races on the same card throughout the summer), Swan's achievement is prodigious. Yet those statistics, the five successive Irish jockeys' titles he has won and the triumphs at Cheltenham that formed the jewel in his champion's crown in 1993 and 1994, are all insufficient to convey the scope of his influence on racing in a country that is stirred more than any other by the beauty, excitement and opportunities for plunder provided by the running, jumping horse. Perhaps the feats in the Cotswolds that made him leading rider at two consecutive Festivals – four winners two years ago, three last March – came closest to encapsulating the unique importance of his contribution to the recent revival in the fortunes of Ireland's hurdlers and steeplechasers.

After decades of being feared invaders on the other side of the water, the Irish discovered that their natural horse-traders' eagerness to sell their best stock in a market awash with extravagant bids had drastically reduced their competitiveness in the great races, and they endured a prolonged, distasteful obligation to be humble at Cheltenham. When the recession's inhibiting effects on English buyers combined with other factors to leave the Irish once again equipped with the kind of machinery they like to take to war on the mainland, there was every prospect that their old rivals would be forced to suffer. But for the revival to be sustained, it needed an outstanding riding talent to carry the banner. The renaissance found its ideal artist in Charlie Swan. He had much more than ability in the saddle to fit him for the role: a clutch of qualities that do a great deal to help a man to be accepted as a true national hero in Ireland. His toughness as a competitor is tempered by modesty, a lack of pretentiousness and an innate civility that evoke warmth as well as admiration in his countrymen. Though there is an anglicised flavour to his background (his mother, Theresa, was born in Rawalpindi, where her father was an officer in the Indian Army, and Swan's father, Donald, was born in London, educated at Gordonstoun and served as a captain in the Queen's Dragoon Guards), the Irish are proud and happy to embrace this son of Tipperary as very much one of their own.

'He is a little fella who knows how to treat people,' said Ted Walsh, who was for a long time the nation's foremost amateur jockey and now brings his uncompromising opinions and earthy eloquence to the screen for RTE. 'It doesn't take a lot of success to cause some young jockeys to get too big for their boots but he's not like that. If a minor trainer with a few horses has one that he fancies and he manages to engage Charlie, he's given more than value for money. Not only does the animal get the full benefit of the best assistance available – the lad is not just an excellent horseman but a real race rider, which can't be said of many who ride over jumps – but he is left convinced that the champion jockey really cared about his horse. Young Swan is a good judge of a horse's capabilities and if he told you yours needed a shorter trip, or half a mile longer, or how it should be used in a race, he would seldom be wrong. So his advice would be worth a lot. And in the case of the small trainer he would try to find something encouraging to say. He would be liable to leave the fella feeling good, so that he might go into the pub that night and say, "I had Charlie Swan riding for me today and he tells me that thing of mine could be a nice horse in a year's time." Well, a year is a long while and at least the man would have a bit of optimism in the morning.'

Swan was always likely to have respect and affection for people who train on a modest scale, the kind who operate from little, homely yards all over Ireland, handling 20 or fewer horses, and are the lifeblood of racing there. His father is such a man, and it was Donald Swan who first launched his only son (there are two older sisters) into action on a racecourse. Final Assault, the two-year-old maiden who was Charlie's debut ride at Naas, had the gumption to win and thus clarify and harden his 15-year-old partner's ideas about what the future should hold. Before that day in 1983, Charlie had not entertained serious thoughts of being a professional jockey, although an outsider might have seen that his boyhood experiences, and the gifts they revealed, had been thrusting him in that direction.

He remembers riding a pony when he was around four and, at the age of nine or 10, walking a two-year-old racehorse out on the roads and then having the confidence to take it through 'a bit of cantering'. Another pony, called Lightning and fast enough to prevent the name from inviting mockery, gave him three victories in a row in a cross-country event held annually in his native corner of Tipperary, where horses compete with hurling for the sporting passions of the locals. By the time he was entering his teens he was learning the basic techniques of race-riding in contests whose designation as pony races could easily mislead the unwary. They involve many thoroughbreds deemed too small to campaign under Rules, and it was in the same serious business that Adrian Maguire made his initial impact. Swan himself had plenty of success, accumulating about 30 wins and developing the skills that drove in Final Assault and led almost inevitably to apprenticeship as a Flat jockey.

Formal education had never been much of a contender for his enthusiasm. He says he enjoyed boarding school in Mullingar but that probably had more to do with the pleasure he took in playing rugby, cricket and hockey than any commitment to his studies. As his headmaster grew increasingly irritated with the budding rider's weekend absences, Swan's parents eventually yielded to his pleas that he should be taken out of school altogether.

In his first year as a licensed jockey, he rode three winners, all for his father, but Donald knew that the nurturing of such a

promising talent demanded a less sheltered environment and for
the next four years he was attached to Kevin Prendergast's stable,
riding a total of 57 winners on the Flat for that and other yards.
Then, in 1986, he fell and broke a leg while schooling a horse for
Prendergast. Inactivity caused his weight to climb and his full-time
career on the Flat was finished. Fortunately, the increase in bulk
was far from devastating and, at not quite 5ft 8in tall, he can still
make 9st 7lb and continues to attract a few good mounts on the
level.

Once he had turned to jumping under the tutelage of Dessie
Hughes, whose credentials are enshrined forever in his deeds on
the magnificent Champion Hurdler Monksfield, Swan swiftly
emerged as exceptional and trainers in England were soon
interested. There had to be soul-searching when he was sounded
about the possibility of replacing the retired Peter Scudamore as
first jockey to Martin Pipe but now he is glad the tentative
approaches came to nothing. He has decided he belongs in Ireland
and has built a handsome bungalow-style house for himself and his
wife Tina on a hill half a mile from his old family home near the
village of Cloughjordan.

After having cleared away the effects of a late and hospitable
night by rising to be awed by a glorious Tipperary dawn, and
watching Donald's horses work out in the half-light against a
backdrop of the breathtaking landscape that rolls away to Offaly in
the north and to Galway and the Shannon a few miles to the west,
the younger Swan's priorities were not difficult for this visitor to
comprehend. Of course, he has more than the tingle of such
mornings to persuade him he is right to stay, more than the
advantages of a lifestyle that is tolerably relaxed compared with the
frenetic hustle of his counterparts in England, the sort of schedule
which affords him enough breaks to give hope of reducing his golf
handicap from 18. What he has, above all, are exciting horses at his
disposal, animals like the creators of his finest Cheltenham
moments of 1993 and 1994, Montelado and Danoli.

Mention of the electrifying change of gears Montelado
produced to overwhelm the opposition by 12 lengths in the
Supreme Novices' Hurdle two years ago spreads remembered joy
across his friendly, boyish face, widening the attractive smile that is
almost permanent. But he can be even more emotional when he
talks of how the Irish punters, who had suffered an early dent to the

rampant confidence they took to last year's Festival, were promptly rescued on the second day by Danoli, the horse they have made their sentimental favourite.

'I had said three months previously that he would win but when the race arrived, and he was carrying so much faith and money, there was terrific pressure,' Swan recalled. 'He is a quick jumper and a tremendous galloper and when he is right he takes me to the front very smoothly, but once he is there he is lazy. Coming up the Cheltenham hill, with the crowd roaring like mad, he was inclined to lose concentration and idle and I can tell you it was a relief when we went past the post. But the truth is that when other horses come at Danoli he can pick up again and beat them off. Losing to Doran's Pride recently doesn't worry me in relation to the Champion Hurdle. Danoli was sick that day – I knew at the three-furlong marker he wasn't right and wouldn't win. People tend to underestimate him now, suggesting he doesn't have the speed for two miles and would be out of it unless the ground was soft. Montelado is absolute class if the going is fast, and I would probably prefer to ride him if we got that surface for the Champion. But Danoli can act on good ground and he has the speed to work with six-furlong specialists, so over a true-run two miles he could surprise a lot of the critics.'

There is no such hint of the unexpected about his declaration that he considers a highly developed sense of pace his most telling asset in the saddle. 'There are plenty of brave jockeys out there but their aggression doesn't help them if they don't know when to attack,' he said. His own judgment of such vital issues can be spellbinding, as he demonstrated in the Whitbread Gold Cup of 1994 on Ushers Island, an erratic jumper he had been warned against riding. Swan hunted Ushers Island round Sandown as if he were a pet, before moving fluently through his field to win at outlandish odds.

As is the norm with National Hunt jockeys, he has a list of injuries as long as his arm (whether you count the right, which is held together by a plate, or the left, which is merely scarred by fractures). But anyone who has watched him galvanise his mount on the way into the last obstacle will know that his nerve is flawless. 'I like to let the horse know he has to be positive there, where the race can be decided by your jump,' he said. 'What's the point of hitting him after he makes a mistake, when he can't understand the reason for the slap?'

Any horse under Charlie Swan will not suffer from a failure of communication. The bookies, too, frequently get the message.

The Sunday Times, 15 January 1995

Cheltenham in the Blood

BARELY HALF AN hour's drive north of Dublin airport, in a training yard so unpretentious and homely that a passing motorist might think it was just another roadside farm, there is a horse-box that could be a shrine. It is old and work-worn, with a sloping ceiling and a small window on the back wall through which light enters as stealthily as a burglar. In any sport other than National Hunt racing, it would be an unlikely repository of dreams.

But that box, and its tenants past and present, embody the incomparable appeal of the jumping game, the blood-stirring excitement and democracy of ambitions which will take tens of thousands of us to Cheltenham this week buoyed up by the certainty that we are about to share not only racing's greatest event but one of the most enjoyable experiences the entire sporting calendar can offer. Thirty years ago those modest quarters housed the horse many regard as the best steeplechaser that ever cleared a fence. Where Arkle stood then, there is today a giant chestnut called Harcon whose status as a dream machine has more to do with potential than achievement, an animal that has yet to prove himself capable of claiming glory in the Cotswolds. However, though the humans who are in charge of Harcon have seen too much of the real stuff to let themselves get carried away, they find it impossible to conceal the swelling of hope he engenders. And when the Dreapers of Greenogue, County Meath, are hopeful, all of Ireland listens. The bookmakers in the Cheltenham ring will hear the name of the big horse shouted at them constantly before the tapes go up for the Sun Alliance Chase on Wednesday afternoon.

For Jim Dreaper, whose father Tom sent out such equine immortals as Arkle, Prince Regent and Flyingbolt to amass the highest total of winners (26) any Irish trainer has recorded at the

Festival, Harcon will be a second string. In the supreme contest of the meeting, the Gold Cup, which Tom won in 1946 with Prince Regent, in 1964, 1965 and 1966 with Arkle and 1968 with Fort Leney, the son will be represented by Merry Gale, a seven-year-old gelding with form that contains jumping aberrations and raises questions about his ability to stay three-and-a-quarter miles on a demanding, undulating course but still makes him dangerous enough to merit third or fourth position in the market. Obviously, the Gold Cup is the booty Jim Dreaper would most like to bring home but a victory for either of his runners would be a tremendous, overdue lift for an admired and popular horseman who has not been in the winner's enclosure at the Festival for 20 years. This is the anniversary of what was a poignantly mixed year, for in 1975 he took the Gold Cup with Ten Up, the Champion Chase with Lough Inagh and the Stayers' Hurdle with Brown Lad at Cheltenham in March, and then had to bury his father in April. Jim was only 24 at the time, having taken control of the stable three years earlier (Tom was 47 before he married to produce two daughters and one son – there is, says Jim, 'a saying in this part of the world that a man shouldn't marry until he is fit for nothing else').

Since he had ridden Black Secret, trained by his father, to be a narrowly beaten second to Specify in the Grand National of 1971, and went on to train Brown Lad and Colebridge to be second and third in the Gold Cup of 1976 and both horses to win the Irish National – by defying loads of weight to succeed in three Irish Nationals, as well as being runner-up again in the Gold Cup, Brown Lad established a special hold on his handler's affections – those seasons in the 1970s provided the high point of the younger Dreaper's career. Apart from the brilliant but erratic Carvill's Hill, Greenogue has not had a genuine star in the intervening years and its master admits that the reduction in impact, especially at Cheltenham, has been painful. 'It becomes more painful as March comes round each year,' he told me in the comfortable kitchen of his home last week. 'I don't lie awake at nights worrying about it. In recent years I've become more philosophical, particularly about the comparisons with my dad, who had such a fabulous record, and nowhere more than at Cheltenham. But the lack of major successes does hurt, and I feel it not so much for myself as for everybody else who works with the horses here.

'At the end of the day, you have to reckon you have failed.

There may be perfectly good excuses. Horses may have broken down or had some other kind of ill-luck, but eventually you may have to face the most obvious and least easily accepted reason, which is that they are not good enough. When the big prizes don't come during a season, it means that what we have been doing for the previous couple of years has not had the required effect, has not led to doing the business out there in the most important races. Just about every horse we buy is meant to be a good horse. I'm lucky in having owners who can afford to go for the animal with the potential and physique to be top-class, the sort of horse that seems at the age of three or four to be the right model with the right specifications. When they don't make it, you feel that ultimately it is your fault, that you shouldn't have bought them. It's all the harder to take because things went so well for me in my first few years as a trainer. Everything was great, and then all of a sudden we forgot how to do it.'

Anyone who knows Dreaper will recognise such utterances not as statements of truth but as confirmation of his tendency to be excessively self-critical, to let an insistence on being realistic spill over into exaggerated modesty about himself and his horses. He is a man of natural warmth and to be welcomed, even briefly, into the life he shares with his wife Patricia and family of two girls and a boy is to appreciate instantly why stable staff who served his father have been inclined to stay with him (Nick O'Connor, who looks after Harcon, has been on the staff for 46 years and another 'lad', Joe Finglas, came to tidy up the yard in 1945, and forgot to leave). But he takes an unfailingly hard line about his own accomplishments. The thin, intelligent face splits readily into an uneven smile but when the subject is how he or his charges have performed it is often a touch sardonic. Praise at such moments is so grudging it appears to be coming from an eye-dropper.

An abiding memory of his father, leaving aside the inordinate flair for preparing steeplechasers, is equanimity, a Kiplingesque balance in dealing with triumph or disaster. Perhaps it is not surprising, after such an example, that his assessment of what constitutes a triumph is particularly stringent. It is not that he does not love or respect many of the horses in his care. He simply regards over-estimating them as next door to a sin: 'I don't like to make a case for horses. They must do that for themselves. There are some owners who are not really concerned with anything written in the papers about their horses the day after a race. They are happiest when reading on the morning of a race that they are going to have a winner. If they are interested in the ego trip, that's their business. But I'd rather not be involved in that kind of hype.'

Dreaper's modesty about his riding days, which brought him around 60 winners, is total. Though many deemed Black Secret an unfortunate loser in the Grand National, he prefers to remember that 'I nearly fell off him a couple of times and was pretty much delighted to complete the course and finish where I did, even if disappointment set in next day'. He also recalls that he was aboard Black Secret only because the deal made when the horse was sold to a schoolfriend of his mother's, someone who was in fact his godmother, stipulated that the price would be £1,000 if the Dreaper boy was the regular jockey, and £1,500 if the job went to the great Pat Taaffe, who steered Arkle to unforgettable glories. 'Being a good Quaker lady, she decided to take the cheaper price and put up with me.'

Arkle has been a magical element in his life – even more so than Tottenham Hotspur – but even that legend does not escape the Dreaper determination to retain an unawed perspective. 'Arkle was not always foot-perfect, you know,' he said. 'He could be a bit flippant about the occasional fence. He was a marvel, and his record supports anyone who calls him the greatest, but it is foolish to say there can never be another steeplechaser as great as Arkle. There may have been one in the yard along with him. It is impossible to tell how fantastic Flyingbolt, who at Cheltenham won Division One of the Gloucester Hurdle in 1964, the Cotswold Chase in 1965, and the Two-Mile Champion Chase in 1966, might have been if he had not contracted brucellosis. Pat Taaffe said that if Flyingbolt and Arkle had met in soft going, he would have stuck by Arkle but wouldn't have been sure he was right.'

He has no hesitation in agreeing that when it came to looks and temperament Arkle had a huge edge. 'Flyingbolt was plain ugly. With his white face and white feet, he was more like something from a circus than a racehorse – and seriously bad-tempered with it. As children, we were told to keep away from Arkle because of what he was but we were warned to avoid the other fella at all costs because he would do you. Arkle had a wonderful nature. Once, when my sister Valerie was about seven, her tennis ball bounced into Arkle's box and, as usual, she didn't think twice about going in after it. He was standing there unruffled with the ball in his mouth.'

Of the horses he has trained, he identifies Carvill's Hill as the one who had it in him to be the best of the lot. But he admits the chaser, who would later be transferred to Martin Pipe in England and have a calamitous ordeal when favourite for the Gold Cup, was always handicapped by stiff-backed jumping, that he 'had a magnificent engine and a faulty chassis'.

He sees Merry Gale as a good jumper, in spite of the odd lapse. Calling in Yogi Breisner, who has emerged as a valued jumping guru at Lambourn, should not be regarded as a sign of anxiety: 'It's like Nick Faldo going back for refresher sessions with David Leadbetter.'

His respect for Merry Gale soared when the horse showed immense courage in going down by just three lengths to Jodami in the Hennessy Cognac Gold Cup at Leopardstown after Merry Gale's rider, Graham Bradley, lost his whip during the hectic finish (a friend told the jockey he had launched the whip further than Fatima Whitbread could have thrown it). Faith in the extraordinarily relaxed, 17.3 hands tall Harcon, successful in all his four chases this season, has also deepened and he is beginning to wonder if winning a Gold Cup, rather than a National, may be the chestnut's destiny. 'If you listen to Nick O'Connor, Harcon could win anything from a five-furlong sprint to a Derby,' said Dreaper. 'But Nick thinks his horses can do no wrong. If you hear a sound from the box that suggests one has coughed, he will say, "No, that was me coughing".'

That kind of commitment will be plentiful at Cheltenham this week. For me, the spirit of this Festival will be diminished by the death last Friday of Richard Baerlein, a great racing correspondent who was for 30 years my colleague on *The Observer*, and a man whose friendship I cherished. But there is no doubt that Richard would have been happy to see a classic horseman like Jim Dreaper get among the spoils.

The Sunday Times, 12 March 1995

Unfortunately, Jim Dreaper didn't.

Often Irritating, Always Irresistible

GOLD CUP DAY at Cheltenham drew precisely 14,000 people more than the 43,804 who formed the Premier League's highest crowd of the season when Manchester United battered Ipswich 9-0 at Old Trafford two weeks ago. Clearly the latest in a rapid succession of record attendance figures at the Festival is proof that each passing year brings a heightened awareness of how exhilarating the peerless celebration of jump racing in the Cotswolds can be.

But an explosion of any kind, even in popularity, always carries risks and Cheltenham may soon reach the stage where it will prove too appealing for its own good. Football clubs are entitled to point out that comparisons with their crowds are unfair, since the limits imposed by the introduction of all-seat stadiums fall well short of the numbers willing to pay to see the more attractive matches. And when it comes to the viewing comfort they are expected to create for buyers of their most expensive tickets, their obligations far outstrip those of the Cheltenham management. Entrance to the Club Members enclosure costs £50 a day at the Festival and admission to Tattersalls, the other main enclosure for the 57,804 who turned up on Thursday, was £20. At football grounds such sums would at least assure the spenders of a seat. At Cheltenham they guarantee nothing beyond the right to join a seething throng of humanity so dense that the glacial slowness of its movement sometimes prevented punters from making their way to the betting ring in time to lose their money. Queues at Tote windows were long enough to suggest that sleeping bags and packed meals might have been in order. Such hardships can have beneficial results and there will be limited sympathy for the bookmakers who were heard complaining that the sheer weight of people severely curtailed the amount of business they were able to handle. But freedom of movement, even if it is towards financial ruin, is essential to enjoyment of a day at the races and the strain applied to Cheltenham's facilities by the increasing enthusiasm for its wonderful sport is in danger of denying us such mobility.

In fact, the 1995 Festival, distinguished though it was by the usual sequence of stirring contests and by unforgettable performances in the Champion Hurdle and the Gold Cup, left some with the uneasy feeling that the charm of the great event might be in peril. No doubt it ill behoves someone who is given free access to all areas of the course, and is further pampered by invitations to several of the most hospitable private boxes, to moan about any aspect of the three-day jamboree. But a lifelong appetite for skirmishing out in the battlefield around the bookies' pitches ensures a continuing empathy with the thousands who are obliged to scuffle for their pleasures. At the very least, the Cheltenham authorities must seek to extend and improve the betting arrangements at the course. Masochists we may be, but we want to choose our own torture, and we prefer being crushed by an avalanche of losers to being squashed in a static mass of fellow victims of hope and ignorance.

An attraction as remarkable as Cheltenham could never, amid the current ethos of professional sport, escape the hazards of rampant commercialisation and much of what has been done at the old arena is commendably restrained. Those operating the racecourse can hardly be blamed if headlong plunder is the blatant objective of so many who are in a position to profit from the annual invasion of the Cotswolds. Even Margaret Thatcher might wince when the principle of market forces encourages hired drivers and hotel-keepers to charge prices that seem to be calculated by thinking of a fancy number and doubling it. At this time of year the West Country throws up a cadre of hard-cases who should have the decency to wear masks and carry guns.

But, the reader of such complaints may ask, will you be ready to face the same problems next year? Could Pele score goals? Could Arkle jump? Yes, there was yet again more than sufficient that was glorious about Cheltenham to make it irresistible. The double triumph of Kim Bailey and his zestful jockey, Norman Williamson, in the Champion and the Gold Cup (a feat that had not been achieved since the greatest of all trainers, Vincent

O'Brien, combined with Aubrey Brabazon to do it with Hatton's Grace and Cottage Rake in 1950) was, in itself, an overwhelming justification for insisting on being there. When Alderbrook won the Champion on only his third outing over hurdles, slaughtering the opposition in a manner that made it hard to believe he was the most inexperienced hurdler to take the title, there was a tendency to herald a new era – to declare that the future would belong to high-class Flat horses who could be converted with skilful suddenness to jumping. However, O'Brien, who was a guest in the royal box on Thursday as his name was honoured by identification with the County Hurdle (where else should such a monarch of horse racing lunch?), thinks it is simplistic to imagine that other outstanding converts from racing on the level will be able to follow smoothly in Alderbrook's path. 'Alderbrook's was a tremendous performance and I feel it may remain an isolated one,' said the 77-year-old Irishman, who made an unrivalled, worldwide reputation on the Flat after a dozen years of pre-eminence in jumping ended in 1959. York Fair, at Cheltenham that year, was the last jumper he saddled and the horse duly won Division One of the Gloucester Hurdle, bringing his total of Festival winners since his first runner at the meeting in 1948 to an astonishing 23. 'Alderbrook,' O'Brien added, 'was able to do what he did because he has exceptional class and courage, toughness to go with his speed. It would be rash to assume that many other horses, even if they are outstanding on the Flat, will manage to switch as convincingly as he has.'

It was natural that after he and Williamson had claimed the hurdling crown, Bailey should shy away from forecasting a repeat of the double O'Brien and Brabazon had completed 45 years before. As the Gold Cup approached, the scale of the dream nudged the Upper Lambourn trainer towards a modesty bordering on pessimism. Though he had a healthy ante-post voucher for Master Oats at 50-1, to set alongside the 40-1 he took about Alderbrook, he began to find cause to be doleful. 'There is every reason to pick holes in the form because it isn't very good,' he said.

Fortunately for countless others who had wagered on Master Oats, O'Brien was on hand to suggest in a television interview that the nine-year-old chestnut was an unavoidable choice to dominate the race the nonpareil himself had won three times in a row between 1948 and 1950 with Cottage Rake and then again in 1953 with Knock Hard. His one reservation, having at that stage seen Master Oats only in a photograph in the *Sporting Life*, was that the gelding's conformation might not be ideally suited to lugging a hefty weight around Cheltenham. 'The photograph was taken with the horse walking towards the camera and I thought he looked a little narrow in front, across the chest,' said O'Brien yesterday. 'But when I saw him in the flesh I realised he was a bigger horse than he had appeared in the picture and I was impressed. I was even more impressed, obviously, by the way he came home 15 lengths in front after such an exciting Gold Cup. He stayed the trip really well in testing conditions and I don't see why he should not go on and win the Grand National.'

As he left at the weekend for a holiday in Portugal, O'Brien admitted that he would love to return to Aintree. Until last week, he had not visited Cheltenham since 1959 and in the case of Liverpool the absence has been even longer. He has not been there since 1955, the year Quare Times became the third of three animals he sent out to win the jumping marathon in successive years. Advanced age does not prevent O'Brien from recalling with absolute clarity almost every important incident in those epic races of 40 years ago and it is Early Mist's victory in 1953 that he remembers with most vividness.

'I had some pretty substantial bets on Early Mist at long odds for the National in the belief that the horse would shorten considerably and I would have no trouble in laying off with the bookmakers,' he told me. 'I had too much on and I wanted to get rid of some of it. He did shorten quite a lot but when I sent the man who bet for me to do the business on the Friday, nobody would let me lay off. Luckily, Early Mist was good enough.'

A more intriguing question is whether bookmakers who refused to let Vincent O'Brien lay off were good enough at their trade to stay solvent.

The Sunday Times, 19 March 1995

Pitman Swaps Agony for Ecstasy

ROYAL ATHLETE IS a horse that Jenny Pitman blames for making her old before her time, but he left the iron lady of Lambourn sounding almost girlish at Aintree yesterday. 'Every year I have had him in training he has cost me five of my life – I was glad when he had a spell off racing last year,' she said, in the euphoric aftermath of one of the smoothest Grand National triumphs anyone in the large crowd at the old Liverpool arena could remember.

It is easy, of course, to say hard things about a favourite protégé when he has excelled himself. And there was no mistaking the affection and pride that ran through the trainer's criticism. She is a woman who relishes a battle and Pitman glowed with the awareness that the struggle to cope with the constant difficulties involved in training the horse she calls Alfie had climaxed in a further dramatic confirmation that she is one of the most effective handlers of jumping horses now at work.

If Jason Titley, the 24-year-old jockey from County Clare who realised the impossible dream of winning the National on his first ride in the race, represented the most romantic story of the afternoon, it was Pitman's reputation that was conspicuously enhanced by the latest running of the historic marathon. She came to Liverpool with the strongest assault force of any stable – six of the field of 35 were sent out from her yard – but there could never be any suspicion that she was merely having half a dozen rolls of the dice. She admits that she would have preferred to aim Royal Athlete at the Scottish National in a fortnight's time, but once the owners had decided they must take their chances at Aintree, her relentless professionalism ensured that the 12-year-old would be trained to the minute to do himself justice.

Young Titley could hardly believe the assurance the chestnut gelding communicated to him from the very first fence. The rider had walked the course in the morning with Mark Pitman, the trainer's son, who was tortured on the brutally long Aintree run-in four years ago when his apparently unassailable lead on Garrison Savannah was annihilated by Seagram. The advice of Mark was that Royal Athlete should be relaxed and allowed to settle early and ridden with extreme delicacy. 'You've got to hold this horse as if he was on a thread of cotton, you need so light a contact on his neck,' he told Titley. 'That way he'll jump.' But Titley, who only learned that he had the mount at Fontwell on Monday and sat on his future partner in glory for the first time last Wednesday, soon learned that his introduction to the National was likely to be blissful.

'Mark had told me that these horses let you know when they have found the right rhythm and as early as the first fence I knew this one under me had got it,' he said after the race. He had made no misjudgment and Royal Athlete jumped as if for pleasure throughout the four and a half miles and made even the most intimidating of the 30 fences appear almost trivial obstacles. He came home an effortless winner to give Pitman her second Grand National celebration (after Corbiere in 1983) and obliterate the disappointment she suffered in 1993 when Esha Ness won the National that never was. Esha Ness fell at the 12th yesterday and none of the stable's other runners did better than Garrison Savannah's ninth. But that hardly mattered. Royal Athlete, the problem boy, had come top of the class.

Obviously, nobody was happier about the result of steeple-chasing's sternest examination than the successful owners, the brothers Libby (for Liberty) and Gary Johnson. They operate a garage business in Wokingham, Berkshire, half an hour from Weathercock House, the Pitman stable, and came in contact with the woman who has put them into Turf history when she enquired about a van they had for sale. Their connection with yesterday's equine hero came some years ago after Pitman suggested, with characteristic lack of diffidence, that a selling-plater they owned was not providing them with sufficient fun and should be replaced by a better-quality novice hurdler she was about to send to the Ascot sales. The one slight complication about her suggestion was that the superior commodity in question happened to have a leg problem at the time. 'When Gary told me that we had bought a horse with a "leg", I said that was a novel twist,' Libby said at the post-National press conference. 'Usually you buy a horse and then find it has developed a "leg".'

Physical ailments have been a way of life for Royal Athlete ever since. 'When the owners phoned about how he was doing, my usual reaction was "Don't ask",' said Pitman. 'If I said he was all right, there would be something wrong with him by the time I'd crossed the yard.' Yet there were plenty of good times with Royal Athlete, notable victories and an honourable third in Jodami's Cheltenham Gold Cup of 1993. He was not sound enough, however, to run in the Gold Cup this year and his taste for Aintree looked limited when he fell in the Esha Ness void race two years ago.

His earlier form this season was unlikely to persuade anybody to grab at the 40-1 starting price at Liverpool. In a Doncaster hurdle on 4 March, Royal Athlete was beaten by 37 lengths. All of which reminds us again that the National is like no other race. Some horses seem to have the most dubious credentials and then, when they are out there facing Becher's, The Chair, Valentine's and the rest of those old monsters, they prove to be transformed on the day. Royal Athlete certainly was, and whenever his name is mentioned from now on, you can expect to discern a trace of reverence in the speaker's voice.

The Sunday Times, 9 April 1995

Celtic Swing in a Class of One

NEITHER HIS LIVE opponents nor the ghosts of greatness past lined up against him could trouble Celtic Swing as he illuminated a damp and overcast afternoon at Newbury with further thrilling evidence that he is a horse for the history books.

With his supremely confident jockey, Kevin Darley, indulging the colt's inclination to pose in the last 200 yards, the winning margin in the Greenham Stakes was an unspectacular length and a quarter at the line. But the distance between the second horse, Bahri, and the third was nine lengths and both that yawning gap and the exceptionally fast time for the straight seven furlongs (at 1 minute 24.31 seconds it was only 0.4 seconds outside the track record) confirmed that this was an impressive trial for next month's Two Thousand Guineas and the Derby in June.

The wider question of whether Celtic Swing will prove capable of joining the company of equine immortals in which his admirers are already placing him can, of course, only be settled in those Classic races at Newmarket and Epsom. And one of the most respected judges of form, Mike Dillon, the principal odds-maker for Ladbrokes, felt the issue had been left sufficiently open to justify a quote of even money for the Guineas and 3-1 for the Derby. 'As a performance, it was definitely OK but I didn't think it was something to frighten any owner of a good three-year-old away from taking on Celtic Swing in the Guineas,' Dillon said. 'The Greenham didn't tell me anything more than I already knew about Celtic Swing and I still have a reservation about how irresistible he will be on firm ground.'

All the other major bookmaking firms were, however, quick to take a more defensive stance in response to this victory on going agreeably softened to an official rating of good by rain that had fallen with gentle persistence on the Berkshire course from around 6 a.m. until lunchtime. Sporting Index cut his price to 4-7 for the

Guineas while Corals went 8-13 and Hills 8-11. There was a widespread feeling that Ladbrokes would not struggle to find takers for the evens. What is undeniable is that those who backed Celtic Swing at 9-4 on in the Greenham never had a moment's anxiety. Not for a single stride was there the slightest prospect that the towering expectations identified with the tall, almost black, son of Damister would be added to the rubble of broken dreams accumulated over the years by all the animals whose extravagant promise as two-year-olds disintegrated when they turned three. Celtic Swing's large white blaze was prominent in second place almost as soon as the field of nine runners had jumped out of the stalls and it was instantly obvious that Art of War was in front only because the 34-year-old Darley was happy to be provided with a lead.

When Art of War started to fall back abruptly about two furlongs from home, Darley asked the favourite to quicken clear and his mount did so with an instant, fluent surge. Willie Carson on Bahri had been tracking Celtic Swing and now he went after the new leader in earnest. There was as much as three or four lengths between them when the Scottish veteran began his charge but the reduction of that distance in the final furlong should not be seen as particularly significant. 'Willie told me that if he had been able to settle Bahri early on, he would have beaten us, but I think when he looks at the replays he will change his mind,' the winning jockey said with a broad smile in the unsaddling enclosure. 'I bounced Celtic Swing out of the stalls to get him travelling sweetly and I was glad to find Art of War giving me a lead. Unfortunately, he couldn't lead me for long enough but I wasn't worried when we had to go on. Once we hit the front, it was all over, although my fella has a tendency to idle when he goes ahead. He was just dossing, not doing a tap. There was a big mass of press photographers on the far side and, as we came into that last furlong, Celtic Swing saw them and he started doing his usual posing, putting his head in the air. But I knew there was no danger and was content just to ease him over the line.'

Contentment was also conspicuous on the face of the owner whose maroon and blue colours Darley had worn. Peter Savill promptly reiterated his declaration that he has no intention of adding to his millions by selling Celtic Swing. 'I have had several offers but I think people have got the message now and given up trying to talk me into a sale. The intention today was not to win by the kind of big margin the horse achieved in his three runs as a two-year-old but simply to get him to the races and win comfortably in a way that would put him right for the Two Thousand Guineas. He is a switched-on horse, one who knows what he is doing and is very alert and aware of what he is about. Naturally, it is a relief to come through this first race of his three-year-old season as successfully. But we realise it is just the first step on a long road.'

Nearby, Celtic Swing's trainer, Lady Anne Herries (daughter of Lavinia, Duchess of Norfolk), who has plainly done a flawless job of handling the horse at her Angmering Park estate in West Sussex, was speaking in a similar vein of total satisfaction. 'He doesn't do anything at home and he wasn't doing a tap when he got in front here. He was just idling. He'll have an easy few days and then we will just step him up again. This race should have put him spot on. You have to respect Diffident, and the way that colt won the European Free Handicap last Wednesday, but I wouldn't swap Celtic Swing for anything.' A glance at the extremely fast times Celtic Swing has recorded in remaining unbeaten through the first four races of his life makes her enthusiasm understandable.

Before the Greenham Stakes, the Queen had a long animated conversation with Lady Herries as they looked over the prospective champion in the paddock. It was a case of two regal presences coming together.

The Sunday Times, 23 April 1995

Darley Stands to Deliver

WHEN KEVIN DARLEY rode his thousandth British winner as a Flat jockey shortly after lunchtime on Friday, the location, the race and the horse involved all reflected the modest nature of most of those successes. It happened at Carlisle in a handicap that was little more than betting-shop fodder and on a three-year-old whose breeding conveys much the same impression of nobility as its name: Busy Banana. There was scarcely anything, other than the fact that Friday's race was over a mile and that Darley was wearing the maroon and blue silks of his principal employer, Peter Savill, to connect that muted triumph in the north-west of England with the moment at Newmarket on Saturday afternoon when the 34-year-old rider will face the most demanding experience of his professional life.

The contest then will be the greatest eight-furlong event in the racing calendar, the Two Thousand Guineas, and the Savill property under Darley will be a colt more feverishly acclaimed than any other thoroughbred in recent decades. Celtic Swing has become the vehicle of an entire industry's dreams and, as he pulls his goggles down over his eyes and enters the starting stalls to look out across the broad, straight ribbon of the Rowley Mile towards the distant stands, the man in the saddle is sure to be tense with the realisation that two talents, his mount's and his own, are about to be tested as never before. Horses obviously cannot familiarise themselves with the special requirements of such challenges, for it is only as three-year-olds that they are allowed to bid for glory in the Classics, but it is highly unusual for a jockey as mature and successful as Darley to find himself riding an odds-on favourite in a race as important as the Guineas when his previous exposure to its uniqueness has been almost negligible. Though he kicked in his first winner on his 17th birthday in August 1977, he did not even secure a ride in a Classic until last season and the partners that ended his deprivation hardly did so in style. Piccolo, from Mick Channon's yard, carried him to 20th place in a Two Thousand Guineas field of 23 runners, and Michael Stoute's Golden Ball finished eighth in the Derby.

His accelerating strike-rate on the racecourses of this country (he had 91 wins in the 1992 season, 143 in 1993 and 154 in 1994) has not brought a corresponding breakthrough in the major races. When Celtic Swing took his third victory in three starts as a two-year-old by storming 12 lengths clear of the opposition in the Racing Post Trophy at Doncaster last October, it was the only time a British Group One has fallen to Darley in his 17-year career. And, inevitably, the bread-and-butter emphasis in his achievements has encouraged many to doubt whether he is ready to dominate in races such as the Guineas and the Derby.

That would seem to be a view as unjust and irrational as the suggestion that Peter Savill and Lady Anne Herries, the trainer of Celtic Swing, neither of whom has tasted Classic triumph, are fatally handicapped by inexperience. Such reasoning is as devoid of common sense as the injunction, 'Don't go near the water until you can swim'. Success is impossible without opportunity and opportunity in racing is the right horse. The fact that the Yorkshire-based Darley has been obliged to spend years driving Ford Fiestas is no justification for doubting his ability to handle a Rolls-Royce. None of the humans associated with Celtic Swing has given the slightest sign of misusing or inhibiting their outstanding prospect's capacities.

Maybe the horse is more vulnerable than his most fervent admirers will admit. Perhaps his natural approach to racing, which appears to involve reaching for his top gear about three furlongs out and seeking to burn off opponents with a sustained surge of power, could invite an effective answer from an animal capable of travelling smoothly in behind him and then striking with a short burst of devastating speed near the line. Perhaps, on the electrifying evidence of the European Free Handicap, the inspired French trainer André Fabre has such a horse in Diffident. But, equally, given the extremely fast times Celtic Swing has recorded, it is possible that his drive when it comes is too searing to permit any rival to remain poised close enough to his quarters to launch that kind of attack. Either way, it is unlikely that the tall, nearly black colt with the devouring stride will be diminished by the quality of assistance from the saddle. Certainly nothing that confronts Darley at Newmarket will be half as unnerving as the hazards which marked the beginning of their working partnership.

The racing world is well acquainted with the story of how, while out on the Herries gallops in West Sussex to try a two-year-old Savill was interested in buying, Darley was irresistibly drawn to another horse who was gangly and unfurnished and yet was surrounded by an aura of something remarkable. When he recommended to Savill that Celtic Swing, too, might be bought, the next stage was that he should return to the stables on the Angmering Park estate for what he calls 'a test drive'. But as he flew into the Goodwood airstrip to keep that appointment, he suddenly had cause to believe it might be his last.

'As we approached, the plane was rocking as light aircraft do,' he recalled the other day, 'but apparently there was a severe windshear problem and before we knew it we were in real trouble. The wind dropped and then, bang, we hit the floor and were wrenched around to the right. The right wheel came off and I can remember seeing it bouncing down the runway and thinking, "This is it". Then the left wheel came off and we started to spin, with mud spattering against the windows. It seemed we went for miles like that before we ground to a halt. Then the pilot opened the door and legged it. I thought, "If it's good enough for him, it's good enough for me". Keith Reveley, the son of the trainer Mary Reveley, was sat in the back. He's a big fella and he had trouble getting out but luckily the plane didn't catch fire and we were able to go back and get our kit out. It was pretty scary and we were shaken up afterwards but I went on to the stable and rode the horse and gave the go-ahead for buying him.'

The resilience he showed through that episode is a positive theme in a life that has interspersed its predominant highs with some sickening lows. It was his father, a Wolverhampton butcher, who first infected him with a passion for racing (mention of Cliff Darley's death two years ago still brings a shadow of pain to the only son's responsive and pleasant face) and his tiny physique as a schoolboy steered him towards a professional link with the Reg Hollinshead yard at Rugeley in Staffordshire that has long been celebrated for turning out well-schooled jockeys.

He was precocious as a rider and after that initial win as a 17-year-old on Dust Up at Haydock, he went to Newbury with the same horse to beat a strongly fancied favourite ridden by Willie Carson in a photo-finish. 'I was barely out of nappies and to beat Willie in a real tight photograph was brilliant,' he said, offering the smile that habitually represents one of the friendliest and least affected personalities in his sport. Intelligence and level-headedness are attributes that virtually all his mentors from Hollinshead to Savill have admired, so it is intriguing to reflect on the deadly lapse of judgment that led him to quit the Rugeley yard prematurely. The ensuing problems were less easily dealt with than the lifelong skin allergy activated in his hands by the effect of horses' sweat on leather. Cotton gloves purchased in boxloads coped with the allergy but it took revised attitudes to get his career back on track.

After completing the 1977 season with 11 winners, he soared to 70 in 1978 and captured the apprentices' championship. It was then, he admits ruefully, that 'I decided I was the bee's knees'. Once out of his apprenticeship, an ill-starred attempt to establish himself at Newmarket saw his fortunes dive and that 70-winner campaign was followed by one that produced 14. His troubles were compounded by a horrible fall at Nottingham and three further lean years followed before he became hitched to the rising star of Jack Berry, and additional boosts from Fulke Johnson Houghton and Mel Brittain thrust him back into prominence.

But it was when Darley teamed up with Chaplins Club – the Savill-owned sprinter who was so consistent that racecourse managements were tempted to hand over the prize money whenever his horsebox swung through their gates – that the graph of his career began to climb relentlessly. An offer to become Savill's retained jockey was eagerly grabbed and the association, now in its seventh year, benefited when the strain of organising the jockey's riding arrangements was passed three seasons back from Darley's wife Debby (they met in their early teens and live with their two daughters at Sheriff Hutton, near York) to the Newmarket agent Nick Babington, who is also Savill's racing manager. The Cayman Islands publishing tycoon accounts for perhaps 25 per cent of Darley's seasonal total of nearly a thousand rides but, since the Savill horses are lodged in stables scattered all over the country, even occasional visits to those yards would be enough to ensure an intimidating amount of travel and a hectic schedule. But it is all well worth the effort and their relationship brims with mutual respect.

At the heart of it, of course, is the glorious promise of Celtic Swing. 'When I first saw him he had a real square, angular look to him, with plenty of muscling up to do,' Darley told me. 'Now he has grown in exactly the right way, not upwards, which we wouldn't have wanted, but outwards to fill his frame perfectly. He has never worked badly at home but at the same time he has never worked well. It is on the racecourse he shows what a serious horse he is. He is so well balanced, has such a good action, that you don't feel the full extent of his acceleration. Look at pictures of him and you'll see he often has all four legs off the ground. He literally floats.'

Kevin Darley expects Celtic Swing to float into history on Saturday afternoon.

The Sunday Times, 30 April 1995

Celtic Swing was beaten in the Guineas and, though he won the French Derby, he turned out to be less of a wonder than his two-year-old career had promised.

A Kingdom for a Horse

THE BEARDED FIGURE in light-blue jeans, patterned sweater and flat cap to be seen striding briskly across the dew-soaked grass of Newmarket Heath at half-past six on Friday morning was not instantly recognisable as either a prince of the desert or the most powerful owner in the history of horseracing. All a casual watcher could have said with certainty was that this was a serious man engaged in serious business. That much is always obvious in the actions of 46-year-old Sheikh Mohammed Bin Rashid al Maktoum, for he is not only the biggest operator in the global thoroughbred industry but one of the most relentlessly professional.

Whether people approve or resent the vast influence exerted on racing by the oil-wealth of the ruling family of Dubai, the one accusation which can never be made is that their approach is at all dilettante. Eight days before the Derby, an owner more amateurish than Sheikh Mohammed might have found it difficult to have thoughts for any animal other than Pennekamp, the three-year-old colt who is a short-priced favourite to fill an increasingly painful void in his generally triumphant experience of the Turf by winning the most magical of all races. But, while Pennekamp was stirring in his box 300 miles away at André Fabre's stables in Chantilly, Sheikh Mohammed was on the Heath to check another strand in his Classic aspirations. He was there to see three representatives of Godolphin, the ambitiously innovative project he has recently established on the basis of training horses six months in the warmth of Dubai and six months in England, undergo their last testing pre-Epsom workout.

None of the three will go out on to the old Surrey track with his famous maroon and white colours. In the Derby, Vettori will carry the blue and white of his older brother, Sheikh Maktoum, the ruler of Dubai, as will Moonshell in the Oaks, while Lammtarra will go for the Derby under the silks of Sheikh Maktoum's son, Saeed Maktoum al Maktoum. But Sheikh Mohammed's identification with all of them will be deep, and not just because of family loyalties. For him, Godolphin is clearly much more than a commercial enterprise, though its viability has been amply confirmed by a remarkable run of international Group One successes in the two years since it was launched. Beyond the statistics, there is an unmistakable sense that Sheikh Mohammed, with significant backing from Sheikh Maktoum, is delivering a statement to the world about the ability of modern Arabs to maintain and extend the formidable traditions of horsemanship associated with their culture.

He has called his training organisation after the Godolphin Arabian, one of the three stallions to whom the bloodlines of every thoroughbred can be traced, and his English stud management company takes its name from another, the Darley Arabian. When his decision to gather a carefully selected group from the 500 horses he keeps in training worldwide into winter quarters at his Al Quoz training centre on the edge of Dubai City caused a ripple of disgruntled concern among trainers who had been in charge of them, he said: 'I am a horseman and I like to see my horses. If I have a yearling in Europe, I don't see it except in the middle of the season and just read small reports about it. I can come over to Al Quoz in the morning or the afternoon, and if I'm tied up through business I can ring my trainer and tell him to delay work until I get there. I like to make the decisions and I always do what I think is best for the horses.' That last sentence does nothing to discourage the widespread belief that he makes a pervasive and decisive contribution to the training of the Godolphin horses. Saeed Bin Suroor, a 28-year-old former policeman, is the official trainer and he is helped by Jeremy Noseda, who previously worked as an assistant to John Gosden, and by Simon Crisford, who switched from being an able lieutenant to Anthony Stroud, Sheikh Mohammed's racing manager. But all three are quick to acknowledge that the man who is Crown Prince and Minister of Defence in Dubai has more than sufficient energy and know-how to be in direct control of every important phase of the operation. 'We are all on the same wavelength,' Crisford said on Friday. 'The Sheikh rode in his first race at the age of eight and he has a tremendous experience of horses. In fact, he has an unbelievable sense of all animals, a feel for them that would put many people who regard themselves as experts to shame. I have witnessed extraordinary examples of that.'

What Mohammed himself witnessed on Friday morning justified hopes that, in addition to the acceleration of the pulse guaranteed by Pennekamp's challenge at Epsom, his commitment to Godolphin will be a matter of pride on the Downs. Over a mile on the watered gallop parallel to the Rowley Mile, Kassbaan, an older work horse noted for speed, provided a lead for Vettori and Moonshell. When Vettori, winner of the French equivalent of the Two Thousand Guineas, strode keenly to the uphill finish a couple of lengths ahead of the Oaks second-favourite there had to be optimism about his chances of running prominently in the Derby. Stamina is the major doubt attached to his name.

Lammtarra is by Nijinsky out of Snow Bride, whose win in the Oaks was by means of a disqualification but represents excellent staying form nevertheless, so getting the mile-and-a-half of the Derby should not be a problem for him. Inexperience probably will be. Victory in a Listed race in this country as a two-year-old has been his only taste of combat so far. However, after Lammtarra performed impressively in his gallop, Crisford argued that his time in Dubai made him more precocious and better prepared for Epsom than he would have been had he remained in Britain. 'Apart from the benefit of the kinder climate, the animals are educated by working on a tight, left-handed racetrack,' he said.

Walter Swinburn, who rode Lammtarra, spoke glowingly of his partner after an exercise session so privately arranged that even the usual Newmarket work-watchers were absent. 'I have always thought a great deal of him,' Swinburn said of his Derby mount. 'He is a strong character with that something special about him that only very few horses have. Maybe the Derby will come a month too soon but I feel sure there are big things ahead for Lammtarra. And even at Epsom, you will dismiss him at your peril.'

The same might be said of Tamure, who will be sent out as an unbeaten contender from John Gosden's yard, and will compete in Sheikh Mohammed's own colours, but everything in the form book suggests that if the Crown Prince is to end his Derby drought on Saturday it will be with Pennekamp. The son of Bering (an honourable second to the marvellous Dancing Brave in the Arc of 1986) is burdened with a far heavier weight of expectation than is

conveyed by his 6-4 betting odds. Apart from satisfying his
owner's hunger for a triumph to set alongside the two provided for
his brother, Sheikh Hamdan, by Nashwan and Erhaab, Pennekamp
is being asked to correct another astonishing omission. Fabre, in
spite of accomplishments that encouraged Henry Cecil to call him
God, is still without a Derby victory on either side of the Channel.

Six wins from six starts, including three at Group One level and
the abrupt demolition in the Two Thousand Guineas of the dreams
of immortality that had been built around Celtic Swing, give
Pennekamp the qualifications to reach for the most glorious heights
a racehorse can scale. Now that Celtic Swing has defected to
today's French Derby, the main worries about the Epsom favourite
are concentrated on his own idiosyncrasies. He has a searing,
hitherto irresistible burst of speed but must be held up for an
extremely late charge, since his response to finding himself in front
is to apply the brakes almost as if a fire had spread across his path.
'In the Guineas he passed Celtic Swing effortlessly, with his ears
pricked,' said one of the most clinical observers, 'but within a stride
they were flat on his head and he was stopping to nothing.'

There has to be profound concern about such a tendency in
relation to the Derby, in which the severe undulations and
awkward cambers of the course and the hectic pressures of the
contest impose nightmare difficulties on a jockey asked to ride a
refined tactical race. And obviously the demands are compounded
when the rider is, like Thierry Jarnet, who will be on Pennekamp, a
Derby virgin. Anthony Stroud, who had a big hand in buying
Pennekamp for Sheikh Mohammed as an incredible $40,000
bargain at the Keeneland September Yearling Sales, recognises the
hazards without coming close to losing faith. 'He is a difficult horse
to ride at Epsom, because he will obviously have to be kept in a
handy position but must not be allowed to hit the front too soon.
When he goes into the lead he pulls up, so his run must be delayed
until he is a furlong-and-a-half or even a furlong from home. Talk
of his exceptional speed implying stamina limitations does not
bother me. If he can be switched off, he'll stay. But having the
manoeuvrability to maintain a tactical position amid the traffic
problems in the heat of the race might be a bigger issue. It's no
advantage that Thierry hasn't ridden a Derby but he has ridden to
three jockeys' championships in France. He knows what he is
doing.'

Of course. Otherwise the man in the jeans and flat cap would have nothing to do with him.

The Sunday Times, 4 June 1995

Lammtarra the Epsom Terror

THE DERBY'S CAPACITY to outreach the wildest imaginings of fiction was dramatically exemplified at Epsom yesterday as Lammtarra, a colt who had run only once before in his life, and whose original trainer was fatally shot last year, came with a pulverising run in the last two furlongs of the one-and-a-half-mile Classic to shatter the course record and give the Maktoum family, of Dubai, a triumph they had expected to take with another horse.

Only three or four rivals were behind the chestnut son of Nijinsky as he came out of Tattenham Corner into the straight and his rider, Walter Swinburn, still appeared to be working hard nearly halfway up that punishing run-in. But suddenly Lammtarra, under the emerald green and white colours of his 19-year-old owner, Saeed Maktoum al Maktoum, was hurtling after the leaders and, although he was still eight lengths down with just a quarter of a mile left, his momentum soon made itself decisive.

The emotional intensity of an unforgettable race was indicated by the fact that the animal that had to be overtaken on the final charge was Tamure, on whom Frankie Dettori believed he was driving towards a first Derby victory for Sheikh Mohammed Bin Rashid al Maktoum. Sheikh Mohammed, the world's most powerful owner, had earlier seen his previously unbeaten contender and 11-8 favourite, Pennekamp, fade completely without ever having threatened to dominate. Pennekamp looked like a horse in pain and before condemnations of him as a non-stayer could harden, there was an announcement from the racecourse vet to the effect that the Two Thousand Guineas winner had finished lame.

But that misfortune could not dilute the pleasure the favourite's owner took in the success for his nephew, a son of the

ruler of Dubai, Sheikh Maktoum al Maktoum, earned by the
extraordinary performance which enabled Lammtarra (at 14-1) to
reach the line a length ahead of Tamure, with Presenting a further
three-quarters of a length away. The time, on what was plainly
firm ground, was 2 minutes 32.31 seconds, compared with
Mahmoud's Derby record of 2:33.80 and Bustino's course-best
2:33.31.

Even John Gosden, the gifted and popular Newmarket trainer,
who saddled both second and third, warmly acclaimed the
training feat achieved by the Godolphin operation set up in Dubai
by Sheikh Mohammed and Sheikh Maktoum. Lammtarra had
wintered at the Godolphin stables and his emergence as a Derby
hero has enriched an already astonishing pattern of success that
has included Balanchine's supremacy in last year's Oaks and
another win in the fillies' premier Classic on Friday by Moonshell.

Little more than a week ago, at 6.30 a.m. on the Newmarket
gallops, Swinburn told me after a workout with Lammtarra:
'Dismiss him at your peril.' The jockey's confidence reflected that
expressed long ago by his close friend, Alex Scott, who had fallen
in love with the chestnut from the moment he started to train him.
After Lammtarra introduced himself to competition by winning a
Listed race last season, Scott instantly asked Mike Dillon of
Ladbrokes to let him have a Derby bet of £1,000 at 33-1. When the
trainer was killed in a shooting incident involving another man in
the autumn of 1994, technically that wager was void. But Dillon
made it clear yesterday that a cheque would be in the post to
Scott's widow Julia on Monday morning. The money will mean
less to her than the happiness that was all around Lammtarra
yesterday. Almost as soon as he passed the post, Swinburn was
blessing himself in thanks for an experience as deep as he has
known in a riding career which had already brought two Derby
successes on Shergar and Shahristani.

Yet there was to be further tension for Swinburn. As he sat on
the scales to weigh in, Willie Carson told him that he was liable to
lose the race as a result of an incident two furlongs out in which
Lammtarra crossed in front of Carson's mount, Munwar. 'I told
Willie that if that happened, he would have to give me mouth-to-
mouth resuscitation,' said the 33-year-old Swinburn. Fortunately,
justice was done and the stewards decided that any hampering of
Munwar, who was already a beaten horse at the time, had been

irrelevant. So Swinburn was free to join Godolphin's principal trainer, Saeed Bin Suroor, and the rest of the joyous Arab circle in their celebrations. 'Let's remember Alex,' the rider said. 'He was the man who believed in this horse even before the first run.' The fact that Lammtarra had just that one taste of combat before yesterday gave him a distinction equalled by only two other Derby winners this century. And by succeeding at Epsom without an earlier race as a three-year-old, he did something not accomplished for 76 years.

Of course, the Derby produced its sad stories, none sadder than the death of Munwar's pacemaker, Daffaq, who had broken a knee. One major surprise was the thoroughly miserable showing of Spectrum, who finished a couple of places behind the struggling Pennekamp – 13th in the field of 15. Another regrettable aspect of the day was that such a modest crowd turned out to see Lammtarra deliver a surge worthy of his magnificent sire. Though a tiny improvement in the paid attendance figure was announced, the switching of the historic festival from Wednesday to Saturday obviously failed to bring about a spectacular revival of public enthusiasm for it.

The absentees on an afternoon that developed from overcast dullness to intermittent sunshine were very definitely the losers. They may have missed a glimpse of greatness.

The Sunday Times, 11 June 1995